DARWIN IN ITALY

DARWIN IN ITALY

SCIENCE ACROSS CULTURAL FRONTIERS

GIULIANO PANCALDI

UPDATED AND EXPANDED EDITION

TRANSLATED BY
RUEY BRODINE MORELLI

INDIANA UNIVERSITY PRESS
BLOOMINGTON AND INDIANAPOLIS

Originally published as *Darwin in Italia* by Società
editrice il Mulino, Bologna © 1983

© 1991 by Indiana University Press
All rights reserved

The paper used in this publication meets the minimum requirements of American
National Standard for Information Sciences—Permanence of Paper for Printed
Library Materials, ANSI Z39.48-1984.

∞^TM

Manufactured in the United States of America

Library of Congress Cataloging-in-Publication Data

Pancaldi, Giuliano.
    [Darwin in Italia.   English]
    Darwin in Italy : science across cultural frontiers / Giuliano
Pancaldi ; translated by Ruey Brodine Morelli. — Updated and
expanded ed.
        p.   cm.
    Translation of: Darwin in Italia.
    Includes bibliographical references and index.
    ISBN 0-253-34287-2 (alk. paper)
    1. Darwin, Charles, 1809–1882—Influence.   2. Science—Italy—
History.   3. Evolution   I. Title
QH31.D2P36313   1991
    575′ .0092—dc20   90-25528
    [B]

1 2 3 4 5   95 94 93 92 91

CONTENTS

LIST OF FIGURES

MANUSCRIPT SOURCES

Darwin Papers	Cambridge University Library
Darwin Offprint Collection	Cambridge University Library
Darwin Library	Cambridge University Library
Papiers C.L. Bonaparte	Bibliothèque du Muséum d'histoire naturelle, Paris
Carte G.B. Brocchi	Biblioteca Civica di Bassano
Carteggio G. Buccola	Biblioteca Comunale di Palermo
Autografoteca Campori	Biblioteca Estense, Modena
Carteggio Canestrini	Museo Tridentino di Scienze Naturali, Trent
Letters of Charles Darwin to Canestrini	Private collection of Dr. Sandro Onestinghel, Milan
Carteggio G. Capellini	Biblioteca dell'Archiginnasio, Bologna
Carteggio E. Cornalia	Museo Civico di Storia Naturale, Milan
Delpino Correspondence and Library	Private collection of Ms. Anna Barone, Rome
Carteggio G. Jan	Museo Civico di Storia Naturale, Milan
Carteggio F. Parlatore	Biblioteca Comunale di Palermo
Carteggio C. Porro	Museo Civico di Storia Naturale, Milan
Carte C. Ranzani	Biblioteca Universitaria di Bologna
Carte Savi	Biblioteca Universitaria di Pisa
Swainson Correspondence	Linnean Society, London

Acknowledgments

My interest in Charles Darwin's work dates back to when I was a student at the University of Bologna. It is a pleasure to recall those early studies under the guidance of Alberto Pasquinelli, Antonio Santucci, and Giorgio Tabarroni. My research was subsequently supported by fellowships from the Domus Galilaeana of Pisa and the British Academy. In recent years a small, active community of Darwin scholars has grown up in Italy, and my frequent discussions with them, especially Pietro Corsi, Mario Di Gregorio, and Antonello La Vergata, have been invaluable. I have also benefited from comments and criticisms emerging from my less frequent, but no less helpful, contacts with John H. Brooke, I. Bernard Cohen, Yvette Conry, Robert Fox, Mirko Grmek, Roger Hahn, Jonathan Harwood, David Kohn, Roy MacLeod, Dorinda Outram, Roy Porter, the late Jacques Roger, Paolo Rossi, Roger Smith, and Valerio Verra. Weighing various points of the American translation with Ruey Brodine Morelli has been instructive, allowing us to come to grips with the formidable difficulties that go along with the transmission of scholarly work across cultural frontiers. I am deeply grateful to all these scholars and to the staffs of the libraries named above. I would like to express my thanks to Mrs. Anna Barone, descendant of the Delpino family, Rome, for allowing me to examine Darwin's letters in her possession and invaluable books from Federico Delpino's library.

The illustrations have been reprinted by permission of the following institutions:

Biblioteca Comunale dell'Archiginnasio, Bologna
   Fig. 3b: Plate facing p. 252, from: 11.R*. I.10

Bodleian Library, Oxford
   Fig. 1a: Plate VI (facing p. 287), fig. 4, from: RR. X.66
   Fig. 1b: Plate VII (facing p. 287), fig. 1, from: RR. X.66
   Fig. 2a: Plate I, from: 18958 c 1(1–2)
   Fig. 2b: Plate IV, fig. 9, from: 18958 c 1(1–2)
   Fig. 3a: Plate XL, from: 18945 d 33(2)
   Fig. 8 top: Plate VII, top left fig., from: 16584 a 1

British Library, London (reproduced by permission of the British Library)
   Fig. 1c: Plate I, fig. 3, from: 39 e 19
   Fig. 4a: Plate V, fig. 3, from: 459 g 6
   Fig. 4b: Plate 22, fig. 75, from: 12215 r 1/27b
   Fig. 8 bottom: Plate III, fig. 4, from: 2228 e 1

Cambridge University Library, Cambridge (reproduced by permission of the Syndics of Cambridge University Library)
   Fig. 5: Title-page, from: MD 51 56
   Fig. 6: Plate XXI, from: MD 51 56
   Fig. 7: Figure III, p. 22, from: CCA 24 25

Introduction

CULTURAL FRONTIERS AND
THE DIFFUSION OF KNOWLEDGE

Science is largely a cosmopolitan enterprise: many of the results to come of it and at least some of the means by which it is pursued belong to the rather narrow sphere of human activities that transcend national boundaries. However legitimate this conviction may be, and there are reasons why it is, it has directed attention away from the tools employed to realize concretely the transnational dimension of science. The understanding of scientific theories has been considerably enhanced by studying the new relations established between different areas of knowledge at important theoretical turning points. Examining how a theory spreads through different scientific communities should similarly improve our understanding of that particular cultural system called science. This may explain why historians of science are showing an increased interest in studies investigating how scientific knowledge is disseminated through different countries and how a theory can interact with traditions other than the one in which it originated.

The main protagonists of the present contribution to that line of inquiry are, on the one hand, Darwin's theory of evolution, or "transformism," as naturalists long preferred to call it, and, on the other hand, the Italian scientific community of the nineteenth century. Although the former is certainly better known than the latter, both deserve an introduction. The best way of getting to know the protagonists of any story is, of course, to watch them in action, which is what we will be doing in the pages that follow, but a few introductory comments are in order.

When talking about "Darwin's theory," the circumstances that prepared the way for it, and its reception after the publication of Darwin's classic work on the origin of species, it is advisable to bear in mind that the expression can be used to refer to more than one thing. Particularly in common nineteenth-century usage, it was rarely specified whether the expression referred to (1) the theory explaining the transformation of species by means of natural selection, (2) the general principle according to which species are subject to transformation in time and are all derived from one or a few original forms, or (3) the methodological rule according to which all living phenomena should be explained without recourse to causes external to nature. These different meanings and the ways in which they overlapped must be taken into account when trying to identify the circumstances that prepared for, favored, or hindered the diffusion of Darwin's theory in a given scientific community.

As for the other protagonist of this volume, the nineteenth-century community of Italian scientists, it must be said above all that this is an area that has remained largely unexplored by historians. Strictly speaking, no national Italian scientific community existed until after the political unification of the Italian states in 1861. According to some contemporaries, even after that date scientists and ideas circulated with difficulty between the various regions of the peninsula. Thus a philosopher addressing scientists gathered in Rome in 1873 could still complain that in Italy "science, rather than breathing a common life, seems to suffocate in the life of each province," adding that "the example set by other countries is judged far too distant, or too high, or one that cannot be imitated." Yet during the twenty years prior to the unification of Italy in 1861, scientists and exponents of the technical professions had already arranged annual scientific meetings in different Italian cities with considerable participation from the preunification states.

It will be seen in the chapters to follow just how widely ideas and scientists from outside the peninsula circulated in these scientific meetings. Still, there are indications that during the Wars of Independence (1848–61) and immediately after unification, the position of Italian science in Europe lost ground perceptibly. About 1870 an outside observer, the Swiss naturalist Alphonse de Candolle, calculated that in the preceding forty years, Italy had dropped from third to sixth place in the European scientific community. Historical surveys confined to the biological sciences seem to confirm that the circulation abroad of work by Italian scientists was less extensive in the second half of the century than in the first.

This book is limited to an exploration of the process of elaboration of knowledge and diffusion of research on transformism. The study of evolutionary theories has, however, proved an effective starting point for a more comprehensive investigation of nineteenth-century Italian science. Moreover, the "peripheral" but singularly receptive community of Italian scientists has proved a particularly favorable ground for testing some general historiographic views on Darwinism and its diffusion.

In dealing with Darwinism in nineteenth-century Italy, it seems appropriate to distinguish between three different groups of intellectuals interested in evolutionary theories. First, there were the professional naturalists, biologists, anthropologists, and geologists, most of them active in the various Italian universities. They could contribute to studies on evolution with original research, and in any event, they guaranteed the circulation of ideas on evolution through teaching. Second, there were the popularizers, "amateur" scientific writers and journalists who kept interest alive in evolutionary theories and their manifold implications outside biology. The many Italian philosophers attracted by Darwinian or, as was more often the case, Spencerian evolutionism could generally be assigned to one of these two groups. And finally there was the general public, which, though having no direct say in the debates in progress, could express its measure of approval of others' initiatives by attending the "popular lectures" that were becoming fashionable, or by buying the popular science books that were being printed in increasing numbers in Italy as elsewhere in Europe.

This study deals mainly, though not exclusively, with the first of these groups, the professional scientists. Of course, they did not live in isolation from others, and on various occasions it will be seen how sensitive they, too, were to the implications of evolutionism in the fields of philosophy, religion, or politics that were being debated.

To avoid, as much as possible and warranted, the uncertainties connected with the definition of what exactly was meant by Darwin's theory and Darwinism in the specific nineteenth-century Italian context, I have chosen to deal with scientists having clear connections with Darwin and his work— i.e., scientists whose ideas had an impact on Charles Darwin himself, as was the case with the geologist Giambattista Brocchi (chapter 1); who shared with Darwin, in the period immediately preceding the publication of the *Origin*, an interest in the fundamental problem of species (chapter 2); who translated Darwin's works and worked out some original hypotheses on the origin of the human species, such as the zoologist Giovanni Canestrini (chapter 3); who debated some crucial aspects of Darwin's conception of nature directly with him, such as the botanist Federico Delpino (chapter 4); or who, like Cesare Lombroso (chapter 5), contributed to the transplantation of purportedly Darwinian concepts from the natural sciences to the social sciences by an operation that also had significant echoes outside Italy. Chapter 6 deals with the reception of Darwinism by the general reader and focuses on the issues of secularization, radicalism, and the Catholic church in connection with the diffusion of evolutionary naturalism in the Italian context.

These particular case studies have been used to explore the wider setting of scientific research in nineteenth-century Italy. They also shed light on some aspects of the "Darwinian revolution" as observed from the standpoint of a specific scientific community and through the contacts this community had with scientists and ideas from various countries, both before and after the publication of Darwin's theory. The following are some of the conclusions to emerge from the research, and to be illustrated in the course of the book.

First, the process that led to a significant affirmation of evolutionary theories in Italy in the second half of the nineteenth century seems to have been the result of the confluence of several lines of research that had developed during the first half of the century in a number of countries. To use a musical image, the affirmation of Darwinian evolutionism as seen from Italy was more like polyphony than a solo. This is something too easily forgotten when attention is focused exclusively on the figure of Charles Darwin, as is done by a number of recent studies.

Second, the "Darwinian revolution" does not seem to conform to certain current images of scientific revolutions. In particular, the view of the nineteenth-century controversy on species as simply a conflict between "fixists," or "creationists," on the one hand, and "evolutionists," on the other, has turned out to be rather misleading when applied to nineteenth-century Italy. In the decades that preceded the publication of Darwin's *Origin*, there were actually only vague traces of a fixist theory of species, whereas after the *Origin* a large number of naturalists adhered to some evolutionary theory of species. Having a theory at one's disposal may well be considered a revolution in comparison with not having one; in this sense as in many others, we can and should continue to speak of a "Darwinian revolution."[1] However, an interpretation crediting Darwin with the establishment of a "synthesis" of nineteenth-century knowledge on transformism—an interpretation modeled with appropriate distinctions on the image of the new "synthetic" theory of evolution established during the twentieth century by a number of scientists—may express the nature of Charles Darwin's extraordinary individual achievement just as well.

Third, the spread of Darwinism in Italy reveals significant differences in the way the various disciplines reacted to the new theory. Noting that systematic zoologists, botanists, and anthropologists reacted differently to Darwin's theory is more than a matter of scholarly curiosity. On the one hand, the phenomenon seems to confirm the "synthetic" nature of the theory just mentioned: Darwin's concepts obliged the different disciplines to meet on ground that was sometimes at the borders between their traditional territories. On the other hand, the phenomenon seems to indicate that the spread of Darwin's theory involved not only the confrontation of rival theories and the discovery of new empirical evidence but also grappling with the particular research traditions rooted in each discipline.

The notion of disciplinary tradition has proved especially useful for a study of the diffusion of science across cultural frontiers. Historians have perhaps not taken into due account the fact that, at least from the nineteenth century on, while or even before adhering to a particular theory or view of nature, scientists have adhered to a body of specialist knowledge shared in the main by all those practicing the same discipline. The set of notions pertaining to the discipline could be called "technical," as they belong to the "art" or "craft" of the scientist in that particular field. Yet the technical notions often involved full-grown, albeit implicit, cognitive strategies, these, too, widely shared by those who practiced the discipline. Thus, for example, those who studied large mammals tended to see the problem of species in terms that were not identical to the terms of the problem for those who studied mollusks. "Technical" or disciplinary notions of this kind can help explain why evolutionary theory had a different impact on systematic zoologists engaged in fieldwork, naturalists working in museums, and physiologists in their laboratories.

Disciplinary traditions, like the pursuit of knowledge itself, are in principle transnational and cosmopolitan. But since besides the study of nature they also involve tools, research facilities, scientific institutions, and the professional figure of the scientist, they seem to be particularly affected by national context. Hence their relevance for an investigation of the development of the scientific enterprise across cultural boundaries. Whereas scientific theories and ideas seem to cross borders with relative ease, this is not quite the case for disciplinary traditions. An article, a book, or a translation can serve to circulate a new theory quickly, even in a cultural context rather different from the one in which the theory originated. Modifying or transplanting a disciplinary tradition, instead, involves many scientists and an adaptation, sometimes a profound transformation, of the organization of research.

Thus when, as in the case of Darwin's theory, new ideas put a wide range of disciplinary traditions to the test and opened the way to new ones, it proved even more difficult to break free of some of the old "technical" and institutional tools embodied in the disciplinary traditions than to abandon old theories. The reason for this is clear enough: like old theories, old disciplinary traditions always contain at the very least some good, and perhaps a great deal that deserves saving. In any event, theory change and the updating of disciplinary traditions often went hand in hand during the phase of accelerated development of scientific enterprise in the last decades of the nineteenth century. Our survey of the impact of Darwinism on nineteenth-century Italian science suggests that what was lacking in Italy was not receptiveness to new theories but rather the capacity to modify old disciplinary traditions or establish new ones promptly and firmly, an inadequacy reflected in both institutions and ideas.

Concepts such as these turned out to be particularly useful for this investigation. Nineteenth-century Italian science, however, has been studied too little so far to permit reliable general conclusions. What I hope to have succeeded in doing is to single out, in a little-known area, some significant points that are solid enough on which to build further investigation. At the same time, it has been my aim to add to the body of knowledge on the Darwinian revolution and the reception of Darwinism, as well as to the study of the diffusion of science across cultural borders.

PART I
Before the *Origin*

A History of Life without Evolution

G. B. Brocchi between Lamarck and Darwin

Some of the fossil remains of animals found by eighteenth-century naturalists were unlike those of any known living beings. Attempts to explain
this fact became the premises of what from then on would be known as
the *species problem*, namely, the problem of their origin, extinction, and
transformation. One of the explanations of the phenomenon advanced at
the time clearly expressed the eighteenth-century naturalists' faith that their
field, which seemed to be lagging behind the physical sciences, was finally
ready to plunge into rapid development. According to Linnaeus, there was
no need to assume that the species known only as fossils had actually
disappeared from the face of the earth. Exploration, which was involving
an ever-increasing number of naturalists, would eventually locate the present-day descendants of those fossil beings in some corner of the earth or
seas. The fact that they no longer inhabited the regions where the remains
of their most ancient ancestors were found simply indicated that those
species had abandoned the regions where they had once lived. This circumstance, along with the fact that many of the fossils found on hills and
mountains far from any ocean were marine animals, led to the recognition
that the earth had undergone momentous transformations in past eras, a
fact that the young science of geology had begun to investigate thoroughly.

Linnaeus's approach to the problem earned widespread consensus. And
yet by the end of the eighteenth century and the beginning of the nineteenth, not many naturalists still doubted that some species had indeed
disappeared. Why did naturalists now concede as demonstrated something
they so long had refused to accept? How did the new fact of extinction
become involved in the reflections, increasingly frequent and daring, on
the relationship between the history of the earth and the history of living
forms?

Giambattista Brocchi, the geologist and naturalist who will be the focus
of this chapter, was one of the first to adopt the idea that some species

had actually become extinct. In this he followed some of the arguments advanced by the celebrated French naturalist Georges Cuvier. Like Cuvier, who was about the same age, Brocchi was soon prompted to explore the causes of extinction, or as he more cautiously termed it, the "loss" of species. Moving from similar premises but following a different path from the one indicated by Cuvier, Brocchi came to formulate some original hypotheses on the laws that governed the succession of different species in the history of the earth.

Brocchi formulated his hypothesis on the extinction of species in various writings published in 1807, 1814, and 1822. At about the same time, Jean Baptiste Lamarck, along with his earliest followers and a heterogeneous movement that included British physicians and philosophers such as Erasmus Darwin and exponents of the German "philosophy of Nature" such as Friedrich W. Schelling and Carl F. Kielmeyer, was restating with new vigor and arguments some eighteenth-century ideas concerning the transmutation of species. These ideas, like the more orthodox tradition represented by Cuvier, also circulated in the Italian peninsula, then divided into many different states, each in the orbit of a different European nation. As we will see, some of these states had extensive contacts with Europe's leading scientific centers. Brocchi was familiar with the writings that then advocated a transformist, or evolutionary, approach to the problem of species and their extinction. He did not, however, consider this approach viable: his hypotheses admitted the successive introduction and extinction of living forms in the history of the earth but *excluded* the possibility that one species might be transformed into another.

This prevents the historian from including Brocchi among the numerous representatives of pre-Darwinian evolutionism. On the other hand, the cautious rejection of the then-controversial transformist ideas seems to have benefited the fortune of Brocchi's hypotheses during the first half of the nineteenth century. The fact that he offered a strategy for dealing with the unsettled problem of extinction, while rejecting both Lamarck's and Cuvier's solutions, helped attract the attention of many naturalists, including the British geologist Charles Lyell. In a work that directly and indirectly had an important role in nineteenth-century developments of the species problem, Lyell gave considerable weight to Brocchi's ideas. That work, Lyell's *Principles of Geology*, would later be of crucial importance in Charles Darwin's intellectual development, influencing his earliest reflections on species. Thus in the 1830s, the decisive years for Darwin's conversion to transformism and for the first formulations of his evolutionary theory, we find Darwin repeatedly pondering Brocchi's ideas, which he learned of through Lyell.

In what follows, the examination of Brocchi's hypotheses on species and some considerations on their reception are aimed at offering new evidence on the history of the species problem in the important period from the publication of Lamarck's ideas at the beginning of the nineteenth century to the first formulation of Darwin's theory three decades later. Adopting as the vantage point Italian science, relatively marginal to the scientific community of the time but peculiarly open to the influences of different cultures, I will highlight the merging of different scientific traditions in the development of the species problem.

EXTINCTION: THE VICISSITUDES OF A SCIENTIFIC FACT

The study of fossil bones and that of shells found in rocks would be sterile and little more than inconclusive if we did not propose to trace what correlation the former has with the zoology of the present world, and the latter with the conchology of today's seas. But when we deliberately undertake this, and with all the careful consideration the subject deserves, we are greatly surprised to discover how many fossil shells and quadrupeds there are that cannot be assigned to known and living species. It thus remains to be seen what can have become of them.[1]

With these words Giambattista Brocchi began his "Riflessioni sul perdimento delle specie" (Reflections on the loss of species), which constituted an important chapter in his influential book on sub-Apennine fossil conchology (hereafter *Conchiologia*), published in Milan in 1814. Behind the abstruse and modest title, Brocchi had concealed the ambitious plan to cast new light on the "ancient history of the globe" and formulate hypotheses on the laws that regulate the "introduction" and "loss" of every species on earth.[2] The uncertain fate of shells and animals known only as fossils was crucial for Brocchi's aims.

Brocchi's *Conchiologia* had the traditional appearance of a classical monograph on the fossil shells found in a particular region. Brocchi had chosen the region comprising the hills and low mountains flanking the higher Apennine range along nearly all of the Italian peninsula from north to south. The choice of this region hinged, as we will see, on some important hypotheses on the history of the earth. The tradition of natural history collecting by regions was still vigorous, but, to use the language of the time, Brocchi's was a highly "philosophical" natural history.

At the beginning of the nineteenth century, one of the most prestigious models for monographs of this kind was Lamarck's *Mémoires sur les fossiles des environs de Paris* (Papers on the fossils in the environs of Paris),[3] and Lamarck was the best-known authority on shells in Europe at that time. Brocchi knew Lamarck's work well, as he did Cuvier and Alexandre Brongniart's on the mineralogy of the area around Paris[4] and James Parkinson's on the fossils found near London.[5] The specific interest in shells, in any case, made Lamarck's work Brocchi's most immediate reference point. Brocchi was also fully aware of the importance Lamarck attached to the comparison between fossil and living shells. In his study on the area around

Paris, Lamarck had found a large number of fossil shells unlike anything known among living species. According to geologists, the Parisian soil where these fossils had been found was of relatively recent origin, although it was of course still covered by the sea when the mollusks in question lived there. On the basis of Lamarck's findings, Brocchi noted, it could be argued that "when the ocean covered the continent, its waters enveloped beings mostly different from those that it nourishes today. This could give rise, as has indeed happened, to some particular system."[6] To what "system" or, to use present-day language, to what theory or wide-ranging speculation was Brocchi referring here?

At the time when Lamarck, Cuvier, Brongniart, Parkinson, and Brocchi were making the first systematic comparisons between fossil and living species, the only fact all naturalists would have agreed on was that some fossil species differed from all known living species. This "fact," however, was accounted for in at least three different ways.[7] The first, already mentioned, was endorsed by Linnaeus and J. E. Walch and had more recently been taken up by a colleague of Lamarck's at the Muséum d'histoire naturelle in Paris, J. G. Bruguière. According to this account, when no living examples of a species were to be found in our regions, this was because the species had emigrated to some distant location subsequent to changes in climate and the earth's surface. The second explanation had been advanced by Cuvier in 1796 and reiterated in the numerous editions of his successful *Discours sur les révolutions de la surface du globe* (Discourse on the revolutions of the globe).[8] He maintained that some species, those of which living specimens could no longer be found, had become extinct as a result of radical changes in the earth's surface, which had encroached on the living world as well. The third explanation, proposed by Lamarck,[9] held that no species had actually become extinct: living species were simply *different* from the fossil species. Lamarck considered this a confirmation of his theory that species are subject to radical *transformations* in time. Lamarck thus resolved the problem of extinction, which he claimed was only apparent, by incorporating it in his evolutionary theory of species. What, then, was Brocchi's attitude toward these three solutions, and what explanation did he himself propose?

As emerges from the first pages of his *Conchiologia*, the study of shells found in Italy yielded results that differed from Lamarck's for the area surrounding Paris. Of the over five hundred fossil species Lamarck had found there, he held that only twenty had living counterparts. Of the fossil mollusks described by Brocchi for Italy, instead, over half were still extant. At that time geologists believed that the Italian sub-Apennine terrains and those around Paris had been formed in approximately the same era. Thus from Lamarck's and Brocchi's investigations it emerged that during the same interval of time, the history of living forms had followed two very different courses in the two areas. Or, as Brocchi implied in the passage mentioned above, the naturalists who had studied the different areas had allowed themselves to be steered by the different solutions to the species problem that each endorsed, a transparent allusion to Lamarck's transformist ideas.[10] In his *Conchiologia*, in any event, Brocchi did not examine in detail the transformist solution proposed by Lamarck for the problem of extinction. Although this may have been the result of a failure to perceive the importance of Lamarck's solution, it might also be a sign of diffidence toward a theory that was meeting with considerable resistance in scientific circles. What is certain is that, in 1814 and afterward, Brocchi's references to Lamarck's transformism remained vague.

Explicit in Brocchi's work, instead, was a rejection of the view that explained the apparent extinction of species by their migration.[11] Linnaeus, Walch, and Bruguière were, like Lamarck, reluctant to admit that some species had become extinct, but they appealed to an account that was much less controversial than that of the transformation of species suggested by Lamarck. In the eighteenth century there had been a great deal of speculation on the changes undergone by climate and the earth in the course of past geological ages. It was thought that modifications of the environment had driven some species to migrate into regions with more favorable conditions. Thus, Linnaeus argued, the large shellfish known as "horns of Amon" or ammonites, found as fossils on European mountains, no longer lived in the seas surrounding the continent, and may have fled to the bottom of the ocean. Bruguière cautioned against making any assumption on the fate of such species until exploration could establish the truth.

Brocchi objected that while there might be doubts regarding the extinction of some difficult-to-find marine shells, there was no doubt that some large quadrupeds and some freshwater shells had indeed disappeared from the face of the earth.[12] As for the quadrupeds, Brocchi adopted Cuvier's arguments, which had shown that of the sixty-eight species of fossil quadrupeds then known, forty-nine had never been found alive on any continent. In the case of large animals such as mastodons and mammoths, it was hard to imagine how their descendants, if they existed, could have been overlooked by naturalists searching for them.[13] As for freshwater shells, whose natural environments are rivers and other easily reached sites, it was unlikely that they might now be located only in inaccessible regions.[14]

Thus, like Cuvier, Brocchi held that the extinction of some species was by then a proven fact. His agreement with Cuvier, however, ended there. Like all those who had tackled the controversial problem of extinction, Brocchi was led to speculate on the causes that could have produced the phenomenon. The search for these causes hinged on each naturalist's general conception of nature, which in turn was the result of a peculiar blend of scientific, methodological, and philosophical convictions. It is not surprising that, though agreeing with Cuvier on extinction, Brocchi diverged considerably in regard to its explanation. To understand Brocchi's account, we must examine the conception of the history of the earth set forth in his *Conchiologia*. We must also consider some general concepts regarding living organisms that Brocchi made use of in formulating his hypotheses on the fate of species. To this end, we can avail ourselves not only of the pages of *Conchiologia* and the other publications where he treated the species problem, with some reticence, as we have seen. We also have the journals Brocchi kept during his travels, his notebooks, his correspondence with many scientists, any many notes on his reading. These materials allow us to follow his thinking even where his published works do not.[15] We may thus be able to understand how he came to propose a fourth, original solution to the species problem, different from those previously advanced by Linnaeus, Cuvier, and Lamarck.

A NATURALIST'S JOURNEY IN THE ITALIAN STATES

Most of the scientific materials Brocchi used in *Conchiologia* were gathered during a trip through the Italian states he carried out in two stages between 1811 and 1813. This trip, on which he kept a detailed diary,[16] is a good illustration of the science he practiced, as well as of the situation of natural history studies in the Italian peninsula at that time. Clearly, both these aspects are relevant for an understanding of Brocchi's approach to the species problem.

When Brocchi undertook the trip, at the age of thirty-nine, he had for about two years been inspector for the Council of Mines instituted by the Kingdom of Italy, patterned after similar French institutions, and having headquarters in Milan.[17] The Kingdom of Italy was a short-lived by-product of Napoleon's control over Italy, comprising a limited portion of present-day northern Italy. Its capital, Milan, and its main region, Lombardy, had been part of the Austrian empire for a century and would again be under Austria from 1815 to 1861. Brocchi was born into a family of the lower nobility in the region near Venice, whose decaying republic had maintained a precarious independence throughout the previous century. Brocchi's works and manuscripts display a mastery of the natural history literature in French, German, and English.

The main duties of the Council of Mines inspectors were surveying mineral resources and perfecting the processes used for ore extraction.[18] This involved carrying out analytical "trials" on the minerals, training engineers and workers, introducing new techniques of extraction, assembling a systematic collection of minerals, and preparing a "mineralogical map" of the kingdom. These last two duties played a part in prompting Brocchi to make his trip, which led him beyond the boundaries of what was then the Kingdom of Italy. A major part of the trip was devoted to surveying the chief mining areas of Italy. Going south from Milan, Brocchi gathered information on the production of "Modena salt"; near Florence he visited the serpentine quarries, in Leghorn a factory for working coral, in Volterra one for the production of alabaster objects, in the Phlegraean Fields the solfatara, in Naples the china works, and around Bari the tufa quarries. On his way back to Milan, he stopped northwest of Rome to study the mining area in the Tolfa mountains and to visit a sulfur quarry and a foundry at Bracciano, as well as saltworks, quarries, and factories along the Adriatic coast.

These were Brocchi's official tasks during his trip, in connection with his post as a mine inspector. In his capacity as a naturalist, former teacher of natural history,[19] and tutor in natural sciences of the young gentleman Alberto Parolini, who was traveling with him, he had yet other interests. Thus in Modena he sought out the optical instruments produced by Giambattista Amici. In Reggio he examined the physics laboratory of the lyceum, equipped with machines built in Paris, and the collection left by the celebrated Lazzaro Spallanzani, though he found the mineralogical part of this disappointing. In Tuscany he visited many private collections of fossil shells. At the Valdarnese Academy near Florence he saw a rich collection of fossil bones, some of which had been identified by Cuvier during a trip to Italy. He also visited natural history museums and botanical gardens in Florence, Pisa, and Leghorn. In Siena he admired a series of wooden models used in a local school to teach the laws of crystal structure, and he deemed them more effective than the models used in Paris.

In Rome he ranked the collection of minerals kept in the laboratory of the "Sapienza" the most complete in Italy. But as for the city's botanical garden, he declared that he had never seen one "so badly kept up, or more miserably stocked." Apropos of the botany lessons sometimes held there during the summer, Brocchi reported with disappointment that they were still based on Tournefort's system, and not Linnaeus's. Nor was the state of the shell collections of the natural history museum of the Collegio Romano, previously run by the Jesuits, any better. Its series of minerals was "very miserable" and the nomenclature employed "either barbarous or nonexistent." The most interesting moments of his Roman stay were his contacts with a brilliant collector of objects of natural history, Giuseppe Riccioli, and his frequent visits to stonecarvers' workshops, where he looked for ancient carved marbles. This search combined his interest as a geologist with his long-standing vocation as a student of Egyptian sculpture.[20]

In Naples he found an important mineralogical collection assembled by students when, under the reign of Ferdinand IV, son of Charles III of Spain, "they were sent at public expense to the main parts of Europe to be instructed in mineralogy and metallurgy."[21] The materials were classified according to René-Just Haüy's method and nomenclature. In Naples Brocchi also met the American geologist William Maclure, with whom he made excursions. Maclure, Brocchi reported, "has been traveling in Europe for twelve years, collecting minerals for the schools of his country, promoting the study of mineralogy there, an undertaking that he conducts at his own expense, motivated by pure patriotism."[22] At the University of Naples he was disappointed in the botany lesson he attended, taught by Michele Tenore. It dealt with the "essential differences between animals and vegetables," but according to Brocchi it was nothing but a superficial amplification of a famous aphorism of Linnaeus's.[23] Among the collections of the Institute of Science in Bologna, he admired the reptiles, shells, and fossils but found the mineral collection poor. He was unable to meet Camillo Ranzani, professor of natural history at the University of Bologna, who was at that time in Paris working with Cuvier.[24]

After his trip through central and southern Italy, in the summer of 1813 he made a trip through northern Italy, to Lombardy, Piedmont, and Liguria.[25] In this new expedition, too, he alternated excursions with visits to natural history collections and meetings with local scientific circles. His encounter with the Turin naturalists may well have been particularly significant: Franco Andrea Bonelli, one of the first in Italy to discuss the Lamarckian doctrine of evolution, was active there.[26]

While Brocchi's first contact with a region was often made through visits to local collections and conversations with the naturalists of the place, his fieldwork was unquestionably the high point of his travels. Fieldwork meant the retrieval, description, and identification of single rocks, as well as surveying a whole region to test some geological theory. The mineralogist's technique and "craft" emerge from this exemplary description of a rock found in the Roman subsoil:

> Its color is a cinnamon yellow with oblong spots of a darker color. The fracture is earthy, with a tufaceous appearance. It is friable, and light in weight. It does not stick to the tongue, and when dampened it gives off a slightly muddy smell. It acts on the needle of a compass, though weakly. It does not effervesce on contact with acids, and it contains a certain amount of heterogeneous parts, which are flakes of black mica, fragments and whole crystals of basaltic hornblend with a vitreous, conchoidal, wavy fracture, rounded grains of white limestone, normally floury. One of these grains, the size of a small nut, was covered on the outside with a floury crust, but when split, inside showed features of transitional limestone with a scaly and semitranslucent fracture. . . . On the basis of Breislak's not very precise identification of its features, I regard it a tufaceous rock formed by water, even if one might assume that the matter it is composed of owes its earliest origin to the action of fire.[27]

The eighteenth-century theoretical controversy between "neptunists" and "volcanists," who maintained that the formation of the earth's crust was chiefly due to the action of, respectively, seas and volcanos,[28] thus oriented the more minute description of single rocks as well. Confrontation with the ideas of his friend and competitor Scipione Breislak, adherent of volcanism, was a thread running through most of Brocchi's field research during his travels.[29]

The following observation, on the other hand, alluding to an audacious hypothesis on the ancient presence of the sea in the plains of central Italy, foreshadowed the general theory of the earth expounded in *Conchiologia*:

> I then climbed the bell tower of the cathedral [of Volterra] to ascertain the extension of the shelly terrains, which offer a singular view from this height, representing a vast open space of ridges like ocean waves, composed of sterile and bare bluish earth, in which you can see only an occasional bush and a few small cultivated fields. This open space includes the hills of San Miniato and all the other hills of the lower Arno valley, which are of the same kind. I previously established the boundaries of this ancient sea bed on the northern side by observing the region from a hill in San Miniato. Now from the bell tower of the Volterra cathedral I was able to identify the borders of the southern part, which consist of the mountains of Frosine, Radicondoli, Gerfallo, Castelnuovo, Serazzano, Monte Rufoli, and Querceto. When I get to Siena I will establish the eastern boundary. Not all the heights included in the area of this basin are composed of sand or shelly silt. Some are of stratified limestone, and of earlier origin; these were once islands. They include the mountains of Montecatino, and Miemo, which are surrounded all around by shelly soil. In the Leghorn and Pisan littoral there was an opening through which the Mediterranean Sea invaded and flooded these lands.[30]

This sort of systematic observation was made possible by the planning of the trip on the basis of a precise geological hypothesis, which was then sometimes contradicted by fieldwork. Thus the discovery of rich shell deposits on the high volcanic mountains of the island of Ischia shook Brocchi's faith in neptunism.[31] A crossing of the Apennines from the Tyrrhenian Sea to the Adriatic at the level of Naples thwarted his hope of finding sandstone hills flanking the highest mountains everywhere: the structure of the Apennines was much more irregular than he had anticipated.[32]

Brocchi's trip through the Italian states between 1811 and 1813 reveals different aspects or "functions" of early nineteenth-century naturalists' travels. As underscored by the title Brocchi gave his journals, his journey was in the first place a "mineralogical trip," devoted to the survey of mining resources and extractive techniques employed in the different regions and states. This was consistent with both Brocchi's position in the Council of Mines and a rich tradition of missions of this kind subsidized by "enlightened" princes and governments during the previous century. It was also, as was mentioned, a trip in which Brocchi was charged with instructing and training the young gentleman Alberto Parolini. For Brocchi it was undoubtedly also a mission of "scientific diplomacy," both personal and in the name of the Kingdom of Italy, carried out with the scientists of the various states he visited, an assignment that furthered the new kingdom's expansionistic ambitions.

But the aspect of this trip that most concerns us is unquestionably the fact of its being "field research" planned and carried out to refine and verify scientific hypotheses. Although these were limited to the structure of the Apennines, they actually aspired to yield an overview of the entire history of the earth. The study of shells and other fossil remains of animals brought the history of life into this overview. Yet the problem of living forms and their history, of which Brocchi was already aware, did not seem to have had a part in the fieldwork he did in those years. That work was for the most part mineralogical, dominated by disputes as to whether particular rocks were of volcanic or marine origin. As far as we know, Brocchi did not do any particular research at that time to test his ideas on the extinction of species. This fact, as we shall see, will have precise consequences for the type of solution that he eventually proposed for the species problem. These consequences did not escape Charles Lyell, whose fieldwork done about fifteen years later in the same regions that Brocchi visited will provide a convenient term of comparison for elucidating the developments of the species problem and of its scientific status during the first half of the nineteenth century.[33]

THE SHELLS OF THE TERTIARY ERA

In his thoughts on the history of the earth sciences that introduced *Conchiologia*, Brocchi observed that, in spite of considerable progress in recent times, "geological science so far boasts of one and only one proven truth; all the rest is doubt, uncertainty, and problems." This truth was that "there was once a time when the sea flooded the earth's entire surface, to a depth that covered the mountaintops."[34] Subsequently the sea dropped to its present level. But how and when the withdrawal of the waters had taken place, where that enormous mass of water had gone, and how the present mountains and valleys had been formed were the focus of hypotheses and conjectures that, Brocchi observed without too much irony, had given rise to "thirty or more systems," or theories.[35] Yet this situation in the field of geology did not deter him from formulating his own theory of the history of the earth, an integral part of which was his hypothesis on species.

To explain the phenomenon of the lowered sea level, Brocchi employed a hypothesis formulated over a century earlier by Leibniz and returned to repeatedly during the eighteenth century.[36] According to it, in the innermost part of the earth there were large caverns, some of whose ceilings had collapsed under the weight; as a result, enormous amounts of water had sunk and caused the sea level to drop.[37] However implausible and "catastrophic" such a notion may seem today, during the eighteenth century it was upheld and used to counter other hypotheses precisely because of its natural and potentially scientific character. Antonio Vallisneri, on whom Brocchi drew for Leibniz's hypothesis,[38] considered it more acceptable than others that attempted to explain the presence of marine fossils on mountains with a "universal Flood," that is to say, a mysterious temporary inundation like the flood in the Bible. Although he did not want to take sides in the controversy, Vallisneri felt Leibniz's hypothesis "would account for all the phenomena without miracles."[39]

Brocchi also found the underground cavern hypothesis acceptable because it provided an explanation for two aspects of the way the sea level appeared to have been lowered all over the world. The distribution of fossils appeared to prove that the sea level had always dropped and never risen; this seemed to contradict the "flood" hypothesis. Furthermore, according to Brocchi the waters had been lowered by stages, *not* gradually and continuously.[40] As a matter of fact, he admitted discontinuity in the history of the earth only after profound hesitations engendered by methodological concerns. Wherever possible, Brocchi preferred explanations that assumed an order of things that was not subject to changes brought on by exceptional causes. Uniformity of phenomena and causes was one of the methodological criteria that guided Brocchi, as it had other geologists during the eighteenth century.[41] Yet because uniformitarian explanations were not always feasible, a conflict emerged in a number of instances in Brocchi's work.

Some had suggested that even in recent times there must have been radical geological transformations, as when the Strait of Gibraltar, previously blocked, was opened, lowering the level of the Mediterranean Sea and altering the whole region. The hypothesis stemmed from testimonies recorded in historical times by Strato, Strabo, and Diodorus Siculus and had recently been reiterated in the *Journal de physique*.[42] According to Brocchi, that sort of hypothesis had the advantage, from a "philosophical" standpoint, of attributing a series of geological phenomena to an event that was well defined and apparently documented by historical testimony. Such testimony may well have appeared more substantial to the geologists of Brocchi's day than the indirect and conjectural evidence typical of their own discipline. Adopting a hypothesis of this kind, Brocchi noted, would "make it unnecessary for us to appeal to extraordinary events, and lose our way in the shadows of remote geological ages."[43] Yet various objections prevented the adoption of that hypothesis. One was the fact that eyewitness accounts of the true extent of natural catastrophes are notoriously unreliable.

It was, however, another difficulty, stemming from the hypothesis's limited range of applicability, which Brocchi felt decided the matter. This objection hinged on certain peculiar features that distinguished the Mediterranean region from the rest of the European continent. What was thought to have occurred in an area characterized by a basin surrounded by water, with the Strait of Gibraltar acting first as a "dike" and then as a "cataract," could not be applied to regions that adjoined the open ocean. And yet geological formations and fossil deposits known to be present in a Mediterranean country such as Italy were found north of the Alps as well. This was the case of the hills rich in fossil shells studied by Lamarck in France and Parkinson in England. Any hypothesis on the formation of these hills should, Brocchi insisted, take into account "the generality of the phenomenon" on the whole European continent.[44] The need to respect a principle of uniformity of causes *in space* thus obliged Brocchi to relinquish reluctantly a hypothesis that fascinated him for its capacity to account for uniformity of causes *in time*.[45] He was inclined to believe that some general upheavals, or "revolutions," in the past had produced the same geological formations throughout the European continent.[46] It was therefore legitimate to claim that the earlier situation revealed "an order of things very different from what we find today."[47]

Similar considerations led Brocchi to reject the idea that the overall lowering of the sea level had come about gradually. One of the adherents of this idea had been Linnaeus, who had considered the gradual changes in the coastline of the Scandinavian countries evidence of the lowering of the sea level.[48] Brocchi had found that his own comparable investigations along the Adriatic coast, which took into account testimonies from different historical ages, were inadequate to demonstrate that supposition. He therefore rejected the version of the underground cavern hypothesis by which a certain amount of sea water filtered continuously into the caverns.[49]

The history of the earth was thus measured off, Brocchi maintained, by the sea level's being lowered at intervals, which had modified the earth's surface by stages. In spite of this discontinuous view of the history of the earth, Brocchi did not advocate the idea that nature was subject to cataclysms ungoverned by uniform laws. This emerges from some important details of his geological system.

One of the issues most extensively debated by eighteenth-century and early nineteenth-century scientists was the problem of how the climate had been modified during geological time. The problem arose as a result of the numerous discoveries farther north of the remains of animals partly or wholly similar to those currently inhabiting warmer regions.[50] Adherents of "floods" held that those remains had been laid down at the time of such catastrophes; that hypothesis seemed to explain adequately the presence in northern regions of animals suited to warm climates without granting long-lasting changes in climate. As we have seen, Brocchi found explanations based on exceptional causes highly unlikely. Others had tried to account for climactic changes by suggesting that the inclination of the earth's axis had been altered by some astronomical cause. Geologist Jean-André De Luc had combined this idea with the underground cavern hypothesis: the transfer of enormous amounts of water from the sea into the caverns, he maintained, must have modified the earth's center of gravity and hence the inclination of its axis.[51]

Compared with hypotheses of this kind, the explanation that Brocchi proposed for changes in climate seems prompted by a pure and simple uniformitarian philosophy. First of all, he took due note of Laplace's criticisms of the assumption that astronomical forces had modified the inclination of the earth's axis.[52] He then called attention to the fact that regions currently near wide expanses of sea had a milder climate than others at the same latitude. And he noted that since oceans once occupied a greater area than now, this must mean that in the past the climate was milder than at present. The subsequent reduction of the waters, a primary agent in Brocchi's geology, had therefore also brought about a series of changes in the climate.[53]

While sudden drops in the sea level had at various times modified the earth's surface, between one geological revolution and another nature had behaved according to laws that were constant and the same everywhere. Brocchi set himself the task of demonstrating this above all for the geological period that he had chosen to study in preference to the others, that of the "tertiary" terrains that composed the sub-Apennine hills in Italy and analogous formations in other countries:

> It goes without saying that when the sea covered the tertiary hills in Italy, the water must have reached the same level in all other countries as well. The matter speaks for itself without need for proof, but it will not be inopportune to show clearly how in various parts of Europe, and indeed of the globe, in locations very far from each other, the same deposits were laid down at that time. This is, it seems to me, a very striking circumstance, in that it shows that Nature's action in this as in other periods was uniform, constant, and regulated by laws conformed to universally. With regard to the state of the materials that compose it, tertiary soil is the same everywhere, just as secondary and primary soils are.[54]

The decision to study tertiary—that is to say, recently formed—terrains was well suited to methodological needs prompted by the principle of gradualism in nature's changes. This is how Brocchi justified his choice:

> These deposits exhibit phenomena so instructive and so singular that the examination of them should serve as the starting point for anyone who wants to construct a reasoned system of geology, rather than beginning, as is usually done, from times so dark and so remote that they verge on primordial chaos. Since tertiary deposits have many similarities to deposits that are formed today, they provide a good term of comparison between the action of the sea in the distant past and that of today. So by backtracking step by step to the earlier deposits, the geologist will be able to discern correctly and appreciate the modifications and the changes that are revealed in the deposits.[55]

On occasion Brocchi expressed his skepticism about theories that claimed to reconstruct the remotest events in the history of the earth. The modern geologist should avoid losing his way "in the labyrinths of cosmogony" to whose perils geologists of the past had fallen prey.[56] It was also better not to propose a precise chronology of the history of the earth, for which, Brocchi said, there was no convincing evidence. It was better to proceed cautiously toward ascertaining the *relative* age of rocks, which

could be done by comparing the stratification and the state of cohesion of
the constituent materials. The systematic study of geological strata was
developing rapidly at the beginning of the nineteenth century.[57] Brocchi
believed the relative age of rocks could be determined by means of two
complementary techniques, in which considerations regarding the history
of life had a significant role.

One dating technique, based on strictly mineralogical principles, entailed determining the different states of aggregation of the rocks.[58] Brocchi
held that in primary, or more ancient, rocks there were always detectable
phenomena revealing "crystallization" of the components. These rocks included granites, grunstein, and serpentine. A less compact state of aggregation with no crystallization was characteristic of later, secondary rocks,
including the "calcaria" that made up the highest mountains in the Apennines. Tertiary terrains were those such as "gray marne" and "calcareous
sandstone," characterized by extreme friability, in which the components
had little cohesive strength. There were also "transitional" rocks with intermediate features, but the subdivision of the rocks into three broad, well-
defined families attested that during each period, nature had behaved
according to constant laws.[59] Over long periods, therefore, the succession
of rocks with gradually decreasing states of cohesion suggested that *there
was a direction or general tendency in the history of the earth*. This consisted in
the gradual progressive weakening of the "energy of the chemical forces"
acting in rock formation. In the world we live in, Brocchi maintained, this
energy has been "almost totally exhausted."[60] As we will see, Brocchi saw
this general tendency in the history of the earth as coinciding with an
analogous tendency in species.

The other technique for determining the relative age of rocks was based
on the identification of the fossil species found embedded in the strata.
The presence in a given stratum of a species of shell identical or similar to
present-day shells was evidence that the stratum was recent, while a large
percentage of extinct species was a reliable indication that the stratum was
ancient. As Brocchi put it, "fossil conchology is the yardstick of geology."[61]

Brocchi was thus well aware that the history of the earth and the history
of living organisms were interwoven. In regard to the history of the earth,
we have seen that with the concept of successive "revolutions," and epochs,
each characterized by uniform laws, he identified some general tendencies.
One tendency was the increase by stages of dry land in proportion to water.
A second tendency, a consequence of the first, was the modification of the
climate, with mild conditions being replaced by colder ones. A third tendency, which Brocchi did not explicitly connect with the other two, was
the progressive weakening of the chemical forces that produced the rocks.
As stratigraphic research was then revealing, there had to be some connection between these tendencies of the history of the earth and the succession of living forms that inhabited it, including the extinction of some
species. But how were the history of the earth and the history of life in-

terlinked? It was in the attempt to answer this question that Brocchi, going "from conjecture to conjecture," was led, as he himself confessed, to a point where "one further step might have made [him] lose [his] way."[62] This was not a risk to deter a geologist who, though very rigorous in his fieldwork, protested that he could not "remain a cool spectator in the theater of Nature."[63]

INDIVIDUAL AND SPECIES: PARALLEL HISTORIES

As some of his early scientific publications and unpublished notebooks reveal, Brocchi had been trained within an eighteenth-century natural history tradition that emphasized empirical research and exercised a calculated restraint toward theories and "systems." One of Brocchi's reference points had been the work of Lazzaro Spallanzani. Some of Brocchi's research on the generation of the microscopic animals observed in infusions was like a continuation, within a new intellectual climate, of Spallanzani's research on spontaneous generation in the 1760s.[64] Brocchi's attitude toward theories and hypotheses, however, was profoundly different from that of the eighteenth-century tradition, and from Spallanzani's legacy in particular. The introduction to *Conchiologia* contained a resounding denunciation of that earlier tradition's abstention from all hypotheses. It was no accident that Brocchi's courageous reaffirmation of the role of hypotheses and "systems" in natural sciences coincided, in 1814, with the enunciation of an original proposal for a solution to the species problem. He declared in *Conchiologia* that

> Nothing is more familiar than complaints against systems, and all the commonplaces that accompany such complaints . . . ; likewise, many allow themselves to be overly swayed by these principles, and when declaiming against the abuse of hypotheses, seem to be ignorant of their use.
> As for myself, I hold . . . that without geological systems, what we know about the structure of the globe would boil down to very little, and that we owe a considerable debt to these variously ingenious theories, as long as they are not merely ideal and speculative, for the knowledge that constitutes the true assets of science.[65]

Brocchi most surely considered his hypothesis on the extinction of species one of those "variously ingenious theories." He had first formulated it, without much emphasis, in his *Trattato mineralogico* (Mineralogical treatise), published in Brescia in 1807.[66] Some pages of this work were devoted to a discussion of the large "horns of Amon" that had been found in fossil form on the mountains of Val Trompia. No shells of this kind, or any as large, were still to be found in the seas of the day. Brocchi proposed to explain their progressive reduction in size and eventual extinction in these terms:

> A constant and general law of Nature seems to have fixed the term of their duration, and this law is still in effect.
> Species die just as individuals do. Now, when Nature has determined that the life of the individual will last for a certain period of time, varying this term to its own liking in the different kinds of animals, who would deny that it has limited the period of time on earth for species as well? And since the individual creature does not pass abruptly from the full vigor of life to death, but is gradually prepared for its end by steadily declining strength and weakening physical faculties, in like manner species slowly deteriorate and move through imperceptibly gradual degradation toward annihilation. With each generation they advance one more step toward destruction, and this final term is marked by the lack of reproductive force and the inability to develop.[67]

The discovery of live mollusks just like horns of Amon only smaller, microscopic nautiluses found by Giovanni Bianchi on the Adriatic beach at Rimini, led Brocchi to think that this kind of nautilus would soon disappear from the "list of beings" (fig. 1).[68] By analogy he surmised that many other species that had been described by early naturalists, but that were no longer observed, were actually extinct. Similarly, other animals described by the naturalists of his day would be sought in vain by scientists in the future.

What in 1807 was a vague conjecture, inserted incidentally into a mineralogical treatise, became one of the central themes of *Conchiologia* seven years later. According to a contemporary who happened to hear him speak of it, Brocchi was thinking of devoting a whole book to the subject of species, but it was never written.[69] Therefore, Brocchi developed his hypotheses on species in *Conchiologia* better than in any other work.

"Without presuming to judge Nature's conduct in the creation of living creatures," he wrote in the introduction, "I seem to have sufficient evidence to venture to say that species perish just like individuals, and that they are destined to make their appearance for a definite period of time."[70] In spite of the caution Brocchi showed here regarding the "creation" of species, in the book itself he furnished some indications concerning the introduction of species as well as their extinction. The individual-species analogy, central to Brocchi's hypothesis, clearly referred to the possibility that just as both naturally "die," so both are naturally "born."

According to Brocchi, recent studies on fossils bore out the hypothesis that in the history of life plants appeared first, followed by herbivorous animals and then by carnivores and human beings. This hypothesis had already been formulated by Linnaeus and was considered compatible with the Biblical account of creation.[71] Brocchi enhanced it with more detailed calculations of the time required after the withdrawal of the seas for the

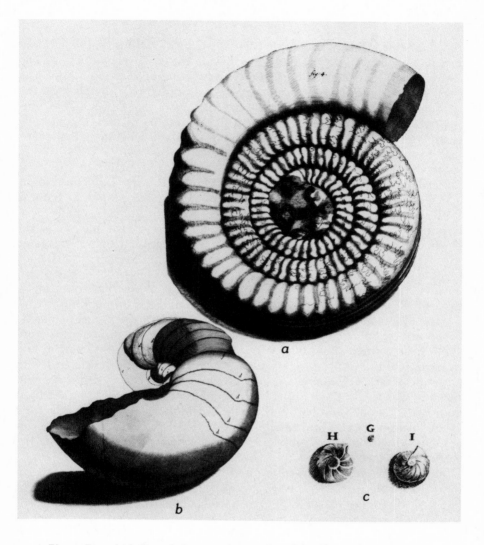

Fig. 1. Brocchi believed that species aged and finally expired, just like individuals. This process implied, inter alia, the progressive decrease in size of the species. He thought that the present descendants of the large fossil ammonites (*a*, actual diameter approx. 45 cm) were the tiny shells found by Giovanni Bianchi on the beach in Rimini, on the Adriatic Sea, in the eighteenth century (*c*, detail *G*, actual diameter approx. 3 mm; *H* and *I* show the two sides of the shell observed by Bianchi under the microscope). Subsequently Brocchi found it more likely that the present descendants of ammonites were the nautiluses of the kind illustrated in *b*.

Figures *a* and *b* are from R. Hooke, *Posthumous Works* (London, 1705), a work containing a hypothesis on the fate of species that was very similar to Brocchi's; *c* comes from J. Plancus (G. Bianchi), *De conchis minus notis*, 2d ed. (Rome, 1760).

development of larger and larger plants.[72] Considerations that would now be called ecological prompted him to reason that rich vegetation was necessary for the existence of herbivores, and that herbivores would not have been able to proliferate if hunted mercilessly right from the start by carnivores: "such a combination would have been too poor a match."[73] Hence his hypothesis of the order in which living organisms had appeared on earth, but one that in any case said nothing about the *causes* that might lead to the introduction of species.

In the search for causes, Brocchi treated the introduction of species in far less detail than their extinction, in spite of the fact that his individual-species analogy suggested that *both* phenomena were altogether natural. With respect to the causes of extinction, Brocchi formulated some precise hypotheses that seemed consistent with his ideas on the history of the earth. Extinction was prepared for by a gradual process of "aging," revealed through the progressive decrease in the size of the species, and it took place with the failure of the "prolific power."[74] This process had many affinities with the gradual weakening of chemical forces that, according to Brocchi, characterized the history of the earth and the formation of rocks.

The points in favor of a possible natural "birth" of species were instead based not on any particular hypothesis but on reference to a general conception of nature. "Nothing on our globe exists in a permanent state," Brocchi noted, and "Nature keeps active with a perpetual cycle and with an endless series of changes." Observation of "the construction of organized bodies" shows that individuals of different species are assigned their own particular size and life span: in producing them, Nature "is governed by calculations of size and time." It therefore seems natural that "species are created with the provision that each must make its appearance on the earth for a particular interval of time."[75]

Conchiologia makes no further mention of the natural causes that might have been able to cause species to "appear" on earth. Nor was Brocchi inclined to employ reasoning derived from religion, convinced as he was that it was inopportune to "mix revealed truth with men's systems, or dogmas of faith with hypotheses subject to examination and discussion."[76]

Yet he tended to rule out that the sequence of different species in the history of the earth was the result of a *transformation* of species, as Lamarck had claimed, although he expressed himself cautiously on this point. Discussing the "decay" that heralded extinction of a species, he admitted that it could produce changes in the "organs essential to vitality and propagation"; but he denied that the whole organism could undergo "a change of structure, [as] this would be a true metamorphosis."[77] This was the declaration against transformism with which Brocchi concluded the chapter on species and theoretical part of *Conchiologia*.

There should be no further doubt at this point that for Brocchi the dynamic conception of the history of the earth and the observation that different species had inhabited it in different ages did *not* signify the adoption of a transformist and evolutionary perspective. The history of the earth and the history of life were indubitably interrelated; the earth's surface had undergone repeated changes, and different species had appeared in different ages. Some of them had become extinct, as had happened in recent times to the large, flightless bird called *Didus ineptus*, or dodo; others would soon disappear, as was indicated by various signs of decline. Decadence of the species brought about changes in the reproductive organs. Brocchi might very well claim that "nothing is in a state of permanence on our globe," but for all that, he would not admit that a single species had been able to change to the point of giving rise to a different species. The broad dynamic conception of the history of the earth and the living world outlined in *Conchiologia* led to no hypothesis of the transformation of species.

This position, which to post-Darwinian eyes may seem paradoxical, was fairly widespread at the beginning of the nineteenth century. Georges Cuvier, writing on the "revolutions" of the globe and on fossil remains, had adopted a similar position. The radical changes in the earth's surface and in climates, the established presence of different species in different geological eras, and the extinction of some of them had not induced Cuvier to adopt transformist positions. Various important aspects, however, set Brocchi's position apart from Cuvier's. His criticisms of Cuvier, which were explicit, unlike his criticisms of Lamarck, clearly revealed how original his ideas were; this originality was largely related to the individual-species analogy.

Brocchi particularly criticized the way in which Cuvier had tried to account for the extinction of species. Cuvier had hypothesized that marine species whose remains were found in the oldest geological strata had become extinct because the sea water in which they lived had acquired properties that were incompatible with their survival.[78] Brocchi found this hypothesis of Cuvier's as untenable as the one, also partly endorsed by Cuvier, according to which the extinction of some species had been caused by great geological catastrophes. What Brocchi rejected in such explanations was the appeal, as he put it, to "accidental and extrinsic causes for the explanation of a fact that can be considered to depend on a general and constant law."[79] We have already seen Brocchi's aversion to "catastrophism" as a strategy for explaining geological phenomena. He appears to have found it even less satisfactory for explaining the living world. This was in view of the peculiar regularities living organisms displayed, on account of the "calculations of size and time" that Nature had, according to Brocchi, followed in creating them. He found events of the physical environment "accidental and extrinsic" to such regularities. This may have been one of the reasons why, in the explanation of the succession of species in the history of the earth, he preferred the model offered by the individual-species analogy. This analogy was not new in the history of scientific thought. In any case, thanks to Brocchi, it exerted a significant role in subsequent developments in the species problem and in evolutionary

thought. It is therefore worth investigating the historical roots of the individual-species analogy, as well as its subsequent reception.

ORIGINS AND AMBIGUITY OF THE
INDIVIDUAL-SPECIES ANALOGY

Brocchi's approach to the problem of extinction in part went back to speculations proposed by Buffon in the latter half of the eighteenth century. In
Les époques de la nature (The epochs of nature) Buffon had connected the
decrease in size of some species with the general process of "degeneration"
that he thought they were subject to, and he had associated such phenomena with the idea of a gradual cooling of the earth.[80] In Brocchi are
found, on the subject of extinction, the themes of both the diminishing
size of species and their "degeneration," in the form of dwindling reproductive capability, paralleling the decrease in chemical forces in the mineral
kingdom. The affinity between Buffon's and Brocchi's strategies for dealing
with the issue of extinction, however, does not extend to the individual-
species analogy adopted by Brocchi: as far I know, Buffon drew no such
analogy.

An author who definitely did inspire Brocchi in his thinking regarding
size and life span in individuals of different species was instead Friedrich
Blumenbach. In his widely read manual of natural history[81] Blumenbach
had emphasized the regularity displayed by living organisms in like phenomena: each species, he said, had its own life span and size, even though
these were not reached by all individuals. From this Brocchi deduced, after
Buffon, that Nature seemed more prone to "corrupt" its works than to
improve them.[82] Blumenbach admitted that some species had become extinct; and yet not even he made the connection, endorsed by Brocchi,
between the fate of individuals and that of species.

Actually, that analogy could be found in the writings of an author long
predating both Blumenbach and Buffon, Robert Hooke. In one of his works,
published posthumously in 1705, Hooke had formulated an individual-
species analogy, in a context apparently similar to Brocchi's:

> we do find that all individuals are made of such a Constitution, as that be-
> ginning from an Atom, as it were, they are for a certain period of Time in-
> creasing and growing, and from thence begin to decay, and at last Die and
> Corrupt. . . . And we see that there are many changings both within and
> without the Body, and every state produces a new appearance, why then may
> there not be the same progression of the Species from its first Creation to its
> final termination? Or why should the supposition of this be any more a de-
> rogation to the Perfection of the Creator, than the other?[83]

It is impossible to say whether Brocchi knew this text of Hooke's; he
does not mention any of the sources on which he might have drawn for

the individual-species analogy. There is no reference to the subject even in that precious collection of his manuscript notes, ordered according to broad topics, *Zibaldone di storia naturale*, in which Brocchi recorded his readings. In trying to discover what these sources might have been, we must therefore turn on the one hand to the rather vague allusions in *Conchiologia*, and on the other to the complex panorama of natural history, philosophy, and medicine that characterized the intellectual milieu of the Kingdom of Italy, particularly in Milan, where Brocchi was active during the Napoleonic age.

Among the images of nature used by Brocchi in *Conchiologia* in his thoughts on species, one that particularly strikes the historian of ideas is that "Nature remains active with a perpetual circle and a perennial succession of changes."[84] Granted, no sooner does Brocchi use this image than he terms it one of those "vague and general axioms" that are not particularly useful to the naturalist. Nevertheless, that image, especially as it refers to the living world, went back to a tradition that enjoyed, during the seventeenth and eighteenth centuries, a considerable, albeit controversial, success in European scientific culture.

In its original form the image of a "circle" of nature dated back to Renaissance natural history and Paracelsus, but in the eighteenth century it had found a new adherent in the physician and chemist Georg Ernst Stahl, whose fame had not died out by the end of the century. It is known that in November 1800 Brocchi, finding himself in the field of the French troops after the Battle of Marengo, had devoted himself to summarizing and reflecting on many of Stahl's writings.[85] In *Conchiologia*, on the other hand, he repeatedly criticized the tradition that accounted for biological phenomena in terms of "plastic forces" or a "vital principle," as Stahl had done.[86] In his early notes on Stahl, however, Brocchi had lingered on some aspects of that "vital principle" that Stahl employed to explain both the general phenomenon of life and its duration in individuals. This is how Stahl-Brocchi dealt with the problem:

> We must therefore begin the discussion by asking why the active Principle that impedes corruption, which is constantly intent on restoring and repairing the organs for such a long time, should cease to carry out its usual functions and leave the machine, leading to natural death. This question is totally insoluble, since we have no way of understanding how the term of activity of that Principle is fixed in such a manner. It would seem that since it was able to sustain the body for thirty, fifty, or one hundred years, it should be able to do so for an unlimited period of time. . . . However, the activity of that Principle not only is generally thus circumscribed, but it also seems that it can release its energies only serially, and within a certain period of time.[87]

Here the idea of a time-limited regulation of the animal "machine" was applied to the individual and to successive generations of the same species, human beings. But in Stahl, Brocchi also found reformulations of the Renaissance analogy between microcosm and macrocosm that were suggestive for the individual-species parallel. One of Stahl's writings summarized by Brocchi dealt with the problem of the movement of blood within the human body, drawing an analogy with the phenomenon of tides. As Stahl intended it, the analogy took the image of regularity, in duration and cyclicity, typical of that physical phenomenon, extending it to living organisms.[88]

Besides thoughts on the duration of life and the restatement of the microcosm-macrocosm theme, Brocchi may have found in Stahl suggestions for the idea of a "circle" of nature, maintained "with a perennial series of changes," which he mentioned in *Conchiologia*. Using various of Stahl's texts, Brocchi had written a manuscript, *Saggio sopra il flogisto* (Essay on phlogiston), which may date back to the same period as the notes on the "vital principle" mentioned above.[89] Phlogiston was the hypothetical element employed by chemists to account for the phenomena of heat and combustion prior to the introduction of the concept of oxygen. In his Stahlian essay Brocchi wrote, "Phlogiston, which exists . . . in all three of the kingdoms of Nature, migrates from kingdom to kingdom, and from body to body. From the vegetable kingdom it passes to the animal kingdom, and from the vegetable and animal kingdoms it passes to minerals."[90] The presumed circulation of phlogiston could therefore be presented as a manifestation of the "circle" of nature.

In assigning the proper weight to the notions that Brocchi could have borrowed from Stahl, it should be underlined that in any case Brocchi seemed interested in arranging them within a new, quantitative framework, hence the insistence on the "calculations of the size and time" that nature observed in regulating the succession of both individuals and species.[91] It is not surprising, on the other hand, given the situation of biological sciences of the day, that he was not able to carry the quantitative side of his conjecture very far.

Another source of the individual-species analogy may have been Diderot. Among the "Questions" posed at the end of his *Pensées sur l'interpretation de la nature* (Thoughts on the interpretation of nature), Diderot formulated the following query: "De même que dans les règnes animal et végétal, un individue commence, pur ainsi dire, s'accroît, dure, dépérit et passe; n'en serait-il pas de même des espèces entières?"[92] This conjecture, which Diderot had pointed to as probably erroneous and contrary to religion, may in turn have stimulated Lacépède, a follower of Buffon. In his "Discours sur la durée des espèces" (Discourse on the life span of species) prefacing the second volume of his *Histoire naturelle des poissons* (Natural history of fishes), Lacépède again took up the individual-species analogy. This work of Lacépède's may also have been known to Brocchi. Yet there are substantial differences between the two in the way the species problem is understood. For Lacépède the notion of species was an eminently conventional one: only individuals had real existence in nature. Brocchi instead did not doubt the reality of species: if anything, he was inclined to view each species as a single large individual. Moreover, Lacépède regarded *climate* as the cause that determined the fate of species, while Brocchi looked for this cause exclusively *within* the organism.[93]

Consideration of the cultural milieu in which Brocchi worked suggests other possible sources for his thoughts on the species problem and the individual-species analogy. An idea of the range of scientific and philosophical themes current in Milan in the early nineteenth century in circles close to Brocchi can be had from a curious work that came out in 1805, by Giuseppe Gautieri,[94] a physician with a vast philosophical culture and, like Brocchi, involved in the legislative bodies of the Kingdom of Italy. Although Brocchi makes no explicit mention of this work in his writings, he corresponded with Gautieri.[95]

"Nature is nothing but one large organism" was one of the mottos with which Gautieri had prefaced his book entitled *Slancio sulla genealogia della terra e sulla costruzione dinamica della organizzazione* (Outpouring on the genealogy of the earth and on the dynamic construction of its organization; hereafter *Slancio*). The work had been printed in Jena, Saxony, and was dedicated to "the founder of natural philosophy, the immortal Schelling." The scientific and philosophical literature that Gautieri made use of, often all too superficially, was more eclectic than that dedication to the founder of German *Naturphilosophie* might lead one to suppose. Gautieri set out to illustrate some very general ideas of the day regarding the progressive development of nature from inorganic to organic, from the formation of the earth to the introduction of human beings.

On the origins of life from water and the subsequent formation of plants and animals, he used eighteenth-century sources, such as *Telliamed*, by the protoevolutionist Benoît de Maillet.[96] On the changes that the inorganic world was thought to have produced in living creatures, the recognized authority was the physician and *idéologue*-philosopher P. J. G. Cabanis.[97] For ideas on the succession of species in the history of the earth, a cherished reference point was the works of the British physician Erasmus Darwin,[98] the author he quoted most frequently. Some of Erasmus Darwin's works had, in fact, been promptly translated in Milan by another famous and controversial physician of the day, Giovanni Rasori.[99] Gautieri invoked, instead, the authority of Franz Joseph Gall and the phrenologists[100] when arguing that the continual use of a person's intellectual faculties produced an increase in the size of the human brain. On the relations between the anatomy of monkeys and that of human beings, Gautieri cited Pietro Moscati, author in the 1770s of a widely read essay maintaining that man had originally been a quadruped.[101] Moscati headed various committees of the Kingdom of Italy in which both Brocchi and Gautieri were active.

The main theme of Gautieri's *Slancio* was Schelling's idea that the natural order of things always proceeded from "synthesis" to "analysis." Gautieri felt the idea could explain, for instance, why in the history of the earth, plants appeared first and then animals.[102] By this line of reasoning he arrived at declarations of faith in the transformation of species that were rather explicit for the times.[103] His transformism, on the other hand, owed much to eighteenth-century evolutionists, to Erasmus Darwin, and to Schelling's natural philosophy, and apparently nothing to Lamarck, whose first transformist writings had appeared only a few years earlier.

It would have been very difficult for Brocchi, with his analytical and empirical mind, to have been converted to transformism by a work such as Gautieri's. Nevertheless, the book may have furnished Brocchi with some elements of his views on species. The conception of nature as one large organism, the basic premise of Gautieri's book, was the most recent version, after Stahl's speculations, of the microcosm-macrocosm analogy. A few years later, the zoologist Lorenz Oken would systematically apply that analogy in his new classification of organisms.[104] Gautieri, moreover, approximated Brocchi's conjectures on the fate of species when he observed that "it is the wisdom of Nature to set the time of the appearance of all beings."[105] It goes without saying that in Gautieri's work these vague suggestions owed very little to the recent developments of geology and paleontology; nor was the treatment they received there in any way as systematic as in Brocchi's *Conchiologia*.

Brocchi's analogy between individual development and the history of the species could perhaps be connected more directly with another theme developed in the context of natural philosophy in Germany. This is the theory that, after Ernst Haeckel's much later reformulations, took the name of the theory of recapitulation, according to which the individual development of an organism (ontogenesis) retraces the evolutionary history of the species (phylogenesis) to which the organism belongs. In its most general form this theory had already been proposed by Kielmeyer in 1793 in a renowned lecture.[106] It suggested a parallelism, and a point-by-point correspondence, between individual development and the history of the species, hence the importance of the study of the development of the embryo as a model for both processes.

What seems to rule out the possibility that Kielmeyer may have influenced Brocchi is the fact that Brocchi never used embryology to illustrate his individual-species analogy. He confined himself to speaking of the "appearance," "old age," and "death" of species, whereas he was not interested in the point-by-point comparison between individual development and the history of life on earth that was the keynote of the first drafts of the theory of recapitulation. As has been seen, Brocchi emphatically denied that the parallelism he postulated involved a "metamorphosis" of species comparable to that produced in the development of some organisms.[107] The example of the metamorphosis of the butterfly, in its passage from the larval to the adult state, was a favorite topic for those exponents of German natural philosophy who adopted some form of the theory of recapitulation and who believed in the transformation of species; but in *Conchiologia* Brocchi did not, as we know, take this last hypothesis into serious consideration. This may also explain why he did not develop the analogy between species and individuals beyond recognizing the regularities in size and time common to both: within those limits, the analogy did *not* involve the uncertain speculations on the "metamorphosis" of species.

The reasons why Kielmeyer's influence on Brocchi was probably very limited also explain why Brocchi was not influenced by an older model that otherwise might have inspired him. As Arthur Lovejoy and more recently Stephen Jay Gould[108] have shown, in the eighteenth century the Genevan naturalist Charles Bonnet had in his *Palingénésis philosophique* (Philosophical palingenesis) drafted a particular version of the theory of recapitulation.[109] Brocchi knew that work well: *Zibaldone* tells us that he had reflected at length on the eighteenth-century idea of a "Chain of Beings," of which Bonnet was a tireless proponent.[110] According to that conception, living beings, if ordered according to degree of complexity, formed a continuous series. In *Palingénésis* Bonnet argued that the stages passed through by any individual in its embryological development informed us about the organisms that once had inhabited the earth, just as they could throw light on the more perfect ones that would inhabit it in the future. For Bonnet the development of forms of life on earth was already encompassed in the initial creation and did not involve a true transformation of species. This was consistent with the hypothesis of preformationism, according to which God had included in the first germs of each species the germs of all future generations.

At the beginning of the nineteenth century, Brocchi had various reasons for not making use of these ideas of Bonnet's. The ascertained fact of the extinction of some species seemed difficult to reconcile with the eighteenth-century image of a "Chain of Beings," as Blumenbach and Cuvier had already pointed out. The extinction of one species, Blumenbach argued, would necessarily eliminate a link in the chain, with the result that "creation would find itself, so to speak, obstructed in its march,"[111] an outcome that the chain's formulators, Bonnet and other naturalists, would have found unacceptable. Brocchi, who in his hypotheses on species started precisely from the phenomenon of extinction, must have noted the incompatibility of extinction and the chain of beings, an image rarely employed in his writing. Moreover, as emerges throughout *Conchiologia*, he was not interested in the blend of scientific hypotheses and theological arguments that were instead typical of Bonnet's work.

Thus Brocchi had good reasons for not referring explicitly to the sources from which he had probably taken the individual-species analogy: he did not fully identify with any of the traditions of thought that are likely to have inspired him. He was set apart from eighteenth-century vitalism and from Stahl by the methodological convictions repeatedly asserted in the historic introduction to *Conchiologia*. The boldest speculations of some ad-

herents of German natural philosophy were certainly remote from the inclinations of the empirical researcher whom we have seen at work on his
geological journeys. As for Bonnet's legacy of "preformationism," it by
then must have seemed incompatible with recent scientific developments
such as the ascertained extinction of some species, the decline of the concept of the chain of beings, and natural history's increasing independence
of natural theology. And still, possibly because he had no chance to carry
out his plan to develop his ideas on species more fully, Brocchi's exposition
in *Conchiologia* owed something to all three of these traditions.

A LAMARCKIAN EXPERIMENT?

In the last two sections we analyzed Brocchi's solution to the species problem and surveyed the ideas that probably inspired him. As we saw, he
contrasted certain essential aspects of his own solution with the one that
Georges Cuvier had proposed not long before. It remains to be seen why
Brocchi did not seriously consider the solution to the species problem suggested at about the same time by Lamarck.

It is quite likely that when Brocchi wrote *Conchiologia* he knew of Lamarck's evolutionary theory. Although his explicit allusions in this regard
may be inconclusive, examination of the sources he employed to write his
book leaves little doubt. While Brocchi adopted Linnaeus's classification in
cataloguing Italian shells, he also recognized Lamarck's important merits
in that area of study. When compiling his own catalogue, Brocchi had to
examine Lamarck's *Système des animaux sans vertèbres*[112] (System of the invertebrates) point by point. Lamarck had prefaced this work with the introductory lecture to his course held at the Muséum d'histoire naturelle in
Paris, where he had expounded some of his evolutionary ideas for the first
time. In 1809 Lamarck's *Philosophie zoologique* (Zoological philosophy)[113] had
furnished a systematic account of his transformist ideas. Although Brocchi
never mentions this work, he was likely to have been aware of it between
1812 and 1814, while he was working on *Conchiologia*. Furthermore, he
knew and respected Lamarck's "uniformitarian" approach in geology and
his aversion to the arbitrary introduction of "revolutions" to account for
geological phenomena.[114]

On the other hand, Brocchi did not share Lamarck's reluctance to admit
that any species had become extinct, and that reluctance was one of the
motives that had induced Lamarck to consider the hypothesis of a transformation of species.[115] Brocchi, moreover, as we have seen, was more
cautious in accepting eighteenth-century ideas on the chain of beings and
the "march of nature," which were instead so important for Lamarck's
theory. Brocchi's attitude toward the action the environment can exert on
organisms was also different: we know from his criticism of the causes of
extinction adopted by Cuvier that he opposed appealing to "accidental and
extrinsic" causes to account for the succession of species. The early for-

mulations of Lamarck's ideas that Brocchi might have known of in 1814 assigned a key role in the transformation of organisms to the environment.[116]

Comparison of Cuvier's and Lamarck's positions can thus further clarify Brocchi's particular view of the species problem. Not only did Brocchi refrain from adopting a transformist solution, he rejected any possibility that the history of the earth might have determined the events in the history of life, as Cuvier conceded at least for the extinction of species. Thus for Brocchi the successive introduction and death of species was a process completely *within* the living world: *he proposed a history of life without evolution, in which the succession of species was essentially independent of the history of the earth.* This was the solution to the species problem delineated by Brocchi in *Conchiologia*, and it remained the reference point for those who, like Charles Lyell and Charles Darwin, would later consider Brocchi's ideas. He did, however, deal with the problem again in a later work. These later views on species seem to indicate Brocchi's growing interest in some of Lamarck's hypotheses that he had disregarded in *Conchiologia*. Although cautiously noting the "entirely hypothetical" nature of his own new ideas, in 1822 Brocchi thought he might be able to set up an experiment to verify a case in which the environment seemed to have modified an individual animal, and perhaps even its species.

The occasion was provided by an excursion to the Adelsberg caverns, during which he had the opportunity to examine the peculiar fauna that inhabited them.[117] As had been known for some time, a very unusual animal, the proteus (fig. 2), lived in one of these caverns. Brocchi described some of its odd features: "its skin is similar to human skin in color, it has the form of a lizard and breathes through gills like a fish, and it lacks visible eyes."[118] The animal had, of course, already attracted the attention of naturalists interested in new links in the chain of being and the environment's action on organisms. In *Philosophie zoologique* Lamarck had cited the proteus, with its atrophied eyes, as an example of permanent effects produced by "disuse" of an organ, by which an animal living in a dark cavern became sightless.[119] The effects of use and disuse of organs were a central point of Lamarck's theory of evolution.

Two Italian naturalists, Pietro Configliachi and Mauro Rusconi, had devoted a detailed monograph to the proteus a few years before Brocchi took an interest in it.[120] They made no mention of Lamarck's hypothesis regarding the proteus's atrophied eyes, but they enlarged upon the description of the animal's rudimentary organs, the two "small bladders" that resembled lungs but did not work like lungs, since the proteus, throughout its lifetime, continued to breathe through gills, which it also possessed; and "if taken out of water, it died exactly as if it were a fish."[121] These features might suggest that the proteus was a salamander larva unable to reach the adult stage. Yet while maintaining this apparent larval state, it was able to reproduce: Configliachi and Rusconi deduced from this that it

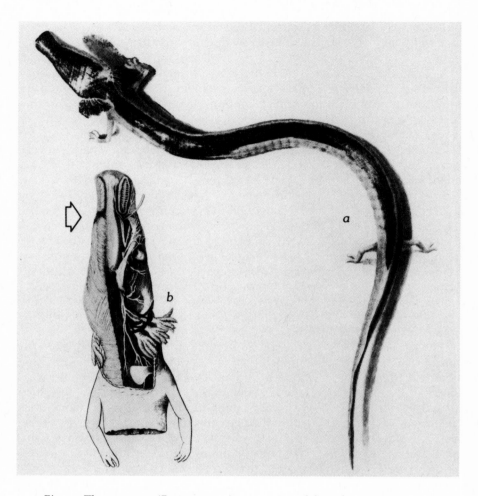

Fig. 2. The proteus (*Proteus anguineus; a*, actual length 20–30 cm), a representative of cave fauna, with rudimentary eyes (*b*, arrow; detail of the head prepared for anatomical observation). The proteus had attracted Lamarck's attention as a possible example of the hereditary effects produced by living habits: he thought that life in dark caverns had produced a progressive loss of vision in the proteus (Lamarck, *Philosophie zoologique* [Paris, 1809], 1, 242). Brocchi conceived of an experiment in 1822 for finding out whether the proteus, instead of being a separate species, might not actually be a salamander larva incapable of reaching the adult state because of unfavorable environmental conditions. In the *Origin of Species* (1859:139), Darwin included the proteus among the organisms that, in spite of the adverse effects of disuse of the organ of sight, had survived because they found themselves in an environment with few rivals, and were now like "relics of primordial life."

The figures are from P. Configliachi and M. Rusconi, *Del proteo anguino* (Pavia, 1819).

was "a perfect animal," and not a larva.[122] They summed up the proteus's peculiarity in these terms: it was a reptile (Amphibia, the salamander's present class, had no place in naturalists' classification at that time), which breathed by making use of "air mixed with water" instead of atmospheric air like other reptiles. Leaving the problem of the presence of the rudimentary organs unsolved, the two authors simply noted that "if it were still legitimate today to return to the inadmissible ideas of the chain of beings, the proteus would be the link uniting reptiles with fish."[123]

In 1822 Brocchi wanted to press his line of reasoning beyond the point at which Configliachi and Rusconi had decided to stop. The proteus's rudimentary organs led him to pose a series of questions:

> Is it so implausible that the proteus might be the larva of some animal of the same genus as the salamander, living in water and breathing through gills, like the larvae of ordinary salamanders? Could it not be conjectured that this larva, hatched in the dark and condemned to live in the dark, was unable to complete its metamorphosis, lacking the action of the light, which has such a great influence on organized beings? And then, as the animal grows and matures in such a state, could it not necessarily follow that the gills, though predestined to perform a temporary function in the circulation, in that emergency become permanent . . . ? So, as proof of how important the lack of the stimulus of the light is in suppressing the development of some organs in these larvae, or supposed larvae, we could point to the example of those two embryonic, or at least very deficient, eyes that remain hidden under the skin. Should we then believe that the proteus was given these eyes and these lungs for them to remain permanently in such a state, or rather that this must be due to accidental and particular circumstances?[124]

Brocchi had begun seriously considering the action on organisms of those "accidental and extrinsic" causes that he had rejected when, in *Conchiologia*, he had dealt with the problem of the extinction of species. He now even thought that the effectiveness of these causes should be verified *with an experiment*, and not simply explained in terms of the supposed "laws of Nature that we often want to generalize on the basis of our prejudices and our ignorance." To find out how things actually stood, Brocchi now argued, "one should carry out experiments raising salamander larvae in the dark at a temperature approximating that of the Adelsberg caverns, and see what happens."[125] Apparently Brocchi now thought it possible that under such environmental conditions, common salamander larvae might, during their lifetime, acquire the attributes of proteuses.

Would these features then be inherited by later generations of the animal? Brocchi does not say, and his insistence on the fact that every proteus was born as a *salamander* larva indicates that he did not credit that possibility. His hypothesized experiment on the proteus therefore cannot be considered "Lamarckian," but Brocchi had definitely become more willing than in the past to concede the important role of the environment and the "plasticity" of animals with respect to it.

There is no evidence that Brocchi took his research on the subject any further. The article on the Adelsberg caverns is one of the last to be published before he left for Egypt and Nubia, engaged as a mining expert by the viceroy of Egypt, on a trip from which he would not return.[126] Brocchi's contribution to the development of the species problem thus rests primarily on *Conchiologia*, and it is the European reception of this work as it relates to the debate on species that will be dealt with now.

A COGNITIVE STRATEGY AND ITS VARIATIONS: BROCCHI, LYELL, AND DARWIN

A reading of *Conchiologia* reveals that the Milan of the last years of the Napoleonic age was very receptive to the ideas developing in the major European scientific centers. Contacts with Paris were particularly intense, as was natural for the capital of a state that was within the French orbit. Although Brocchi was one of the rather few scientists of his day who did not go to Paris, he was kept in active contact with intellectual circles there through the naturalist G. Marzari-Pencati of Vicenza, who regularly sent him books and scientific materials from Paris, and later through his former pupil Alberto Parolini.[127]

To judge from the European success of *Conchiologia*, even after the restoration of Austrian power following the Congress of Vienna in 1815, Milan and Lombardy maintained solid relations with European scientific circles. In Brocchi's case it was now England that was particularly receptive and generous in its recognition of his work. In 1816 he met the geologists George B. Greenough and William Buckland on their travels in Italy and gave Buckland a copy of his recently published book.[128] In the same year Augustus Bozzi-Granville, a physician and naturalist of Italian origin who lived in England, informed Brocchi that Brocchi had been elected a foreign member of the London Geological Society.[129] That was also the year that a long review of *Conchiologia* appeared in the prestigious *Edinburgh Review*.

The author of the review was Leonard Horner,[130] a member of the Geological Society who was very active in London scientific circles. In presenting Brocchi's work, Horner took into account what he felt was the orientation of the British scientific community. He noted with satisfaction Brocchi's defense of theoretical reflections in geology, which he felt was opportune at a time when the geologist was too often invited to limit himself to mere descriptions of the facts: "Theory," Horner insisted, "is the main goal of every geological research."[131] And yet he found it expedient to restrict his own exposition for the English audience to the "questions of fact" in *Conchiologia*.

Horner was well aware of the great importance that Brocchi's analytical description of tertiary terrains had for the geology of the whole European continent. The comparisons between the tertiary formations of the Italian peninsula and those of France and Great Britain naturally attracted his attention. These comparisons, which, as we have seen, revealed considerable differences in the relationships between living and fossil fauna found by Brocchi in Italy and by Lamarck around Paris, offered Horner the occasion to cast a few aspersions on Lamarck's work. Horner's endorsement of Brocchi's preference for Linnaeus's system of classification over the more recent ones formulated by Lamarck and the French conchologists had, apparently, a similar aim.[132] Horner was evidently also reassured by Brocchi's resolute stand against the existence of human fossil remains: he found the *recent* origin of man an "extraordinary fact, perhaps the most important ever established in the geologists' research."[133] It is well known that at that time this "fact" appeared to be a guarantee that geologists' theories would not come into conflict with religion on the question of man's origin.

Horner did *not* mention Brocchi's hypothesis on species: it was evidently not one of the "questions of fact" to which he had decided to confine himself. In any case, Horner's review and recognition by the scientific community favored the circulation of Brocchi's ideas on species in Great Britain,[134] and discussion of them by Charles Lyell, as well as their significant presence, via Lyell, in Charles Darwin's early speculations on the species problem.

The importance of Brocchi's book for Lyell's *Principles of Geology*, a significant text in the history of geology and fundamental in the prehistory of Darwin's theory of evolution, has often been noted by scholars.[135] The scientific journey that Lyell carried out in Italy in 1828–1829 was partly a result of his decision to visit the tertiary terrains described by Brocchi. Although disappointed to find no trace in Milan of the Council of Mines for which Brocchi had worked, and no one continuing his work, Lyell found expert conchologists in the Italian states willing to collaborate on his ambitious project.[136] This consisted essentially in demonstrating the principle of "actual causes," according to which remote and recent geological transformations must have been produced by causes still in operation, and not by exceptional catastrophic events. Observing important changes produced in even the most recent terrains, namely, the tertiary, was fundamental to Lyell's project.

Lyell's detailed discussion of Brocchi's hypothesis on species has attracted less attention from historians of science. Yet this discussion occupied, in *Principles*, a key position in Lyell's arguments against the idea of the transmutation of species and at the same time in favor of the notion of some general laws that might regulate their successive introduction and disappearance.[137]

Lyell took up Brocchi's ideas on species mainly to demonstrate that the causes of extinction were not to be sought in hypothetical exceptional events, as maintained by the tradition going back to Cuvier. He appreciated

Brocchi's attempt to explain extinction "through the action of regular and constant causes": within this methodological perspective, Lyell accepted Brocchi's individual-species analogy to a certain extent.[138] He disagreed instead with Brocchi's attribution of extinction to the gradual decline of the species' reproductive capabilities, a conjecture that Lyell found "merely hypothetical."[139] Once he had accepted Brocchi's methodological approach and rejected the essence of his conclusions, Lyell went on to delineate his own solution to the species problem. He considered extinction a result of the continual changes produced in the relations between different species, and between species and the physical environment; such changes could eliminate the place traditionally occupied by a certain species, causing its extinction. The tradition of eighteenth-century environmentalism, recent studies on the geographical distribution of species, and in particular the ideas of Augustin-P. de Candolle on the "war" in progress between living creatures[140] induced Lyell to adopt an explanation for the extinction of species that today would be called ecological.

Such phenomena were not unknown to Brocchi: he was familiar with eighteenth-century naturalists, particularly Linnaeus, who had laid the groundwork for the study of the geographical distribution of organisms. Brocchi did not, however, appeal to such ecological factors: he probably found distribution "accidental and extrinsic" to living beings, just as he did the changes in the physical environment. Brocchi, we know, preferred to refer to causes *within* the living world, conceived of through the individual-species analogy. But that made Brocchi's explanation of the extinction of species more speculative than Lyell's solution, which rested on evidence offered by geographical distribution. The difference emerges clearly from a comparison of the fieldwork done by the two geologists in the same areas of southern Italy. Lyell's attention to problems of geographical distribution gave him the opportunity to test various hypotheses on the "creation" and the extinction of species. Through the questions of geographical distribution, the species problem acquired a prominent place in Lyell's fieldwork in southern Italy, leading to *Principles*.[141] As we have seen, the same cannot be said for Brocchi at the time of the journeys preceding the writing of *Conchiologia*. Brocchi's explanation of extinction, resting upon causes within the organism, was less suited to being empirically tested.

Although their solutions to the problem of extinction differed, there were many resemblances between the images of the history of the living world offered by Brocchi and by Lyell. For both, because of phenomena such as extinction, "a complete change in the state of organic creation" was in progress.[142] This was occurring, according to Lyell, as for Brocchi and Cuvier, without any transformation of species taking place, in contrast with Lamarck's claim made at the beginning of the century. Like Brocchi, Lyell preferred to avoid definite statements as to "whether new species were occasionally introduced, as others were lost."[143]

The singular theoretical convergence that we find in Brocchi, Cuvier, and Lyell on the species problem was, of course, later shaken by Darwin. Darwin's theory, in fact, endeavored to account for both the extinction of species, which the transformist Lamarck refused to allow, and their transformation, which Lamarck's opponents refused to allow. Still, the new cognitive strategy conceived by Darwin had a place for Brocchi's individual-species analogy, at least in Darwin's earliest steps leading to the theory of natural selection. As David Kohn has established,[144] before adopting the theory of selection, Darwin considered and reformulated the individual-species analogy several times.

Darwin showed interest in Brocchi's analogy as early as the time of his trip around the world on the *Beagle*, before he had adopted any hypothesis involving the transmutation of species. In 1835 he was searching for a cause to explain the extinction of the large mammals that once had inhabited South America. What was known of those regions indicated that there had been no changes in the geology of the country great enough to cause the extinction of those mammals. This fact led Darwin to surmise that some cause of extinction must exist *independent* of geological events, and Lyell's discussion of Brocchi's ideas suggested a possible solution. As he then recorded in his geological notes, Darwin thought that extinction might have been produced in "the ordinary course of nature," through the "gradual birth and death of species," according to Brocchi's principle by which "species may perish as well as individuals."[145]

That Darwin gave this kind of hypothesis careful thought is confirmed by the fact that he went back to it in the scientific diary of the *Beagle* journey, published a few years later. Once again with reference to extinct South American mammals he observed there:

> On such grounds it does not seem a necessary conclusion, that the extinction of species, more than their creation, should exclusively depend on the nature (altered by physical changes) of their country. All that at present can be said with certainty, is that, as with the individual, so with the species, the hour of life has run its course, and is spent.[146]

Darwin went back to the individual-species analogy in March 1837, in a period that was crucial to his conversion to transformism. At that time he wrote that he was "tempted to believe animals were created for a definite time:—not extinguished by change of circumstances." This emphasized a certain predilection of his for Brocchi's analogy: "there is no more wonder in extinction of species than of individual."[147]

As Kohn and M. J. S. Hodge have noted, during this phase Darwin's thinking reveals more willingness than Lyell displayed to share Brocchi's idea of species' natural "aging," which Lyell had basically rejected.[148] Like Brocchi, Darwin seemed interested in seeking causes *within* the species to explain their vicissitudes in the history of the earth. For Darwin, however, unlike Brocchi, those causes had to account not only for the extinction but also for the *transmutation* of species, of the possibility of which Darwin was by then convinced. Hence Darwin's insistence on a part of the individual-species analogy, that of "birth," which Brocchi and Lyell had refrained from developing fully. According to Darwin, there could be *"generation* of *species* like generation of *individuals."*[149]

Kohn has maintained that Darwin's reworking of the individual-species analogy was concomitant and connected with his criticism of "natural theology."[150] In that tradition of theological thought, still very much alive in the early nineteenth century, especially in Britain, organisms' adaptation to their environment was believed to be perfect, as a religious conception of nature seemed to demand. The possibility that there might be causes of extinction independent of the organism-environment relationship, such as those hypothesized by Brocchi, appeared to be an alternative to that tradition and to the "creationist" solution, according to which species had been created in a state of perfect adaptation to the environment. According to another of Darwin's interpreters, Camille Limoges,[151] the critique of the idea of perfect adaptation was decisive for the very formulation of the theory of natural selection.

What has been seen in this chapter apropos of the individual-species analogy, both in Brocchi and in the sources of which he availed himself, points to a further aspect of the question. That analogy linked Darwin with a long and heterogeneous tradition that had attempted to explain some fundamental features of living beings (birth and death, life span, the size of individuals and of species) *independently* of the organism-environment relationship. It would be reductive for the historian to construe this tradition as the antithesis of the one that instead emphasized the action of the environment on organisms. The relations between the two traditions of thought were already complex and interwoven during the eighteenth century, as is shown by Buffon's work, to name just one instance. And yet Brocchi, as we have seen, defended his individual-species analogy precisely by setting it against the explanations of extinction in terms of causes "extrinsic" to the living world. And Darwin, when he declared he was "tempted to believe" in that analogy, was himself seeking an alternative to environmentalism.[152] As a strategy for resolving the problem of species, environmentalism may well have seemed inconsistent to Darwin, since it was adopted in some form both by the transformist Lamarck and by the opponents of transformism such as Cuvier and Lyell, as well as by the adherents of "natural theology."

It can therefore be said that by offering an alternative to environmentalism, reflections on the individual-species analogy contributed to the originality of Darwin's solution to the species problem, a solution in which the relationships between organism and environment were peculiarly *indirect*, though by no means as irrelevant as Brocchi had supposed in his speculations on extinction. In Darwin's solution, furthermore, the succession of species, and hence the course of evolution, were complex and unpredictable to an extent that was highly incompatible with Brocchi's analogy of the regular, "prearranged" development of the individual. For both these reasons the individual-species analogy, despite the role it had played in Darwin's early steps toward natural selection, in the end had no relevance for Darwin's theory as expounded in the *Origin of Species*.

And yet interest in Brocchi's analogy was not thereby exhausted. It was returned to when, starting from the 1870s and 1880s, natural selection and Darwin's conception of evolution began to come under fire. Then the analogy was proposed again by those who were interested in conceiving of the history of living organisms as a *necessary* process, and not essentially random, as Darwin believed. The Swiss paleontologist Oswald Heer[153] employed the individual-species analogy in his campaign in favor of a history of life determined by *causes internal to the species itself*, a dispute in which he made use of some of Carl Nägeli's and Rudolf Albert von Koelliker's arguments that converged with his own.

In Italy, too, the analogy enjoyed a new surge of popularity, though there is reason to maintain that in this new phase Brocchi's direct influence was limited, even among Italian biologists.[154] What did last, evidently, was the tradition of biological thought that has been delineated here by tracing the origins of the individual-species analogy and its development by Brocchi, a tradition that seemed to promise what Darwinism and neo-Lamarckism no longer seemed able to offer. According to Daniele Rosa, who returned to the individual-species analogy in the new context of early twentieth-century biological theories, the idea of evolution as a *necessary* process, due to causes *within* living creatures, had from Lamarck's times "continued to smolder under the ashes, awaiting only a vigorous puff to flare up and burn again."[155] For Rosa evolution was "a biological necessity as much as individual evolution"; in it "every species is predetermined in the previous one as an individual organism is in the egg."[156] According to Rosa, the *entire* evolutionary process ("hologenesis"), phylogenetic ramifications included, was predetermined, produced "as a simple consequence of life": the role of factors external to living organisms was still more limited than in Nägeli.[157] Rosa obviously did not share Brocchi's nontransformist conception and rejected his idea of the "aging" of species.[158] But the cognitive strategy adopted was abundantly convergent with Brocchi's: it, too, sought necessary biological laws and was averse to acknowledging the role of random circumstances or ones external to living organisms.[159]

Brocchi's thoughts on the extinction of species may rightly be said to occupy a crucial place in the development of nineteenth-century biological theories. With their roots in the life sciences of the previous centuries, and their Darwinian and post-Darwinian ramifications, Brocchi's ideas expressed a current of thought that was highly influential in the history of biology. It conceived of organisms as subject to necessary, internal laws that governed their development in time, their essential functions, and their size and life span. The search for laws of this kind aspired to making the science of living beings an enterprise comparable to that of physical sciences. The existence of such biological laws was deliberately postulated along the lines of what already had been established for the physical world. The tradition that expressed itself through Brocchi, on the other hand, conceived of living organisms as highly organized bodies, and for that very reason, as relatively autonomous of their physical environment: it could not allow that organisms were at the mercy of the myriad physical agents that geology was revealing to be at work in the history of the earth. Brocchi's proposal to extend to species the laws and the "calculations of size and time" that were beginning to be detected in the development of each individual organism was aimed at satisfying both these requirements. It gave reason to hope that there would soon be found, for species and for their successive appearance on and disappearance from the earth, laws as certain as those displayed in individual development, and at the same time it ensured that the living world was not subject to the "accidental" and "extrinsic" influences of the physical environment.

As its developments during the nineteenth century confirm, this conception of the living world did not necessarily entail either a transformist or a nontransformist solution to the species problem. In Brocchi, as we have seen, it was incorporated in an essentially "fixist" conception of species. Darwin, on the other hand, made use of it in key moments of his conversion to transformism, as an antidote to the vague environmentalism of the previous century and to the concept of perfect adaptation typical of natural theology. Some post-Darwinian biologists considered it compatible with an evolutionary conception of life. In any case, the tradition that expressed itself through Brocchi was opposed to the idea of the random, indeterministic evolutionary process that many late-nineteenth-century observers assumed was a fundamental tenet of Darwin's theory of natural selection. This circumstance may explain why Brocchi's old ideas enjoyed a new burst of popularity among evolutionary biologists at Darwinism's critical moment in the decades at the turn of this century. The same circumstances suggest that the appeal of Brocchi's solution to the species problem may not even yet have run its course.

Mapping the Labyrinth

The Italian Scientific Community
and the Species Problem

Between February and April 1830 the Académie des sciences in Paris was caught up in a celebrated controversy that was destined to have a symbolic role in the development of evolutionary theories and in the history of science.[1] The immediate object of the controversy was not the idea of evolution itself but a more limited issue. The two contenders, Georges Cuvier and Étienne Geoffroy Saint-Hilaire, debated some recent observations that seemed to establish analogies between the structure of fish—i.e., vertebrates—and that of cephalopods, classified at that time as invertebrates.

For the contenders and their contemporaries, however, and even more so for scientists of the Darwinian age, those analogies assumed a significance that went beyond the case under discussion. By negating the analogies, Cuvier was reiterating his conviction that there existed a few basic, unrelated patterns or types of organization of living organisms. Geoffroy, by accepting the analogies, was arguing that organisms revealed a "unity of composition," in other words, that they shared a common basic structure. In defending their respective positions, both of which were expressions of the extraordinary recent progress in comparative anatomy in France and Germany, the two contenders drew more general questions into the dispute. Proclaiming himself a staunch supporter of positive facts, Cuvier also aimed at eradicating from the domain of science Lamarck's views and those of German natural philosophy, which had recognized the possibility of species transmutation. Geoffroy, instead, defending a sometimes speculative approach to comparative anatomy, found himself more or less deliberately endorsing transformism.[2] According to some historians, the controversy of 1830, or rather the situation in natural history that it reflected, later influenced the French scientific community's attitude toward Darwin's theory. This was in fact countered in France by arguments and a conception of science similar to those Cuvier had used against Geoffroy.[3]

To understand the Italian scientific community's reactions to Darwin's theory, we also need to consider the kind of research and the images of science current there prior to the publication of the *Origin of Species* in 1859.

A good starting point for doing so is an episode having affinities with the famous Académie des sciences debate. When in February 1830 that controversy exploded, Carlo Luciano Bonaparte, a naturalist born in France and educated in Italy and the United States, who had for some time been living in Rome,[4] was concluding a blistering critique of Cuvier's latest work, the second edition of his basic treatise, *Le Règne animal* (The animal kingdom). Bonaparte's critical examination, which appeared early the following year in the most important natural history journal then published in the Italian states,[5] was a withering attack on Cuvier's scientific prestige. Bonaparte did not, however, side with Cuvier's Parisian adversaries: he did not subscribe to the "unity of composition" of living organisms, nor did he adopt any of the ideas of Lamarck or German natural philosophy upheld by Geoffroy. A comparative evaluation of the arguments used by the participants in the Parisian controversy, on the one hand, and by Bonaparte and his Italian colleagues, on the other, reveals the different traditions that in different countries, but often within the same scientific community as well, guided naturalists in the search for the best possible classification of living forms.

Since Linnaeus's day, naturalists had been engaged in the search for a "natural" classification that would identify the true relationships between species in nature and provide an "Ariadne's thread" leading through the "labyrinth" of the thousands of living forms.[6] It was Darwinian evolutionism that eventually would furnish a new solution: the theory of evolution asserted that the labyrinth of forms had been built up gradually in time, starting from a few initial species that little by little had been transformed and proliferated.[7] Thus a natural classification of present-day species could be attained by reconstructing the route followed by the evolutionary process through the ages. This solution to the classification problem was not altogether new, unlike Darwin's special theory accounting for the causes of the transmutation of species. But before 1859 scientists had delineated and discussed many other approaches to the classification problem in addition to the transformist explanation. It was by no means obvious to naturalists before Darwin that the best method for tracing a map of the labyrinth was to establish how it actually had been built up in time.

In the decades from the affirmation, at the beginning of the nineteenth century, of Cuvier's works as widely accepted guidelines for the classification of living forms, up until the turning point determined by Darwin, a large number of possible "maps" of the living world were elaborated and evaluated, and modified or rejected. This intense though often little-noted activity was a significant reference point for Darwin himself. For naturalists of his generation it represented a crucial and very delicate aspect of their daily work, as well as of the "philosophy" of natural history. It is no mere chance that in the *Origin* Darwin underscored naturalists' uncertainties in the classification of living forms as the best means of laying the groundwork for his new theory.[8] The way the different national scientific communities pursued the examination of the numerous proposals for species classification advanced in the twenty or thirty years preceding the publication of Darwin's *Origin* has not yet been studied in detail, except in the important cases of Paris and Britain.[9] During the period in question, Parisian naturalists indubitably had a leading role compared with other countries; but as we will see, their supremacy did not go unchallenged.

This chapter traces developments of the species problem within the Italian scientific community, establishing points of convergence and difference with what was happening in other countries. An examination of Carlo Luciano Bonaparte's criticisms of Cuvier is followed by a consideration of the discussions of the problem of species classification during the meetings the Italian scientists held annually from 1839 to 1847. Although Bonaparte also had an important role in those meetings, it will be chiefly interesting to observe the interaction of international, national, and individual factors in the work behind the proposal, discussion, and evaluation of the theories involved in the classification of organisms. As will be seen, reflection on these complex transactions reveals that some members of the Italian scientific community, which was taking shape at the time of those very conferences, displayed a preference for conceptions of nature that could be termed evolutionary. However, because of the wide range of scientific traditions prevalent in naturalists' circles and the lack of centers like Paris or London with the prestige to impose research programs and research styles, the Italian debate on the species problem turned out to be, above all, eclectic. On the whole, the prevailing position among Italian naturalists in the decades preceding Darwin's *Origin* can be described as a third alternative between fixism and evolutionism, a phenomenon to be kept in mind when considering the reception of Darwinism in Italy, as well as the earlier diffusion of Lamarck's ideas.

CARLO LUCIANO BONAPARTE VERSUS CUVIER: SCIENTIFIC CONTROVERSIES AND CULTURAL BOUNDARIES

Carlo Luciano Bonaparte pointed out at the beginning of his scathing criticism of Cuvier's *Règne animal* that the need for a synthesis of the knowledge accumulated in zoology was strongly felt around 1830.[10] But the expectations raised by the new edition of the *Règne animal*, the most popular work by an author whom some saw as a modern Aristotle, were not fulfilled. The criticisms Bonaparte leveled at Cuvier in his painstaking 170-page "review" were very serious and called the work into question from a number of standpoints.

To start with, there were reservations on the general criteria proposed for the classification of living forms. Cuvier had conceived of his work as a compendium of systematic and descriptive zoology, capable of ordering everything known about the entire animal kingdom.[11] The order depended in the first place on an appropriate subdivision of organisms into groups made up of similar forms; but, Bonaparte objected, some of the main groups, for example the "genera" established by Cuvier, did not satisfy current criteria for classificatory studies. Cuvier's genera were too broad, embracing very dissimilar animals.[12] Moreover, the principle of "assigning the same rank to equivalent divisions in the same kingdom"[13] had not been respected. This meant that in the case of some animals, rather minor features were deemed sufficient to distinguish one group from another, while in other cases, similar characteristics were considered inadequate for that purpose. Thus in birds Cuvier had identified and distinguished the order of Grimpeurs (climbers), whereas among mammals he had not grouped the Chéiroptères, or bats, as a separate order, although, Bonaparte observed, they "seem more important in comparison."[14] In the choice of the finer divisions of the classification system, matters were no better: "the Insectivores in mammals are divided into many genera, whereas in birds the Dentirostres (sickle-bills) are divided into subgenera, so that the subgenus turns out to be more important in the latter case than the genus in the former."[15]

One of the anomalies of Cuvier's classification that particularly struck Bonaparte was the case of human beings. What had led Cuvier to eliminate the order of Primates, where Linnaeus had placed the human species and monkeys together?[16] Surely there were no valid reasons from the standpoint of the philosophy of classification: why should two-handed "bimana" and four-handed "quadrumana" be considered two separate orders when the former order then included only one species, humans?

Cuvier had taken other apparently arbitrary steps in choosing the "transitory species," or "links" between one group of forms and another.[17] Even without subscribing to the eighteenth-century idea of a continuous series of living forms, or chain of beings, which Cuvier rejected[18] and which Bonaparte did not explicitly support, the passage from one group of forms to another—Bonaparte maintained—should avoid juxtaposing forms that were totally different. It was inappropriate, for example, to put pigeons at the end of the order of Gallinacés (gallinaceans), so that they were next to the Échassiers (waders), or cranes, storks, and woodcocks, instead of next to the Passeraux (sparrows), with whom they had much more in common.[19]

Yet another debatable aspect of Cuvier's work was, according to Bonaparte, his treatment of the geographical distribution of species. Cuvier tended to attribute a very wide distribution to the single species, often implying that the same specific form was identical all over the earth. Bonaparte instead thought it proper to distinguish, for instance, between American species and the corresponding European species. This did not depend only on Bonaparte's experience as a naturalist working on both continents. It also signified a different conception of the relationship between species and environment: it presupposed a different way of understanding the probable origin and diffusion of species on earth.[20]

Alongside these criticisms of Cuvier's philosophy of classification, Bonaparte leveled serious charges of inaccuracy. In spite of the extraordinary means that Cuvier had at his disposition in Paris—at that time the unchallenged capital of zoological studies[21]—the *Règne animal* was, according to Bonaparte, full of factual errors and omissions.[22] Given the author's great prestige and the predictable circulation of the work, Bonaparte feared that such imprecision would have lasting detrimental effects on zoology.[23] By attacking both the underlying philosophical principles of Cuvier's work and his competence, Bonaparte expressed major doubts as to the legitimacy of the prestige that Cuvier still enjoyed in 1830 in European scientific circles.[24]

But who was Carlo Luciano Bonaparte to dare to launch an even more ruthless attack than Geoffroy's against the leading authority of the time in the field of zoological studies? How could such an attack be published by a journal, the *Annali di storia naturale*, that, like other European scientific periodicals of the day, mustered naturalists who had deeply felt Cuvier's influence, when they had not actually studied with him in Paris? And finally, to what extent can it be said that Bonaparte's attack, like the contemporary Parisian controversy at the Académie des sciences, indirectly brought out the problem of evolution?

In 1830 the scientific reputation of Carlo Luciano Bonaparte, then twenty-seven, was already quite well established. It rested on a series of writings published during his stay in the United States between 1823 and 1828.[25] While participating in the work of the Philadelphia Academy of Natural Sciences, he had become one of the leading ornithologists in America, along with Alexander Wilson and John James Audubon. Bonaparte's interest in natural history went back to an earlier stay in Italy, when his father, Luciano,[26] the brother of Napoleon I, had moved to Rome during the early years of the Restoration. One of his first endeavors as a naturalist had been the compilation of a flora and fauna of the Viterbo area, north of Rome.[27] Shortly afterward he wrote an introduction to a fauna of the region around Rome, whose classification was ordered "according to Linnaeus's system, updated and amended on the basis of the most recent systems of classification."[28] The double interest in the study of local fauna, as in the tradition of amateur naturalists, and in the more philosophical aspects of classification would continue to characterize Bonaparte's research. His appreciation of the importance of geographical distribution for species' classification can be considered a consequence of this combination of interests, and his writings on geographical distribution[29] are significant in the history of an area that, through the studies of Augustin-Pyramus de Candolle, Alexander von Humboldt, and Charles Darwin, contributed decisively to seeing the species problem in a new light.[30]

Bonaparte's most important theoretical work before 1830 had been carried out while revising Wilson's *American Ornithology*.[31] The revision had prompted him to verify the principles of classification, which was generally less sophisticated in the work of the earliest American ornithologists than in that of French, British, or German naturalists. Bonaparte discerned better than many of his American and Italian colleagues the need to order the species described within a coherent system of classification. In this he approached a working style that in those years was mainly typical of French and German naturalists. But exactly how a rigorous systematic classification of living forms, reflecting their presumed natural order, might be established was as controversial a topic as one could find in zoological studies.

In this earliest phase, Bonaparte maintained that the pursuit of a natural classification should adopt as a guideline the concept of a "linear series" of organisms, in a suitably corrected version of the preceding century's conception of animal series. A number of eighteenth-century naturalists had claimed that species, when arranged according to their characteristics, would constitute a continuous, gradual series of forms, each distinguishable from the contiguous forms by minimal differences.[32] At the turn of the century the idea of a series or chain of beings had been disputed by such authoritative scientists as Blumenbach and Cuvier.[33] Other naturalists, however, were not averse to keeping the concept in a more or less modified form. Among these were Lamarck, Isidore Geoffroy Saint-Hilaire, and Henri de Blainville;[34] Bonaparte's ideas were akin to those of the last two naturalists. This is how he described some of the principles he had adopted in revising Wilson's ornithology:

> We have endeavored to dispose the species as nearly as possible in a natural series. We are, however, fully aware that organized beings cannot be arranged in a regular and continuous line, but that their relations with each other would be more accurately represented by lines radiating from different centers, uniting and crossing in various directions.
>
> Notwithstanding this general intricacy of affinities, there are, however, several genera, families, and especially orders, that will admit of a disposition in a regular series, and yet remain in strict conformity to nature. It is obvious, for instance, that the ANSERES must terminate the series of the feathered tribes (as the CETE that of the pilose), that the GRALLAE should immediately precede them (occupying the relative position of the BELLUAE), then the GALLINAE (which may be compared to PECORA), and still ascending in the natural series, we arrive at the families of the passerigalli and columbini, which form an excellent link between GALLINAE and PASSERES, and thus connect our two subclasses.[35]

Arguments such as these aptly illustrate the state of studies on the classification of organisms in 1830. The image of living nature for those who studied it from the standpoint of classification had changed since the previous century. Even those who, like Bonaparte, continued to believe in a natural series of organisms no longer conceived of it as a uniform sequence. By this time the series was not necessarily thought to connect all beings from the most complex to the simplest, as many had claimed, or from the simplest to the most complex, as the transformist Lamarck preferred to envision it. Rather, lines starting from different points intersected in various ways. The growing number of known forms and the increasingly detailed investigation of their morphology and anatomy had led naturalists to modify their strategy for seeking an order within the labyrinth of nature. But while comprehension of the general scheme of living forms seemed to many more difficult and elusive than ever, not all agreed with Cuvier that the search for a single connecting thread should be abandoned. Cuvier's caveats notwithstanding, Bonaparte continued to feel that the identification of the most appropriate "links" between the different groups of forms was an important part of the naturalist's philosophy and "craft."[36] Thus, when uncertain as to how some groups should be arranged within a class of forms, the naturalist could establish useful comparisons with groups belonging to better-known classes. This was the point of the parallel between birds and mammals drawn in the passage quoted above.

The geographical distribution of organisms, which naturally attracted the attention of a European-trained naturalist working on American species, was also the source of some of Bonaparte's reflections on the "links" connecting groups of different forms. Thus he reasoned that a certain species of vulture might represent the "transition" between a subgenus of American vultures and the corresponding European subgenus.[37]

Bonaparte had left the United States for good in the spring of 1828, taking rich zoological collections and the works of American naturalists with him to Italy, and leaving his American colleagues the European publications he could easily replace. Anxious to establish contacts with Italian scientific circles, upon his return to Europe he turned to Camillo Ranzani, who was the author of the only large-scale zoological work published in Italy in those years, and who had studied in Paris with Cuvier.[38]

The picture of Italian natural history studies that Ranzani drew for Bonaparte on this occasion was not promising. "As far I see," Ranzani wrote, "in this fine country of ours the natural sciences have few advocates who sincerely try to promote their advancement."[39] As exceptions to this grim rule, he mentioned Franco Andrea Bonelli of Turin and Giambattista Guidotti of Parma for zoology and conchology, Tommaso Antonio Catullo of Vicenza for mineralogy, Nicola Covelli and Teodoro Monticelli of Naples for geology. The overview that Ranzani sketched was impassioned and aggrieved: "I must reluctantly conclude that very little is being done for natural history in Italy, especially for zoology." The appraisal of Charles Lyell, who was traveling in Italy that same year, was less drastic, as we saw in chapter 1.[40] But the area Lyell was interested in, conchology, probably constituted a fortunate exception. Foreign scientists' estimation of the state of zoological studies apparently coincided with Ranzani's. Upon reading Ranzani's *Elementi di zoologia* (Elements of zoology), Henri de Blainville, a respected Parisian zoologist, could not disguise his amazement that such an ambitious and serious work should have come out of Italy, "which we consider so backward in zoology."[41]

After two years in Rome, Bonaparte himself had arrived at a similarly pessimistic view of the state of Italian zoology. In 1830 he tried to encourage William Swainson, a London naturalist of some repute, to visit Italy again, but his desire to bring Swainson to Italy did not induce him to misrepresent the unsatisfactory state of natural history collections and scientific societies. In the panorama Bonaparte outlined for Swainson, only the museum of natural history in Turin and the one recently created in Pisa were deemed acceptable. The museums in Florence and Bologna were deteriorating, and in Rome both the collections themselves and institutions such as the Accademia dei Lincei were in a state of woeful neglect.[42]

For approximately a year after his return to Italy, Bonaparte abandoned all natural history studies, for reasons that may well have been connected with the unfavorable situation. But in July 1829 the new edition of Cuvier's *Règne animal* arrived to "rouse him out of his lethargy." Reading that work prompted him to write some critical notes, originally in the form of a letter to Ranzani to appear in the *Annali di storia naturale*, publication of which recently had begun in Bologna under the guidance of Ranzani and others.[43] A first draft of his comments on Cuvier was ready early the next September,[44] several months, that is, before the famous Cuvier-Geoffroy debate erupted at the Paris Académie des sciences.

In addition to the reasons already mentioned, Bonaparte's private correspondence suggests others that led him to attack Cuvier, disclosing grounds that were not quite so evident in the review that eventually was published. In Bonaparte's opinion, Cuvier had made "some egregious blunders" in his treatment of American species, as a result of his having systematically underestimated the work of American naturalists.[45] In advancing these charges, Bonaparte was on the one hand vindicating his own personal competence, and on the other defending the young American scientific community against the influential Parisian naturalist. Strictly scientific considerations regarding American species were mixed with critical estimates of Cuvier's authority, judged excessive and dangerous for the development of zoology. "When Great Names slip up," Bonaparte wrote, "the greater and more widespread their prevailing authority, the greater and more widespread the harm they succeed in doing."[46]

The figure of Cuvier evoked the idea of authority for reasons that were not exclusively scientific. His extraordinary scientific prestige was matched by administrative responsibilities and political power to a degree virtually unequaled among scientists of the time.[47] Such a blend of scientific eminence and political authority was highly questionable in the eyes of Bonaparte and some of his American colleagues. Bonaparte had no qualms about suggesting that the causes of the inaccuracies in the new edition of the *Règne animal* must have included an overload of political obligations that had diverted Cuvier from his "patient attention to a long, minute work."[48] The figure of Cuvier thus took on a peculiar ambiguity. Bonaparte, vindicating the worth of a zoologist friend, Thomas Say, could therefore call him "the American Cuvier," only to specify immediately, "Cuvier for his science, not for his honors!"[49] Say himself, notified by Bonaparte of his intention to attack Cuvier, displayed his satisfaction with the way political and scientific arguments were mingled:

> So Cuvier has published a new edition of his Regne [sic] anim. And I am much pleased to hear that you have undertaken to review it, it could not fall into better hands. A man who has partially deserted N. History for the grovelling, and vulgar ambition of ministring [sic] to a stupid, and besoted [sic] bedevilled king, deserves to have evry [sic] error held up like a mirror [uncertain] in alto rilievo [in high relief; in Italian in the original] to his eye.[50]

At the time Say was at New Harmony, Indiana, taking part in Robert Owen's experimental socialist community. Bonaparte regarded this experience with interest: "New Harmony, that colony of *superhuman beings*, where the Owens, the Maclures and the Says invest their money, their science and their philanthropy."[51]

In launching his attack on Cuvier's prestige, Bonaparte could therefore count on the solidarity guaranteed for various reasons by a number of members of the American scientific community to which he had belonged until a short time before. But what was the attitude of his new colleagues, the Italian naturalists? Their support of the attack on Cuvier was less wholehearted than Bonaparte thought it should be. In tracing the causes of this lukewarm response, an important point is that few naturalists in Italy around 1830 were involved in the sort of wide-ranging, philosophical systematic zoology of which Parisian naturalists were so fond, and which Bonaparte himself to some extent espoused. An Italian naturalist such as Paolo Savi,[52] for instance, with a certain celebrity in European scientific circles, did not hide his lack of enthusiasm for the "philosophical" side of zoology. In his *Ornitologia*[53] he had deliberately opted for an artificial classification rather than a natural one. The work was primarily intended to help amateurs recognize species; it did not necessarily have to respect the presumed natural order of living forms.[54] Savi's approach to zoology was shared by other Italian scientists, both those who, like Savi, were writing for a wide audience, and those who (as was increasingly the case) were illustrating new species for their naturalist colleagues alone.[55]

There were, however, exceptions on the Italian scene, and the most significant was Ranzani's *Elementi di zoologia*,[56] mentioned above, which, not surprisingly, was largely inspired by Cuvier's *Règne animal*. Furthermore, in Ranzani's hands Cuvier's principles became singularly explicit: likes and dislikes on the scientific, philosophical, or religious level were rendered with a forthrightness often lacking in the writings of the more diplomatic Cuvier. The results were often interesting, as in the treatment of the species problem or in the discussion of transformist hypotheses.

Regarding the problem of the actual existence in nature of the groups of individuals called species, Ranzani adopted a version of the Aristotelian doctrine of essences that took into account the age-old philosophical dispute over "universals."[57] According to Ranzani, "real essences"—that is, the sets of natural characteristics that define the different zoological species— unquestionably existed in nature. However, "real essences" are known only through the "mental essences" that are made of them, and these may vary from one naturalist to another. This variability should not raise doubts as to the existence of real essences, and the fact that they are "immutable,"[58] just as one must not be misled by the numerous varieties of each species in nature, which seem to thwart naturalists' desire to distinguish clearly one form from another.

Following Cuvier's philosophy of classification, Ranzani attacked the idea of a gradual, continuous chain of beings, and he also very plainly cautioned against the tendency to use variation as evidence supporting species transmutation. As Ranzani admitted more candidly than Cuvier, the adversary to overcome on this terrain was no longer just Lamarck.[59] He admitted that analogous ideas were circulating in Europe through the works of many naturalists, among whom he mentioned Gottfried R. Treviranus, Georg Prochaska, Sprengel (probably Kurt Polykarp), and Mihaly Lenhossék.[60] Furthermore, he recognized that the new popularity enjoyed by the notion of the "spontaneous" generation of elementary forms of life from inanimate matter moved in the same dangerous direction.[61] All these ideas were disseminating a pantheistic and materialistic view of nature that Abbot Ranzani, a professor at the papal University of Bologna, regarded with as much alarm as the Protestant Cuvier.[62] Ranzani, however, was not one to avoid sensitive issues: in the 1830s he held crowded university courses on the history of the earth and the antiquity of the human race, and he came to support the hypothesis of a remote origin of the human species not granted by Cuvier.[63]

When in September 1829 Bonaparte sent Ranzani the first part of his adverse review of the *Règne animal*,[64] he was well aware that the person he was asking to publish it was a former student and an adherent of Cuvier's. Some of the criticisms in those first pages implicated Ranzani as well: apropos of the human species, for example, Ranzani's *Elementi* adopted Cuvier's distinction between bimana and quadrumana that was sharply criticized in the review. Furthermore, Bonaparte knew Ranzani's peculiar view of the role of criticism in scientific work, namely, his extreme caution in employing a tool that Bonaparte considered essential to scientific life. When on an earlier occasion Ranzani had informed Bonaparte of his determination never to respond to criticism leveled at him and never to criticize others,[65] Bonaparte had countered that "one cannot pay greater homage to a scientist's work than to undertake to criticize it."[66] These opposing views of the role of criticism suggest another likely reason for the tepid response that greeted Bonaparte's attack on Cuvier in Italian scientific circles. It was not just that relatively few naturalists shared an interest in the broader philosophical principles of classification, and that those few still felt Cuvier's influence. There was also a limited appreciation of the role of criticism in scientific work, perhaps due to the situation of the Italian scientific community, which was divided into many small centers and lacked adequate forums where scientists could engage in debates.

Bonaparte in any case interpreted the delay in publishing his critique of Cuvier in *Annali di storia naturale* as evidence of reservations against it.[67] Ranzani had warned him that the zoologist and anatomist Antonio Alessandrini and the botanist Antonio Bertoloni might counter his attack with a defense of Cuvier in the journal.[68] Cuvier's prestige in Italian scientific circles was still high in 1830. As for Ranzani, it must be recalled that he was in contact with the network of personal relationships that Cuvier adroitly maintained through correspondence.[69] Although the direct exchange of letters between the two had become sporadic after Ranzani's stay in Paris, they had remained in contact through their mutual friend J. B. Pentland. Incidentally, in 1824 Pentland had informed Ranzani of the very poor relations—personal as well as scientific—between Cuvier and Étienne Geoffroy Saint-Hilaire.[70]

At any rate, Ranzani never dealt directly with the criticisms of Cuvier in writing to Bonaparte, although of the editors of the *Annali*, he was the one most directly responsible for their publication. Nor did the rejoinder ever appear in the journal. Even when Bonaparte invited Paolo Savi to express his opinion elsewhere, Savi circumspectly refrained from doing so.[71] Thus what might have become a chance for the Italian scientific community to discuss the situation in zoological studies and weigh the validity of the tradition led by Cuvier against other traditions current in the field came to nothing. Some circumstances that may have contributed to this outcome have been singled out. Now the scientific motivations prompting Bonaparte will be examined in greater detail: ultimately, what conception of natural history did he set against Cuvier's?

There is reason to think that Bonaparte conceived of his critique of Cuvier as a kind of "manifesto" that on the one hand assessed a scientific tradition whose supremacy seemed illegitimate, and on the other sketched new guidelines for the development of systematic zoology. That these were Bonaparte's aims is confirmed by the publication, immediately after the *Règne animal* review, of a lengthy work in which he proposed his own "systematic distribution of vertebrates," a work that he presented as a "necessary complement to the observations on Cuvier."[72]

Neither the review nor the subsequent work, however, tackled the philosophy of classification Cuvier propounded in the preface to the *Règne animal*. This philosophy had been, of course, one of the matters at stake in the Parisian controversy with Geoffroy; but Bonaparte preferred to conduct a point-by-point appraisal of Cuvier's actual choices in classification, confining himself to general comments on Cuvier's principles.[73] He even refrained from recapitulating the methodological criteria he had clearly delineated in his revision of Wilson's work. Rather than focusing on philosophical and methodological choices, Bonaparte's point-by-point criticism of Cuvier aimed at emphasizing empirical data on all sorts of animals and the rapidly growing literature on zoology. Bonaparte's view was that the ongoing contribution of naturalists and the rigorous, critical verification of their work facilitated, better than any debate on principles, the elaboration of classifications increasingly reflecting the true distribution of living forms in nature. Bonaparte felt that this goal was not unattainable, and not even overly remote: the "systematic distribution of vertebrates," which he proposed as the constructive side of his criticism of Cuvier, arranged 5,353 species of mammals, birds, and reptiles in order.[74]

Bonaparte's "empirical" approach to the problems of classification embodied, of course, its own philosophy, which it may be worthwhile to compare with Cuvier's and Geoffroy's. Bonaparte was confident that a classification could be established that was not merely useful for the recognition of living forms but "natural" as well, and he thought that this should be the naturalist's main goal: "I always keep my sights on the natural method, however chimerical this may seem to many."[75] And on this point both Cuvier and Geoffroy surely would have concurred with him. Bonaparte thought, however, that the means for reaching this natural classification was provided by an eclectic set of norms that were not principles of a philosophy of classification but rather the norms of the "craft" and, in a sense, the "ethics" of the naturalist.

To cite just one more instance: in classification, Bonaparte asserted, "there is no virtue to clinging to a characteristic that exists only in the adult male but is never found in the female."[76] Again, both Cuvier and Geoffroy would have agreed on the adoption of such general, empirical norms. But they would have added that there existed a superior route to a "natural" classification. This was comparative anatomy, that is, the comparative examination of the internal organization of animals and their principal apparatuses. Bonaparte would not willingly have conceded that this was the principal, much less the only, route, though he did not deny the importance of comparative anatomy.[77] In fact, he saw no reason to emphasize certain features of organisms rather than others: in a spontaneously empirical conception of zoology, the weight to assign to the various data (e.g., external features, anatomical organization, geographical distribution) should be established instance by instance, on the basis of what the naturalist's experience and expertise suggested.

The eminently empirical, practical norms of the naturalist's craft, however, contained significant fragments of theories and ideas that had dominated the natural history of an earlier period. Thus, as we have seen, while Bonaparte did not explicitly claim to be a proponent of the eighteenth-century concept of a chain of beings, his search for the most appropriate links between groups of forms revealed what deep traces this idea had left in naturalists' craft. Even when it was not adopted as a theory or a working hypothesis, it made itself felt in classification work.[78] Cuvier was well known to be a resolute opponent of the chain of beings, so here he and Bonaparte parted company. Geoffroy, on the other hand, though he repudiated Cuvier's portrayal of him as a tardy adherent of that eighteenth-century idea, did not reject new and more sophisticated versions of the chain of beings. Cuvier, too, for that matter, displayed some interest in developments of that old idea, as when he established certain parallels between different classes:

> Marsupials could be said to form a class of their own, parallel to that of ordinary quadrupeds, and divisible into similar orders. So if we arranged these two classes in two columns, the opossum, the dasyure, and the bandicoot would be opposite the insectivorous carnivores with long canines, such as the tenrec and the mole: the cuscus and the potoroo would be located across from the hedgehog and the shrew. Strictly speaking, the kangaroo is not comparable to anything else, but the wombat should correspond to rodents.[79]

Bonaparte claimed to admire such parallels devised by Cuvier.[80] He himself, however, proposed images based on circles rather than parallel lines: "The naturalist should strive to single out the typical species in the continuous mass [of living forms], suitable to serve as a center around which to arrange the other more or less similar species, allowing the circumferences to touch and even intersect. . . . "[81] It should also be remembered that in the eighteenth century the chain or linear series of forms was only one of several images to be proposed by naturalists. Vitaliano Donati, for instance, envisioned the relations between living organisms as a network rather than a series.[82]

Bonaparte's insistence on the need to take species' geographical distribution into account in their classification also presupposed some highly "philosophical" considerations.[83] His conviction that American species should be distinguished from the equivalent European species, and that the number of genera and species common to the two continents would decrease as studies proceeded,[84] denoted a belief in a closer relationship between organisms and environment than Cuvier would admit. Nevertheless, Bonaparte refrained from developing a conception of such relationships that went in the direction of Lamarckian transformism, which Geoffroy instead to a certain extent endorsed.

Bonaparte's insistence that the human species be classified according to criteria that conformed to those adopted for other species was also an expression of a basic orientation. His preference for Linnaeus's order of primates, which—unlike Cuvier's—comprised *both* bimanous (human) and quadrumanous species, signified a choice in favor of the study of humans carried out according to the ordinary criteria adopted by naturalists.[85] But

Bonaparte did not in this case, either, make this choice a research program, and unlike Geoffroy, he apparently had no interest in a systematic, comparative study of humans and animals.

As was said, the principles of Bonaparte's implicit philosophy largely coincided with the norms of the naturalist's "craft" as he conceived of it. The fact that these principles often differed from Cuvier's confirms that Bonaparte adhered to a research tradition that essentially diverged from the one that evolved in Paris under the aegis of both the celebrated rivals involved in the 1830 controversy at the Académie. Naturalists such as Bonaparte had not been influenced—or at least not to the same extent—by important innovations developed in Paris. They had adopted very few of the most sophisticated tools of comparative anatomy, and they displayed a limited interest in the study of fossils and their role in the search for a natural classification of living forms. Reluctant to engage in disputes on the larger philosophical principles, they did not enjoy debating general and poorly defined theoretical positions such as creationism and transformism: although Bonaparte's critique of Cuvier occasionally drew on the transformist tradition, it constituted neither an attack on Cuvier's philosophy nor a defense of transformism. Bonaparte's primary targets were, rather, inaccuracy and insufficient supporting evidence. These expressed the ideals of a scientific routine that dated back to Linnaeus, and that numbered such staunch adherents as Bonaparte's American friend "the precise and modest Say."[86]

It would be mistaken, however, to suggest that the tradition exemplified by Bonaparte looked more toward the past than toward the future of natural history. Naturalists such as Bonaparte did not abandon the goal of finding a natural classification. Following on earlier speculations on the chain of beings, they succeeded in framing new classificatory models. They advocated a non-Eurocentric stance in the study of living forms and a naturalistic approach to the study of the human species. They eclectically emulated some lines of research prevailing in the main scientific centers, though without forgoing their own role in verifying and criticizing them, at times severely.

Such characteristics indicate that the sort of natural history practiced by Bonaparte was the product of settings that lacked scientific institutions capable of dictating rigid research programs, imposing research styles, or forming true schools of thought. That is one reason why this kind of natural history was more likely to be found at the periphery of the scientific community than at its center.[87] To call it "amateur," however, distinguishing it from the "professional" sort practiced in public scientific institutions or universities, would be misleading.[88] At that time wealthy "amateurs" such as Bonaparte could compete with professionals working in such institutions, at least in countries such as the Italian states.

The day-by-day work documented by Bonaparte's correspondence is enlightening in this regard, as a few examples will show. The assistant who prepared Paolo Savi's zoological collections for the new natural history museum at the University of Pisa was more experienced than Bonaparte's. In vain Bonaparte asked Savi to be allowed to send his own technician to Pisa to gain experience:[89] working in an institution created by the grand duke of Tuscany evidently had its advantages. At another level, however, Savi conceded that Bonaparte's competence in the philosophy of classification was superior to his own:[90] Savi's scientific training was not, in some important ways, as sound or as up to date as the "amateur" Bonaparte's. Comparison with Ranzani provides another example. Ranzani succeeded in reading the new edition of Cuvier's *Règne animal* before Bonaparte did:[91] his contacts with Paris were evidently more direct. But to fill the gaps in his zoological collection at the University of Bologna, Ranzani often had to turn to Bonaparte for new specimens.[92] Bonaparte was able to procure ample materials, thanks to his network of correspondence with naturalists in many countries, incomparably wider than Ranzani's.

How widespread was the research tradition illustrated by Bonaparte's early works and his criticism of Cuvier? We know his early training as a naturalist had taken place in such outlying contexts as the English countryside around Worcester and the papal states. His first publications of note had taken shape within scientific circles such as the Philadelphia Academy of Natural Sciences, which had not yet attained a recognized position in the international scientific community.[93] Bonaparte's correspondence, in any case, shows that the type of natural history he practiced was representative of much of the work carried on at a distance from the major scientific centers, both in Europe and in the United States. Furthermore, the extensive correspondence he maintained with naturalists working in public institutions and universities indicates that there were still strong ties between the "amateurs" and the professionals of natural history. The former's rivalry with the latter—itself exemplified in a sense by Bonaparte's attack on Cuvier—reveals, however, that the amateurs and the naturalists of the periphery of the scientific community were concerned about their future. In 1830 Bonaparte expressed this anxiety, still mainly on behalf of American naturalists.

But these same worries soon bolstered his intention to promote natural history studies in the Italian states. He felt that the best way to achieve that aim would be the institution of annual itinerant meetings of scientists, patterned after those that had existed for some time in Switzerland, Germany, Britain, and France.[94] At such meetings, embodying a new model of scientific institution, the "amateurs" would encounter the professional scientists, and the scientists of outlying areas would meet those of the center of the scientific community. Above all, participants would finally have a forum where they could compare and assess research programs and work styles.[95] Bonaparte's failure in 1830 to spark a critical debate on Cuvier's natural history contributed to his determination to promote annual congresses of Italian scientists, which were then held from 1839 on, thanks to his initiative. The work carried out in the zoology and botany sections during these meetings offers a good observation point for following the developments of the species question, as well as the interaction of different research traditions within the new Italian scientific community. And in the 1840s, many of the naturalists that later would either support or oppose the Darwinian revolution in Italy were trained.

THE SPECIES PROBLEM AND THE ITALIAN SCIENTIFIC COMMUNITY BEFORE THE *ORIGIN*

The work conducted during the Italian scientists' congresses from 1839 to 1847[96] reveals important developments in the reflections on the species problem, developments that were gradually reshaping natural history, as exemplified by Bonaparte's work around 1830. An element that carried over from an earlier tradition, on the other hand, was the search for a "natural" classification of living forms. The most significant moments in the work Italian naturalists carried out during the congresses between 1839 and 1847 were generated by the debate on this topic, which more than any other polarized the scientists' attention. In fact, there were major innovations in the conceptual tools being used to pursue that traditional objective.

The new "tools" came from new or renewed disciplinary areas, particularly embryology, paleontology, and teratology, or the study of monstrosities. Ongoing attempts to establish a natural system of classification could not fail to compare notes with these fields of research. The geometric images used up to about 1830 to describe the entirety of living forms—a linear series or chain of beings, parallel series, a network, or variously intersecting circles—no longer satisfied naturalists' need for order unless they took into account the embryological development of the different species, the growing number of known fossils, and "monstrous" abnormalities. Morphology and comparative anatomy, in the form cultivated by both Cuvier and Étienne Geoffroy Saint-Hilaire, still provided the essential notions for dealing with classification problems. However, the front line of knowledge considered relevant to formulating a natural system of classification had opened up toward the new disciplines. Of these, it was embryology and the study of monstrous variations that particularly attracted the attention of Italian naturalists.

This shift in interests was matched by changes in the concern for what was going on outside Italy. Many still looked to France, and in particular to the work of Henri de Blainville, who in a sense was continuing the work of both Cuvier and Geoffroy, but the studies of German naturalists were gaining increasing prestige south of the Alps and furnished new research models. Along with the diffusion of Lamarck's transformist ideas, which— though challenged—were significantly present, these circumstances were gradually modifying the terms of the species problem within the Italian scientific community.

Italian scientists' first chance to take a stand, in their periodic meetings, on the great issue of "the natural system in zoology" was during the Turin congress in September 1844. The twenty-seven-year-old Filippo De Filippi, who in the 1860s would become one of the leading Italian supporters of evolution theory, read a paper on the natural system on that occasion.[97] This offers indications of how earlier positions were interlaced with new ones in the development of this old problem.

De Filippi expressed dissatisfaction with recent attempts to replace the idea of a single "series" of organisms with the image of more than one parallel series, each corresponding to a class of beings, as was suggested, for instance, by Étienne Geoffroy Saint-Hilaire's son Isidore:

> The parallel series hypothesis that today has so many adherents can lead only to artificial systems. Animate beings constitute a line, or rather a ladder, reaching from the simpler animals to the most perfect being, man; but this line cannot offer the systematic regularity to which some try to reduce it. The natural classification of animals is nothing but their arrangement according to the inviolable norm of their degree of organic perfection.[98]

With statements such as this, De Filippi seemed simply to restate, with some adjustments, the eighteenth-century notion of a chain of beings; but the old idea was combined with new views stemming from recent biological research. The proceedings of the Turin congress reported that "Dr. De Filippi admits the existence of a primitive animal substance that forms the basis of the organism in the simplest animals, and that is changed in the higher tissues and varies as the organic ladder is ascended." This alluded to studies that recently had been carried out in Germany by Theodor Schwann on the cell structure of animal tissues, found to be common to all living organisms. Another new element that De Filippi added to the old idea of the organic chain was taken from embryology. De Filippi, the proceedings reported, "drawing on the observations of some modern embryologists, especially Dr. Rusconi's and his own, introduces into the zoological system the consideration of the different ways in which embryos develop."[99] Cell theory and embryology thus offered new "Ariadne's threads" leading through nature's labyrinth.

Reflections on embryonic development did not only introduce new elements that would have to be taken into account in classifying organisms. The study of individual growth was an indirect stimulus to conceiving of species, too, as subject to development in time. During the same Turin congress, Mauro Rusconi concluded his paper on fish embryology by suggesting a parallel between the development of the individual and "the life cycle of the species." This was reminiscent of Brocchi's earlier individual-species analogy, although Brocchi[100]—as we know—refrained from embryological considerations, which now provided a new impetus and brought new implications to the analogy. The parallel between the two kinds of development was now more especially seen in the light of what was later termed recapitulation theory, according to which the embryonic stages of development of the individual retrace the animal series, which is in turn conceived of as the result of a process of development in time.[101] Not all embryologists, and not even the most illustrious of them, Karl Ernst von Baer, accepted this theory and adopted its evolutionary implications.[102] In Italy, in any case, it circulated to some extent, thanks, for example, to the work of Johann Friedrich Meckel, one of its most outspoken supporters. A manual by Meckel had already run to two Italian editions by the 1820s.[103] In it was to be found, inter alia, the statement that "the degrees of development that human beings follow from their earliest origin to the moment of perfect maturity correspond to constant formations in the animal series." Meckel maintained that in its development "the embryo truly resembles the animals on the lower rungs, including those very far down the ladder."[104]

Belief in some version of the chain of beings and commitment to recapitulation theory were shared by other protagonists at the Italian scientific congresses, including Filippo Parlatore.[105] In his botany lectures at the Florentine Museum of Physics and Natural History in the 1840s, Parlatore devoted considerable attention to those concepts.[106] In Paris he himself had attended the lessons of Blainville, who affirmed yet another version of the chain of beings, and those of E. R. Serres, a French supporter of recapitulation theory.[107] And yet Parlatore was anxious not to sever his ties completely with Cuvier's tradition, now represented by Cuvier's student Pierre Flourens, whose criticisms of chain-of-beings theories Parlatore carefully took into account when outlining the core of a new discipline that he suggested be called "comparative botany."

In Parlatore's case as in De Filippi's, French natural history was no longer the only point of reference for those interested in the "philosophy" of classification. Parlatore numbered F. W. J. Schelling, Wolfgang Goethe, and C. G. Carus among the leading inspirations for his comparative botany. He gave Schelling and Goethe credit for having established precious new links between different scientific disciplines, and with philosophy. He felt that Goethe's work on plant metamorphosis had led to a true "revolution" in the natural sciences. As for the theory asserting the unity of composition of all organisms—the theory for which Étienne Geoffroy Saint-Hilaire had defied Cuvier at the Académie in 1830, obtaining Goethe's support—Parlatore thought it was confirmed by Carus's speculations. Carus had theorized that living forms could all be traced back to a "primordial living being," spherical in shape, from which the other forms were derived by successive modifications.[108]

Parlatore combined these elements from recent French and German natural history and philosophy into an original system of ideas. According to it, the form, structure, functions, and fossil remains of plants were evidence of a "vegetable series," that is, a "successive progression of plants" that was part of the "general series of organic beings."[109] It could be demonstrated, moreover, that "in their ensuing development higher plants pass through stages corresponding to the lower plants." The law of recapitulation was thus as true for the vegetable as for the animal kingdom and seemed to establish a connection between the two. As Parlatore put it, "Is it not arguable that animals, being largely higher and more perfect organisms than plants, replicate plant development as they themselves develop?"[110]

The relationships between the vegetable and the animal series led Parlatore to propose yet another variant of the idea of an organic series. He thought that the vegetable series and the animal series were parallel, since in both, more complex beings succeeded simpler ones. The parallelism, however, continued only up to a certain stage, since the vegetable series never managed to develop some of the more complex apparatuses such as motor or nervous apparatuses, or, of course, the corresponding functions. The organic series as a whole was therefore discontinuous: there was no link joining the most complex plants to the simplest animals.[111] There was, however, an affinity between the "lowest extremes" of the two series. Very simple plants such as "red snow" corresponded to elementary animals such as *hematococcus*, similar and nearly spherical in shape, the very shape of Carus's "primordial living being." Nor should the vegetable series be thought of as a "single, continuous series, comparable to a chain, whose links are represented by organisms." Granted, nature must have progressed from the simple to the complex, "but in this progression it did not always follow a single plan of organization, but rather promoted the development first of one and then of another system of organs."[112] Organs, modified in the different species, provided a guide for classification, as Aristotle and Cuvier had suggested. Thus Parlatore tried to reconcile the boldest speculations on the organic series and recapitulation theory with the Cuvierian tradition.

Concepts such as De Filippi's and Parlatore's, inspired by French and German natural history, met with the skepticism of traditionally trained naturalists, such as the dean of Italian entomologists, Massimiliano Spinola,[113] and Carlo Luciano Bonaparte himself. During the annual congresses of the Italian scientists, they both seized every opportunity to express their apprehension about some of the more audacious theoretical conclusions reached by the younger generation of naturalists. According to Spinola, it was wholly premature and perhaps impossible to proceed from the analytical description of organisms to a comprehensive vision of the entire living world. Spinola ridiculed the innumerable geometric images introduced to give order to the labyrinth of nature. His polemical reductio ad absurdum of such attempts is reported in the proceedings:

> Marquis Spinola . . . ironically proposes that attempts at wider or narrower syntheses be replaced by an infinitely recurring system, no longer based on lines, single or parallel, or polygons, but on true solids—indeed, on spheres, in which each point of the periphery and the interior is the site of a different creature, each of which resides in the center of another sphere, identical to the first, in such a way as to maintain every relation between beings. Marquis Spinola proposes such an impossible system in order to arrive at the conclusion that this would mean proceeding as if at random in the shades of primitive ignorance. . . . [114]

Bonaparte, in spite of his well-documented approval of some versions of the chain of beings and his interest in the introduction of parallelisms and circles in classification, declared on that occasion that he "completely agreed" with Spinola.[115] Skepticism toward all-too-"philosophical" natural history was probably one reason behind this declaration. It is also likely that both Bonaparte and Spinola looked with misgivings on the most radical formulations of the unity of composition of all living beings, which Bonaparte feared now also had adherents in Italy. The renowned German zoologist and philosopher Lorenz Oken, who had an important role in the Italian congresses, attending some and sending papers that were read in public by Bonaparte, perceived this inclination in Italian scientific circles.[116] Oken was diffident toward the more extreme forms of the hypothesis of the unity of composition: he held that there existed more than one fundamental type of animal organization, even if all types—he thought—were then summed up in the single human species.[117]

In any case, Oken willingly apprised Italian scientists of his speculations on the natural classification of organisms, which suggested new analogies with chemical classification as well as with geometry. As Bonaparte reported to the scientists meeting in Naples, Oken expressed in a letter the hope that

> the time will come when it becomes possible to calculate the genera in botany and zoology, as we now calculate the stoichiometric combinations in chemistry. Only then can we be certain how to put aberrant genera into their proper places. . . . We already have, however, a substitute for this in the parallelism of genera in tribes of the same degree in the different classes. And this is why [Oken] insists that families should contain the same number of genera. Any classification that does not take this into account should be regarded as unacceptable. It does not, however, follow from this that all the classes must actually have the same number of genera, but rather that those genera have the same value. There are philosophical grounds, for instance, for there being more genera in the class of insects than in that of mammals. . . . A mammal genus may well be worth more than all the genera of insects. Geometry provides a telling analogy of this. The equilateral triangle is individual and unique in that it bears no modifications, whereas an isosceles triangle is an individual only when the vertical angle has been defined. There are many of these individual triangles, which all together are worth no more than the single equi-

lateral triangle, which is of a kind with no transition. This is why some genera have few and others many species.[118]

That through the contributions of De Filippi, Parlatore, Bonaparte, Spinola, and their foreign interlocutors the Italian congresses of the 1840s offered a forum for significant debate on classification was noted by the British zoologist and paleontologist Richard Owen.[119] He attended the 1845 Naples congress, where he also participated in the work of a committee working to establish the place of the amphioxus, or lancelet, in the "natural system." The amphioxus was a chordate whose particular structure suggested it might be an intermediate form between vertebrates and invertebrates. Others taking part in the commission included Ernst Weber of Leipzig, who also had come to Naples for the congress, De Filippi, and Stefano Delle Chiaje, while Oronzio G. Costa, a zoology professor at the University of Naples, cooperated by keeping his colleagues supplied with a good number of live amphioxi every day for their observations. The commission's conclusions were not recorded in the proceedings of the congress, but the very fact that this task was assigned is indicative of the kind of interests cultivated by scientists attending the congress.

The next year the naturalists meeting at Genoa were informed, again through Bonaparte, that Owen had delivered a series of lectures supporting "homological" theories, according to which the same basic organs were present in the different classes of animals. Bonaparte reported that according to Owen, the doctrines of Carus, Oken, Geoffroy, and L. H. Bojanus inspired by that principle were "the groundwork for a philosophy that deserved a better fate than it had received at the hands of Cuvier, L. Agassiz, and Johannes Müller."[120]

That a number of naturalists participating in the Italian congresses adhered to the "philosophy" defended by Owen is confirmed by the case of O. G. Costa.[121] In his lectures at the University of Naples in the early 1840s, Costa displayed a certain indifference toward the large number of systems of classification in fashion among naturalists, and the continual revisions to which they were subject. He adopted Blainville's system, however, and above all took advantage of the uncertain state of systematics to restate the principle of an "order or successive graduation in the series of living beings."[122] The series outlined by Costa took into account recent research that made the mere reiteration of old, linear models unacceptable. A series in a strict sense, he warned, is discernible only within single classes of organisms. And yet, he insisted, naturalists must always look for connecting links between one class and another. The model for such research was provided, according to Costa, by astronomy:

What has been found for the relationship between planets in astronomy may also turn out to hold for the animal series: i.e., that the discovery of living animals in unknown lands, or buried in the bowels of the earth, furnishes the intermediate links between classes or orders that seemed unrelated; just as the discovery of Uranus and then Ceres, Pallas, Juno, and Vesta came to demonstrate the validity of Kepler's law.[123]

In the wake of such speculations, Costa proposed yet another geometric form, the spiral, to represent the organic series: "I seem to be able to glimpse in the series of living forms of each class a successive depression and elevation in the degree of animality, building a link whose boundaries do not touch: and yet where one stops the other starts, creating a spiral. . . . "[124]

Thus adherence to the notion of an organic series, in the revised forms that recently had been proposed by French, German, English, and Italian naturalists, was quite widespread in the Italian scientific community of the 1840s. For the most part the adherence manifested itself through new proposals on the overall structure of the organic series or significant segments of it. Such proposals often suggested some geometric form to represent better the features that current anatomical, embryological, and paleontological studies were meanwhile attributing to the supposed organic series. Whatever the shape attributed to it, the series was principally conceived of as a response to the general problem of classification. It had to provide a general "map" to the "labyrinth" made up of the increasingly numerous known living and fossil species; it did not necessarily describe how the labyrinth had been constructed *in time*, or explain how species might eventually be modified or transformed.

During the 1840s, however, at least one Italian naturalist dealt directly with the problem of the boundaries of variation, and hence of the possible transmutation of species. Carlo Porro, a malacologist from Milan, noted that the study of the laws regulating the uncertain limits between species and varieties would eventually lead to a solution to the problem of classification itself, while the proliferation of new models to describe the entire organic series, or large portions of it, seemed incapable of attaining conclusive results. He noted, and announced during the congresses of the Italian scientists, that it was worthwhile to study in depth "the laws of variations to which animals of the same species are subject."[125] He then undertook the task by examining a large number of forms of shells normally classified by naturalists as different species, and focusing on the genus *Helix*. He eventually concluded that the fifty or more forms generally thought to be species of *Helix* could be reduced to just three basic species. The dozens of known forms ascribable to those three species should be considered not separate species but the result of variations, whose laws remained to be ascertained.

According to Porro, variations could be the result of different factors. There were variations that depended on environmental circumstances: thus in the species of *Helix* it could be noted that "the more southern the climate, the more pronounced the characteristics that develop."[126] There were also variations that seemed independent of the environment, determined, in ways that were as yet inexplicable, by the organism itself. These first two kinds of variations were as a rule found in many members of the same species.[127] And there were the ones that Porro called "individual varia- tions." These were the "anomalies" or "monstrosities" studied by tera- tology, then cultivated in particular by Isidore Geoffroy Saint-Hilaire, by whom Porro's research was to a large extent inspired[128] (fig. 3).

These elements of a general theory of variation were the result of the minute study of the extraordinary variety of forms of shells of the single genus *Helix*. Porro intended to extend this study to a systematic exami- nation of the data provided by the enormous literature that was being published on every genus of shell.[129] The result of this research strategy was highly significant from the theoretical and methodological standpoint, although not entirely new in the history of classificatory studies. According to Porro, the research on shells showed that the term *species* had to be considered wholly conventional.[130] Previously Linnaeus, and more explic- itly Buffon, had expressed the view that at least some of the classificatory groupings used by naturalists (class, order, genus, species . . .) were con- ventional,[131] since in nature only individuals are actually observed, and reliable empirical definitions of classificatory groups were possible at best only for species. Now, however, the context in which the conventional nature of the term *species* was to be understood had changed. Not only was a concept basic to the endeavor of classification itself being called into question; at the same time a promising *theory of variation* was being delin- eated. Porro was aware of the new situation and expressed the consequent "need for an innovation" in natural history:

> Some will accuse me of an excessive tendency to destroy some of the means used up to now to acquire historical knowledge of natural objects. . . . But I address myself to those who argue that knowledge of the facts is inseparable from the laws emerging from them, if we are to arrive at the truth. Such persons should note that whenever I destroy without at the same time proposing sub- stitutes, replacements are postponed only until further study can be made of the little that I have managed to accomplish so far. They should also note that it is a constant norm that one advances only by destroying; that sketched here and there in these studies are ideas that, if better developed, would achieve the desired end; that the need for innovation is not simply based on my own unsubstantiated assertion but rather emerges from a long series of facts; and that the perfection of natural science lies in the solution of this problem: how to understand the greatest number of facts in terms of the simplest, most natural principles.[132]

In spite of Porro's concern over criticisms that might be raised by his research on variations, his studies were favorably received by Italian sci- entists at the 1842 congress in Padua. Interestingly enough, generous en- couragement came from the very naturalists such as Bonaparte and Spinola

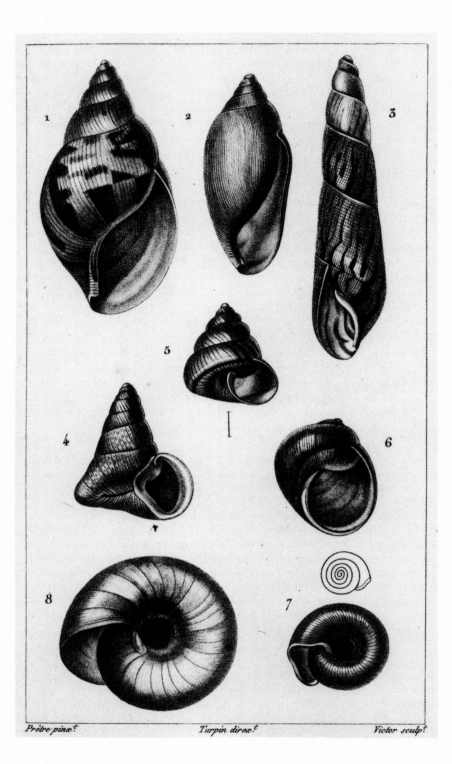

Prêtre pinx.t   Turpin direx.t   Victor sculp.t

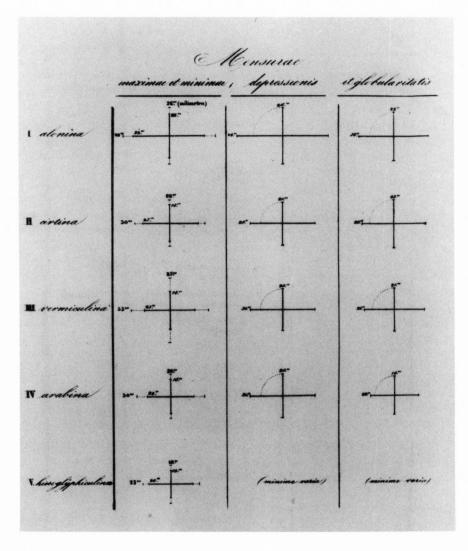

Fig. 3. Carlo Porro thought the notion of species was to a certain extent conventional. By meticulously measuring variations observed in the genus *Helix* (specimens 5–8 in 3a), he came to the conclusion that the over fifty "nominal species" described by naturalists could be reduced to just three "specific types." According to Porro, the variations that accounted for the approximately fifty forms originating from the three types were caused by (i) "topographical conditions," (ii) causes internal to that type of organism, and still inexplicable, or (iii) freakish aberrations of the individual organism. Figure 3b shows the sizes of some of the second kind of variations observed by Porro in *Helix vermiculata*. Fig. 3a comes from H. de Blainville, *Manuel de malacologie et conchyologie* (1825–27); 3b from *Atti della quarta riunione degli scienziati italiani (1842)* (1843).

who were known to look with some suspicion on other proposals for re-forming the classificatory system.[133] They may well have seen in Porro's detailed study of variations evidence of the "analytical" spirit, which they thought preferable to the excessively "synthetic" aspirations of those in-spired by the French or the German "philosophical" tradition.[134] Porro's research could indeed be considered a continuation of the empirical tra-dition of natural history illustrated by some of Bonaparte's ideas expressed around 1830, though it certainly represented a development in a notably more sophisticated direction.

In any case, to understand the debate on the species problem in progress in the Italian scientific community in the 1840s, we need to take into account a circumstance that never emerges explicitly in the proceedings of the con-gresses but that nevertheless underlay much of what was going on there. It is the diffusion of Lamarck's ideas on the transmutation of species, which continued to circulate despite the aversion to them of some or the silence imposed by prestigious scientists such as Cuvier. Discussions on the "natu-ral" system of classification examined so far concerned the "map" of the labyrinth of living forms, either its overall structure (the organic series) or its fine details (variations). Even those who, like Porro, investigated the uncertain boundaries between species and varieties avoided explicitly pos-ing the problem of the fixity of species. It was implicitly conceded that the map of the labyrinth could be studied without asking how the labyrinth had been built over time. Granted, keeping the two problems separate may have been advantageous from various standpoints. But how much longer could this be kept up?

LAMARCK'S LEGACY

"Lamarck believed that animals change in response to the influence of external circumstances, so he said that they change in form and function as required by those circumstances, and that therefore species do not exist in nature. This is a very mistaken opinion . . . , but one that has never-theless acquired many adherents."[135]

These are the words with which Filippo Parlatore opened his botany course as professor at the Florentine Museum of Physics and Natural His-tory in 1842. Not confining himself to pointing out and condemning the phenomenon, he attempted to situate it within what seemed to him the two basic philosophical orientations then competing in natural history, which he referred to as "pantheism" and "spiritualism." By pantheism Parlatore meant the school of thought "maintaining that beings were cre-ated at random and that one being generated another." He considered this school to be derived from German natural philosophy and more specifically from the work of Schelling, the expression of "pure idealism." In the hands of Goethe and Carus, however, that idealism was translated into a "posi-tive" research program and had exerted "an immense influence on natural history."[136] Étienne Geoffroy Saint-Hilaire had transplanted "pantheism" to France, where, among other things, it had provoked the famous debate between Cuvier and Geoffroy at the Académie in 1830. In Parlatore's historical reconstruction, Lamarck's ideas, too, could be traced back to the pantheism of the German school, and represented their most debatable development.

The "spiritualists'" front, with which Parlatore sided, included, he claimed, "the advocates of the series or chain of beings endorsed by Leibniz and Bonnet." He placed here Cuvier and Blainville, who "recognized in the creation of beings a creative force that established a principle by which these beings are formed and that acted with intelligence to reach a goal," which was the very opposite of the "random" creation attributed to the pantheists and Lamarckians.[137]

Whatever the strictures of Parlatore's historical reconstruction, it is clear that he feared Lamarck's views were as great a threat as ever in 1842. This led him to devote an entire chapter of his comparative botany course to a discussion of "whether plant species are fixed or variable."[138] The chapter ended with a denunciation of Lamarckian views, accompanied by arguments for the fixity of species borrowed in toto from Cuvier. Parlatore may have chosen Lamarck and pantheism as polemical targets to reassure his audience as to the religious orthodoxy underlying his lessons. If this had been his only aim, however, there would have been no reason to emphasize so strongly Lamarck's dangerous but "celebrated opinion" and his "many advocates."[139] Nor was the situation in the 1840s new in regard to the circulation of Lamarck's ideas in Italy.

In his *Elementi di zoologia*, which began coming out in 1819, Ranzani had given considerable emphasis to Lamarckian ideas on transmutation, rebutting them with detailed arguments. According to Ranzani, Lamarck recognized "a force in nature from which all bodies have received or will receive existence, so that no body is produced directly by God."[140] He regarded these "very pernicious errors," which risked casting a shadow of irreligion over the whole field of zoology, as a consequence of Lamarck's transmutation theory and the ideas of various exponents of German natural philosophy.[141] Our examination of the debate on the philosophy of natural history in the Italian scientists' congresses has shown the profound impact of French natural history after Lamarck and of the German tradition. But how widespread were Lamarck's ideas in Italian scientific circles for Ranzani and Parlatore to refer to them, in different periods, in such contentious tones?

In the first half of the nineteenth century, Lamarck's influence and prestige came not so much from his views on transmutation as from his basic texts on invertebrates. In the Italian states interest in the study of shells, widespread among both amateur collectors and those with scientific ambitions, naturally meant that his works were read extensively. In addition to Porro, Brocchi and Guidotti might be recalled in this connection. As we have seen in the case of Brocchi, those who were interested in Lamarck as a malacologist did not necessarily support his evolutionary ideas.[142] Still, some of Lamarck's writings obliged his reader to deal with both aspects of his work.

The prompt translation of Lamarck's *Recherches sur les causes des principaux faits physiques* (Research on the causes of the major physical phenomena), published in Venice between 1795 and 1796, confirms that there was interest in his "natural philosophy" in northern Italian scientific circles as early as the late eighteenth century.[143] However, at a time and in countries where educated classes habitually read French, a translation should not be regarded as proof of the wide circulation of ideas, and in any case, *Recherches sur les causes* did not yet contain evolutionary themes. A translation is more significant as evidence of the penetration of ideas into foreign countries when the text is proposed as a teaching tool or as a basic introductory reading. And this was the case of Lamarck's *Histoire naturelle des animaux sans vertèbres* (Natural history of invertebrates), translated in an abridged version by Francesco Baldassini in 1834.[144] By presenting Lamarck's work as a teaching tool, Baldassini no doubt aimed at exonerating himself with respect to Lamarck's controversial ideas. He insisted that the order Lamarck used to describe living forms, from the simplest to the most complex, and not the other way around as most naturalists did, was just more practical for teaching purposes. The order from simple to complex, Baldassini warned, should be looked on "as a method of study best suited to instruction, and not as the order actually existing in nature." But elsewhere Baldassini did not disguise his inclination to think that this must also be the order that nature actually followed in *producing* living forms.[145]

Works that may have favored the spread of Lamarckian ideas on transmutation in Italy include the *Dictionnaire classique d'histoire naturelle*[146] (Classical dictionary of natural history), published in Venice in an Italian translation between 1831 and 1843. The dictionary had been compiled in the 1820s by Bory Saint-Vincent, who showed himself in numerous articles to be a follower of Lamarck. There is evidence that some of Bory's articles on the "natural history of man" for the *Dictionnaire* had attracted the attention of Ranzani, who discussed them in his courses at the University of Bologna.[147]

For nearly two decades before Baldassini's translation and the *Dictionnaire* became available to Italian readers, Franco Andrea Bonelli[148] had been giving considerable emphasis to Lamarckian transmutationist ideas in his zoology courses at the University of Turin. Although he never published anything on Lamarck's theory and dissented from it on some basic points, Bonelli discussed it and illustrated its basic concepts in his zoology courses, from the idea of a progressive development of living forms to the action of environmental circumstances and the virtually unlimited variability of the forms produced by different circumstances.[149] In Bonelli's case Lamarck's personal influence also played a part: he had met Lamarck in Paris in 1810–1811, when he had also attended Cuvier's, Geoffroy's, and Blainville's courses. At that time, Bonelli appears to have told Lamarck that he endorsed transmutationist ideas, and to have received encouragement.[150] The prestige that Bonelli and the Turin zoological museum enjoyed suggests that Bonelli's lessons must have been a significant tool for the diffusion of an interest in Lamarck.

Lamarckian themes are also found in a kind of "discourse on method" published in the mid-1830s by Carlo Matteucci,[151] a young physiologist who would have an important role in the Italian scientific community in later decades. His original *Discorso sopra gli elementi del progresso della scienza dell'organismo* (Discourse on elements of progress of the science of the organism),[152] a methodological "manifesto" in favor of experimental physiology, espoused the Lamarckian theme of environmental action on living organisms, as well as more recent developments in embryology and paleontology. Advances in physiology, Matteucci claimed, would shed light on

the most sublime fact revealed by philosophical zoology, namely, the series of progressive complications followed by animal life, a series that represents beautifully the various phases of embryonic life. If we then examine the fossil remains that have been spared in the great revolutions of the globe, and compare the succession of geological epochs where they are found, their structure, and the series revealed in animals' embryonal development, this will stand as supreme proof of secular transformations that progressively modified animal organization in response to external conditions.[153]

First published in Florence, Matteucci's *Discorso* was reprinted in the Vatican states in 1839, with some curtailment of his intentions to apply the scientific method to the higher intellectual, affective, and volitional functions that became manifest in the transition "from the last to the first link in that chain of beings."[154] When, at the beginning of the 1840s in Florence, Parlatore declared his opposition to "pantheists" and denounced the popularity of Lamarckian ideas, he may well have been thinking of writings such as Matteucci's and the difficulties they might create in the relations between science and religion. Parlatore preferred to follow Flourens, the Parisian advocate of the Cuvierian tradition who aimed at conciliating science and religion.

But in the 1830s and 1840s, Italian naturalists received other indications from Paris, besides those from Cuvier's heirs. Porro, for instance, looked chiefly to Isidore Geoffroy Saint-Hilaire, who was advocating a revival of the doctrines taught by his father, Étienne, and by Lamarck, supporting them against the denigrations of Cuvier's followers. In the book that inspired Porro's research on variations in shells,[155] Isidore Geoffroy declared that "Lamarck's works on the influence exerted by external circumstances and their power to modify organization may well be his foremost claim to

distinction in the eyes of posterity,"[156] their chilly initial reception notwithstanding. When Porro spoke of the "need for innovation" in natural
history called for by recent research on the laws of variation, he was re-
peating almost verbatim Isidore Geoffroy's plea for a revival of Lamarck's
ideas, although he refrained from mentioning Lamarck's name.

The suspension of the Italian scientists' annual congresses after 1847
makes it difficult to trace further research developments introduced on a
nationwide basis during the late 1840s. Porro, for one, died in 1848, during
the political turmoil that took place in Milan as in many other European
cities. There are testimonies indicating that between 1848 and 1861, political
and military events connected with the unification of Italy led to a general
reduction in the activities of the Italian scientific community.[157] A perusal
of the literature produced during the 1850s, however, leaves the impression
that when the topic was the species problem, Lamarck's alternative still
exerted a certain attraction. Only two examples will be considered here:
one a zoology manual printed in Milan, the work of De Filippi, who was
then teaching at the University of Turin; the other a popular text produced
in Florence, the work of F. C. Marmocchi, who wrote on geography and a
variety of other subjects.

De Filippi's manual can be considered a good example of how com-
fortably tradition and innovation could coexist in natural history, at least
in books meant for teaching. Intending it "for use by Italian youth," De
Filippi entitled it *Regno animale* (Animal kingdom), after Cuvier's famous
work.[158] He reproposed Cuvier's four basic subdivisions or types of living
forms, though he added a fifth group, protozoa, as new findings in research
demanded. The definition of species, too, was apparently fixist. A species,
De Filippi stated, is "that complex of individual animals that, going back
toward the origin of things created, comes from two common parents. . . . "[159] This definition and the manual's overall design were traditional, and so indeed did the whole work seem at the beginning of the
twentieth century to Lorenzo Camerano, who was the first to write a history of the diffusion of Lamarck's doctrine in Italy.[160] And yet, although
the part devoted to systematics allowed no glimpse of the non-Cuvierian
tendencies of which De Filippi had made himself the proponent in the
previous decade, a long, conclusive chapter on the geographical distribution of species did restate Lamarckian themes.

De Filippi deemed the study of the relations between animals' characteristics and the settings in which they live "of prime importance" for
biology.[161] He pointed out that different species living in the same region
often had common characteristics, traceable to the action of the environment, e.g., the bright colors typical of many tropical species. In the wake
of considerations such as these, and not wishing to relinquish the stability
of species, De Filippi came to a singular compromise, which might be
designated with the paradoxical term *Lamarckian creationism*.[162] He formulated it as follows:

Because of these relations [between organisms' environment and their characteristics], we may assume that the act that populated the different regions of the globe with animals took place under the influence of factors specific to each region, tending to impress an overall character on the various and multiform species of the same class. This influence was instantaneous, and then ceased to be exerted; indeed, animals transported from one continent to another have never been observed to develop characters typical of the new country, or to lose those they had in their native country.[163]

Considerations of this sort led De Filippi to conclude that "a critical discussion of the notion of species" was indispensable as a basis of zoology.[164] It is worth recalling that in the early 1860s De Filippi would be among the first Italian naturalists to adhere explicitly to evolutionism, and to favor the circulation of Darwin's theory, though he still aimed at safeguarding the harmonious relations between science and religion.[165]

The case of Marmocchi is rather different. A geographer and popular writer, he did not, strictly speaking, belong to the scientific community as De Filippi did, and his work, which came out in installments between 1844 and 1853, was aimed at a wider audience than just students of zoology.[166] His commitment to Lamarck's transmutation theory was explicit, nevertheless, and he gave a lucid exposition of it. Marmocchi declared that two great hypotheses confronted each other in biology in those years. One assumed "an order of successive births of individuals always similar to their parents with invariable constancy." The other admitted the "direct generation" of some simpler individuals out of inanimate matter, giving rise to all the other species through progressive improvement. This improvement process was the result of the factors Lamarck had identified: the action of circumstances, a "growth force" within organisms, and the hereditary transmission of organic features,[167] including those acquired by the individual. To demonstrate the effectiveness of such factors, Marmocchi adduced as examples domestic breeds and species produced in a very short period of time compared with the geological eras available to nature.[168] As for the "animal series," he maintained that the irregularities and the gaps that were found were ascribable to the same action of circumstances and to "lost species."[169]

The historical background against which Marmocchi set the theories favorable to the transmutation of species illustrates the strictures affecting the circulation of Lamarckian ideas. He defended Lamarck's views by setting them against those of the *philosophe* Buffon, whom he called "our adversary." Lamarck's ideas were never attributed to him alone but also to Pascal, de Maillet, and Goethe. In fact, Marmocchi organized his arguments in such a way that it was Pascal, "that great man whose religious faith was nothing less than genius," who endorsed the transmutation hypothesis and showed that it was reconcilable with religious tradition.[170]

The strategy that Marmocchi thought it fitting to adopt is not the only evidence to indicate that objections of a religious nature and the accusation of "pantheism" were still an important obstacle to the spread of Lamarckian ideas. In the 1850s, Lamarck's Italian translator, Francesco Baldassini, by then elderly, confirmed this in a comment on Flourens's celebration of the achievements of Cuvier and his school.[171] Baldassini firmly rejected the accusations of pantheism leveled by Cuvier against Geoffroy and Lamarck's views during the famous 1830 debate at the Académie, and now reiterated by Flourens. He considered those accusations evidence that in the debate Cuvier had violated the rules of serious scientific discussion by raising a theological question for the purpose of discrediting his adversaries. According to Baldassini, if by charging Geoffroy with pantheism Cuvier had meant to accuse him of espousing a conception of nature ruled by "random" circumstances, then Geoffroy's ideas on the rigorous laws of animal organization were enough to fully exonerate him from the charge.[172]

Baldassini, himself early won over to Lamarckian views, was naturally interested, in 1856, in refuting Cuvier's old views and Flourens's revival of them, and he suggested his own version of the events that had characterized natural history during the past twenty-five years. In his reconstruction, Geoffroy and Lamarck were set side by side with exponents of Naturphilosophie such as Goethe and Carus. Baldassini acquitted all of them of the charge of being the heirs of the discredited eighteenth-century protoevolutionists such as de Maillet and Robinet with whom Flourens had associated them. The concepts of unity of composition (Geoffroy) and progressive development of organization in response to changing circumstances (Lamarck) were represented as strictly connected. Baldassini traced a long series of studies and ideas developed during the first half of the century back to those two basic concepts. Baldassini's reconstruction brought Brocchi's earlier speculations on species together with recent developments of embryology and teratology. It juxtaposed Porro's studies on variations in shells and the studies done by Henri Milne-Edwards on crustaceans and J.-L.-A. Quatrefages on *Synaptidae*, a family of holoturians. As for the Lamarckian mechanism of species transmutation, Baldassini speculated that some recent work by the physicist Domenico Paoli on the molecular motion of solids gave a fairly accurate explanation of how external agents could modify organisms.[173] Himself a malacologist, Baldassini thought of shells as the typical example of the action of circumstances on organisms.

His version of the recent history of biology had much in common with Isidore Geoffroy Saint-Hilaire's, and with Richard Owen's as outlined in Owen's letter to Bonaparte read at the Genoa congress of Italian scientists. Such historical reconstructions no doubt oversimplified what had happened in recent decades, but they bolstered many naturalists' conviction that research in the 1840s and 1850s was at last tackling issues that Cuvier had disposed of in the famous 1830 dispute at the Académie.

Thus from their appearance at the beginning of the nineteenth century up to the publication of Charles Darwin's *Origin of Species* in 1859, Lamarckian ideas were familiar to a good many Italian naturalists. Few of them, however, claimed to be Lamarckians. Various circumstances, scientific and otherwise, made it advisable for them not to do so. Carlo Porro's attitude clearly illustrates the scientific side of these qualms. What was concretely known about variation—that is, about the extent of the variability of living forms—was accelerating the critical revision of the concept of species. For the moment, however, Porro did not find this entirely adequate to bring about the radical "innovation" that he felt to be urgently needed.

As for the qualms attributable to problems of a religious nature, the attitudes of Parlatore and Baldassini, different as they were, are significant. Ever since the 1830 controversy, and even before, the accusation of pantheism launched by Cuvier had threatened Lamarck's and Geoffroy's ideas, which tended to be seen as the same, thanks to a polemicist's stratagem employed by Cuvier. What he presented as pantheistic, and therefore deplorable according to Christian tradition, was the idea of an autonomously developing nature, capable of producing an infinite number of forms merely as the result of "random" changes in circumstances. The marvelous laws of animal organization established by Geoffroy, Baldassini retorted, provided ample arguments for refuting that accusation, without having to give up the idea of a progressive development of living forms. On the other hand, Parlatore, whose position was incomparably more prestigious and more representative within the scientific community than Baldassini's, found it more opportune to stick to the laws of organization while forgoing the hypothesis of the natural production of species. Yet—and this was a crucial change—even in the eyes of those who, like Parlatore, deliberately rejected the transmutation hypothesis, the new disciplines gaining ground in the first half of the century (comparative anatomy, embryology, paleontology, teratology, biogeography) were delineating a picture of organic nature that was richer, more varied, and above all more dynamic than anything earlier generations of naturalists could have conceived of, even when they allowed themselves to be guided by the old notion of the chain of beings or by Lamarck's ideas on transmutation.

BETWEEN IMMUTABILITY
AND EVOLUTION

Through several episodes—Bonaparte's attack on Cuvier in 1830, the debate on classification in the congresses of the 1840s, and the circulation of Lamarck's ideas—we have explored the attitude of the young Italian scientific community toward the species problem. What has emerged makes it possible to specify above all in what sense scientists perceived the existence of a "species problem" before the introduction of Darwin's theory. Only for a limited number of Italian naturalists did the alternative between a transformist conception and a nontransformist conception of species take the form of a radical choice. It was perceived in such terms only by those who decided to deal explicitly with Lamarck's legacy, either to adopt it in part, as Bonelli, Baldassini, Marmocchi, and Matteucci did, or to reject it, wholly or in part, as did Ranzani, Parlatore, and others. The rest of the naturalists—and the first group, too, when they were not expressly involved in confrontations over Lamarck's contested hypotheses—followed research traditions that managed to sidestep the immutability/transformism alternative. Thus Bonaparte's attack on Cuvier was not in any direct sense an attack on Cuvier's creationism, just as the concurrent Parisian controversy between Cuvier and Geoffroy turned not so much on the issue of transformism as on a host of other questions.

Likewise, it would be reductive to describe the debate over the "natural system" among Italian scientists in the 1840s simply as a conflict between a static and a dynamic conception of nature. The debate was carried on for the most part within a complex classificatory tradition, in which the problem of the limits of species variability was just one of many. The reformulations of the long-standing idea of an "organic series," proposed in the light of comparative anatomy, embryology, or paleontology, could in fact be linked to a variety of "dynamic" or "synthetic" conceptions of nature; but these did not necessarily imply adherence to a theory of species transmutation of a Lamarckian type. In any case, in Italy naturalists with an adequate "professional" competence and an interest in the phenomena of organisms' adaptation to the environment and the study of variations and their causes—that is, the kind of research most pertinent to Lamarck's and Darwin's evolutionary theories—were a tiny minority, represented in two different generations by Bonelli and Porro.

It might be conjectured that interest in this kind of problem was limited because Italian culture lacked the sizable tradition of "natural theology" that elsewhere, especially in Britain, kept a concern for the question of organisms' "providential" adaptation alive among naturalists.[174] By the same token, the fact that the theme of "war" in nature was fairly infrequent in the writings of Italian naturalists might be linked to the relatively static social context in which they lived.[175] Elsewhere, under the pressure of social concerns, the theme was creeping into studies on biogeography (a field that was also cultivated by some in Italy).[176] But this sort of "negative" evidence is notoriously shaky ground for the historian.

The events in the Italian scientific community between 1830 and 1859 seem rather to confirm the existence and diffusion of a substantial *third alternative*, in addition to transformism and nontransformism, in pre-Darwinian biology. Examples of a similar third alternative have been pointed out by Martin Rudwick in the work of Richard Owen and by Toby A. Appel in that of Henri de Blainville.[177] We have seen the influence of both these naturalists on their Italian colleagues, but the phenomenon appears wider than is suggested by the personal influence of an Owen or a Blainville. The case of Carlo Luciano Bonaparte indicates that the traditional naturalist's

empiricism and some theoretical remnants of the eighteenth-century notion of a chain of beings could combine in a mixture incompatible with
Cuvier's classificatory divisions, while the cases of De Filippi, Parlatore,
and Costa indicate that even those who, unlike Bonaparte, accepted the
teachings of comparative anatomy and Cuvierian systematics, engaged ea-
gerly in reflections on the organic series or the unity of composition that
Cuvier had firmly resisted. Among Italian scientists, what brought about
the eventual decline of Cuvier's proscriptions was, in addition to Bonaparte's kind of eclectic empiricism, the circulation of the works of German
naturalists. This circulation had been promoted in various ways by the
success of Goethe's morphology, by Naturphilosophie, and especially by
the impressive new findings emerging from embryology, recapitulation
theory, and cell theory.

The success of a third alternative beyond fixism and transformism was
undoubtedly fostered by the charge of "pantheism" that had stalked Lamarck's ideas in Italian scientific circles at least from 1819, as Ranzani's
writings show. Cuvier had polemically intended the accusation to implicate
both Lamarck and Geoffroy's and the German naturalists' speculations on
the unity of composition, an association that from the historical standpoint
was debatable, to say the very least. In the 1840s and 1850s, however, the
accusation had come to be directed mainly at Lamarckian views. By then,
in any event, it was the Lamarckians themselves, given the success of
"synthetic" or "dynamic" speculations on the natural system dating back
to Geoffroy, who willingly conceded the affinity between these and transformist, Lamarckian views, though with historical justifications no more
solid than Cuvier's.

In this situation an interest remained alive among naturalists for the
distant controversy of 1830 between Cuvier and Geoffroy. New interpretations of the old dispute were subject to the needs of the moment. A
critical assessment drafted by Bonaparte in 1854 is indicative of the new
situation.[178] He stressed what great changes had occurred in the discussion
of the issues that had been at the center of the controversy twenty-four
years earlier. Yet in effect he still summoned up that episode again precisely
to demonstrate that Cuvier, the apparent victor in 1830, should in the end
be considered the loser.

The tangible signs of Cuvier's defeat, according to Bonaparte, also included the by-then-definitive decline of the old and poorly defined idea of
the immutability of species. In an 1856 paper, which thus preceded Darwin's *Origin* by three years, Bonaparte could emphatically state—in harmony with views that Isidore Geoffroy Saint-Hilaire had upheld for a long
time, though with greater caution—"*the hypothesis of the fixity of species is
simply absurd, of an absurdity that strikes even those who are least versed in
science.*"[179] In a parallel fashion, in Bonaparte's opinion the idea of a transmutation of species was becoming imperative, limited within the span of
the single geological eras but virtually unlimited in the course of the entire

history of life. At this point one might wonder: did the decline of the old, spurious notion of the fixity of species unequivocally amount to a victory for evolutionism?

For the reasons we have seen in this chapter, Cuvier's posthumous defeat cannot itself be said to have implied the victory of transformism. While many obstacles had been overcome and an enormous amount of new information had been accumulated, potentially usable in an evolutionary perspective, few naturalists—as we have seen in the Italian scientific community—found it desirable or urgent to adopt an evolutionary perspective. Few naturalists were capable of formulating and imposing an orientation of this kind in their own particular discipline. There may have been no one, ultimately, whose competence was broad enough even to conceive of a synthesis, from an evolutionary perspective, of all the knowledge amassed by biology in the previous thirty years. And this, precisely, was the extraordinary goal that Darwin would soon pursue with the *Origin of Species*.

PART II
After the *Origin*

Introducing Natural Selection

Innovation and Tradition in Zoology: G. Canestrini

"I have heard it said," Darwin wrote in his *Autobiography*, "that the success of a work abroad is the best test of its enduring value. I doubt whether this is at all trustworthy, but judged by this standard my name ought to last for a few years."[1] Darwin was evidently convinced that one indication of a scientific theory's validity is the extent to which it is adopted in cultural areas other than the one in which it was conceived. However, the process by which a scientific theory is transplanted from one cultural context to another has not often been studied by historians.[2] This may be a result of the common and largely legitimate conviction that the validity of scientific theories tends to transcend cultural boundaries, possibly more easily than any other sort of intellectual work.[3] The opportunity to test that conviction is one of the facets that make the study of the diffusion of Darwin's theory beyond the English-speaking world so fascinating.

The reception of Darwin's theory in Italy might be said to offer a particularly severe test of the transnational nature of the scientific enterprise.[4] The situation of research and scientific institutions in Italy in the second half of the nineteenth century clearly differed from that in England in a number of ways.

For one thing, the two countries' standing within the international scientific community was very different. In contemporaries' estimation,[5] England was vying for first place, whereas Italy was plummeting from third to sixth place. The role of science in national life also differed, as is indicated by the way institutions such as the British Association for the Advancement of Science flourished, while the fate of Italian scientists' annual itinerant congresses remained uncertain.[6] As for the disciplines most relevant to the diffusion of Darwin's theory, Italy did have a solid tradition of natural history studies in the many universities and academies throughout the peninsula, but it had been slow to establish new, specialized societies of the kind that in England had been providing fresh impetus to studies in

geology, zoology, and botany ever since the turn of the century.[7] And
beyond the limited circles of experts, the audience of laymen interested in
the questions debated by naturalists had been expanding at different rates
in the two countries. In England a lay audience existed prior to the diffusion
of Darwin's theory, as is shown by the success of the *Vestiges of the Natural
History of Creation* (1844).[8] In Italy the diffusion of popular science books
coincided with the arrival of Darwin's *Origin of Species*. It is no accident
that the first Italian naturalist to be successfully involved in the popularization of science was one of Darwin's most energetic supporters, Michele
Lessona.[9] Finally, England and Italy were manifestly dissimilar in the traditions of philosophical and religious thought with which scientists had to
come to terms when dealing with wide-ranging theories such as evolutionism.

In what way and to what extent did these differences influence the
Italian reception of a scientific theory generated in England? Did they only
shape the perception of the wider audience and the many who were re-
sponsive to the theory's appeal? Or did they also influence the more limited
scientific circles that aspired to be part of the international scientific community, and that made positive contributions to the development of Darwin's theory? In view of how little nineteenth-century Italian science has
been studied up to now, some of these questions may seem premature. In
fact, for the time being, the most appropriate approach for drafting some
answers is to lay down a limited number of case studies focusing on authors
or moments especially relevant to the reception of Darwin's theory in Italy.
One such case is represented by Giovanni Canestrini and his work.[10]

The first Italian translator of the *Origin of Species* and editor of many of
Darwin's other works in Italian, Canestrini contributed an early application
of Darwin's theory to the problem of the origin of human beings in the
1860s. Over the next thirty years, with a competence grounded in a solid
preparation in natural history, he recorded and evꜜ ꜜated criticisꜟ ꜟ
amendments, and alternatives to Darwin's theory that were emerging o.
the international scientific scene. Some aspects of this work brought him
directly into contact with Darwin. With his combination of declared loyalty
to Darwin's ideas and tendency to circumvent, like Darwin himself, the
most heated disputes over evolutionism, Canestrini acquired the reputation
of being "the most Darwinian of the [Italian] Darwinists."[11] To borrow
Thomas Kuhn's well-known expression, he might be said to represent better than anyone else in Italy the "normal science" practiced by the Darwinians,[12] that is, the routine research that thrived among biologists after
the "revolution" precipitated by Darwin. But how did the direction of
Canestrini's research actually change with the adoption of Darwin's theory?
Did adherence to Darwinism also modify his conception of biological science, its objectives, and its basic methods of investigation? In which fields
did Canestrini feel that Italian scientists could contribute to transforming
into a proven theory what he continued to regard as a hypothesis?

Addressing these questions will entail some considerations of a more general order. One has to do with how different disciplinary traditions within biology—for example, systematic zoology, as distinct from experimental biology—reacted to Darwinian innovation. Another concerns how the different development of single disciplinary traditions in the different national contexts affected the diffusion of Darwin's theory in each country. The picture of the "Darwinian revolution" that will emerge from consideration of this kind based on the Italian case departs form the current image in a number of ways.

THE EARLY IMPACT OF THE *ORIGIN OF SPECIES*: EVOLUTIONISM AND ZOOLOGY

If a prompt translation is any measure of the country's receptivity to the theory expounded in the work translated, then in the case of the *Origin of Species* Italy ranked as the third most receptive, along with Russia and the Netherlands.[13] The first Italian edition appeared in 1864, following a German translation in 1860 and a French one in 1862. Before Darwin's death there would also be translations into Swedish (1869), Danish (1872), Polish (1873), Hungarian (1874), Spanish (1877), and Serbian (1878). By 1977 the *Origin* had been translated into twenty-nine languages. As R. B. Freeman has noted, by this yardstick the only scientific works to surpass Darwin's were Euclid's.[14]

But, of course, how promptly a work is translated provides only a very rough measure of its impact and recognition. A more revealing picture emerges from information indicating who took the initiative for the translation, how those persons fit into the scientific community, and what use was made of the work once it became accessible to a wider audience than those who could read it in the original language. Particulars of this kind are especially important because Darwin and other contemporaries felt the first translations of the *Origin* were not reliable. Darwin was dissatisfied with the German version,[15] and the French edition was quickly challenged because of Clémence Royer's long preface,[16] which placed greater emphasis upon the controversial philosophical, religious, and political implications of Darwin's book than upon its scientific content.

Cognizant of the disservice that some thought Royer had rendered Darwin, the Italian translators, Giovanni Canestrini and Leonardo Salimbeni, announced in 1864 that they intended to refrain from adding "untimely annotations" to Darwin's theory.[17] They warned Italian readers against the French translation, "in many points erroneous and generally too free and imprecise."[18] Canestrini and Salimbeni's proclaimed neutrality toward Darwin's theory and their insistence on rigor in translating it did not prevent them from stressing the exceptionally wide philosophical scope of the *Origin*. They felt it brought substantial "changes to nearly all the natural

sciences" and tended to "strictly limit the immediate influence of a su-
pernatural force." Bearing in mind the potentially wide audience that the
work might reach in Italy as it had in England,[19] they pointed out that "the
conclusions developed with so much common sense in this book are such
that they may interest not only the positive scientist and the rationalist
philosopher but also all those who enjoy, out of simple curiosity, pondering
the difficult subject of the genesis and the development of animal and plant
species."

The attributes of the *Origin*'s potential audiences referred to here coincided in part with those of the two translators. Canestrini could at that
time aspire to being described as a "positive scientist," while his occasional
contributions to the press propagandizing secular "freethinking" showed
his penchant for "rationalist" philosophy.[20] Twenty-nine years old, he had
been director of the Museum of Natural History at the small University of
Modena for two years. He had had a thorough preparation as a naturalist,
acquired during seven years at the University of Vienna,[21] from which he
had graduated in 1860, and an initial scientific training period at the Museum of Natural History in Genoa. In both Vienna and Genoa, Canestrini
had focused on ichthyology. Since 1861 he had participated, with a role of
increasing responsibility, in editing the only periodical specifically devoted
to zoology then printed in Italy.[22] These activities had brought him into
frequent contact with the leading Italian naturalists of the day, including
Giorgio Jan and Emilio Cornalia of Milan, Filippo De Filippi, then of Turin,
and Michele Lessona, with whom he had worked in Genoa.

Canestrini's cotranslator of the *Origin*, Salimbeni, who did much of the
actual work, resembled instead those amateur naturalists who were also
expected to have an interest in Darwin's book. A teacher of natural history
and "terrestrial physics" at the Collegio San Carlo in Modena, Salimbeni
published articles on a variety of natural history topics in local newspapers,
revealing a taste for subjects that were also of practical value, such as how
to raise silkworms. Some of his more theoretical articles, published prior
to the translation of the *Origin*, revealed him as a proud opponent of spontaneous generation and a partisan of Louis Pasteur in his controversy with
Félix-Archimède Pouchet.[23] Salimbeni's pride in this position was all the
greater because at the Collegio San Carlo he occupied the chair held at the
beginning of his career by Lazzaro Spallanzani, the fiercest Italian opponent
of spontaneous generation in the previous century. In these articles Salimbeni showed a Christian conception of nature governed by Providence,[24]
a notion completely absent from the writings of the "rationalist" Canestrini.

The positions and personalities of the two translators, and the fact that
the work was printed in Modena rather than in one of the leading national
centers of publishing, seem to indicate that the Italian scientific community
did not usher in Darwin's theory in 1864 in a particularly impressive way.
The characteristics of the publisher confirm this: Nicola Zanichelli had
founded his publishing house only five years before, and Darwin's was its

first book of outstanding scientific relevance.[25] Furthermore, of those involved in the first Italian translation, only Canestrini remained loyal to Darwin's theory. By 1866, Salimbeni had already expressed some reservations,[26] and Zanichelli would soon publish some of the severest of the Italian attacks on Darwin's theory.[27]

These being the promoters of the first Italian translation of the *Origin*, and their expectations, how did the general public react to the initiative? Unfortunately, the sort of detailed information on the English editions is not available for the Italian translation.[28] There is reason to think, however, that it did not circulate widely. When in 1875—eleven years later—Canestrini edited a new translation for another publisher, based on the sixth English edition, he did not mention that the first edition had sold out.[29] He only alluded to the corrections that Darwin had meanwhile made in the original text. The conviction that Darwin's writings were generally more often debated than read was expressed by many, including another of Darwin's Italian translators, Michele Lessona.[30] This situation will obviously be taken into due account when dealing with the popular reception of Darwinism.

Here, however, we are interested in the events of the narrower Italian scientific community, consisting of those with the competence to attempt a detailed appraisal of Darwin's theory and possibly contribute to its further development. Canestrini is a representative figure for this purpose. When the *Origin* appeared, he was young enough to adhere enthusiastically to the new theory but mature enough to have a background as a pre-Darwinian naturalist. What impact did the new theory have on his scientific investigations?

As a student of philosophy and natural sciences in Vienna during the second half of the 1850s, Canestrini had taken part in the work of the Viennese Society of Zoology and Botany. With its rich natural history collections, its library, and its periodic meetings, the society provided a favorable environment for the formation of a young scholar, even though there were no scientists of European stature in the field of natural history. Canestrini worked mainly with Rudolf Kner, one of the society's vice-presidents, and professor of zoology at the university.[31] The proximity of German universities and the common language in any case favored contacts with the German scientific community, which was among the most active and prestigious at that time.

In his earliest projects Canestrini was engaged in a critical revision of the classification of fishes, particularly teleosts, proposed by the renowned Johannes Müller.[32] A source of inspiration for Canestrini's critique of Müller were the recent works of Rudolf Albert von Koelliker and André Duméril, while the guiding idea for the "reform" of fish classification remained the stipulation that classificatory subdivisions be as "natural" as possible. Establishing a taxonomy of living forms that reflected all their features as faithfully as possible was the classic aspiration of pre-Darwinian natural history. The amendment of classifications in accordance with this ideal proceeded through the study of new specimens, sometimes employing the minute observation afforded by the microscope, and, more important, through a critical appraisal of the features selected in order to distinguish between the different groups of organisms. In his early works Canestrini used these procedures, avoiding broader theoretical questions such as those raised by the notion of the organic "series." Moreover, he worked mainly on specimens of fish preserved in the Vienna museum, i.e., on just a few individuals per species, and not usually live specimens.[33] This had long been a standard research style in natural history.

An example of the limited "reforms" of the classification system that were possible with such methods is provided by Canestrini's first studies of "labyrinth fish."[34] Systematists had created this family to cover all fish with a labyrinthine cavity located above the gills. More accurate studies, however, were revealing that in the fish traditionally assigned to this family, the "labyrinth" did not always fulfill the same function. Moreover, a labyrinthine organ recently had been discovered in another order of fishes. In the light of all this, the family that up to then had been believed to be adequately identified by the presence of a labyrinth no longer seemed *natural*: a different classification of the genera and species contained in it would have to be found.

It is not known when Canestrini read the *Origin* for the first time.[35] What is known is that a number of his writings, even subsequent to his translation of Darwin's book, show no signs of the sort of radical change we might expect would be produced by a scientific "revolution." This at least holds true for his research in systematic zoology of the type mentioned above: the writings that Canestrini published in Italian in the early 1860s maintained the same approach as those that had appeared in the Viennese society's *Verhandlungen* prior to the publication of the *Origin*.

The examination of the external form and proportions in, for instance, pleuronectids (a family of fishes that included the flounder) observed in the Gulf of Genoa, near which Canestrini lived from 1860 to 1862, permitted him to identify six species in addition to those already known.[36] The observation of a number of specimens of flying gurnard, ranging from young fish to adults, on the other hand, permitted him to dispel misapprehensions that had arisen when different-aged specimens of the same species were mistakenly classified as different species.[37] Such mistakes were frequent, because of the practice of identifying new species on the basis of very few observed specimens. Unlike in Vienna, in Genoa Canestrini could carry out observations on a large number of fish: for the time being, proximity to the sea modified his work at least as conspicuously as the new theoretical framework.

The first signs of Darwin's influence appear in Canestrini's work not in the adoption of a radically new perspective but in a heightened awareness of issues that systematic zoology had already identified as critical for some time. His works of the 1860s stress the uncertainties attending the definition of the boundaries of single species, or the presence in some genera of a particularly large number of varieties of the same species. For example, the study of a common freshwater fish, the rudd, showed that this species is subject to considerable variation, confirming, Canestrini noted, "the view of A. Candolle, Darwin, and others that very common species tend to vary a great deal."[38]

The phenomenon of variation was familiar before Darwin, of course. In chapter 2 we saw that in the 1840s Carlo Porro, following in Isidore Geoffroy Saint-Hilaire's footsteps, tried to establish the "laws of variation" of some genera of mollusks. In the case of fishes, there had for some time been attempts to systematize the multiplicity of forms by carefully measuring and calculating the ratios between the different parts of the body thought to be typical of each species. Canestrini's study of many specimens now revealed that such relationships varied with age, sex, and even location. In this respect, the new Darwinian standpoint encouraged the systematist to assume an approach that already had been adopted by naturalists such as Geoffroy Saint-Hilaire and Porro: reduce the number of "true" species, and try to order the varieties belonging to each. As Canestrini now warned, "allowing varieties to be incorrectly called species not only makes classification of our fishes difficult but also curtails a priori the investigation of the causes that give rise to many varieties."[39] This investigation of *causes* was the top priority pointed to by Darwin's theory, but systematists had a great deal of work yet to do before they could begin to handle the various hypotheses put forward on the causes of variations.

Canestrini perceived that the evolutionary perspective launched by Darwin's theory definitely required that the traditional concept of species be revised, but not that it be radically transformed, much less that the concept be abandoned. Canestrini would later severely criticize excesses in that respect:

> the incontrovertible fact that there are no distinct boundaries between species and varieties has led some of Darwin's followers to an extreme and erroneous conclusion. They claim that species do not exist, that the study of species is a waste of time and effort, and that systematic zoology is a useless science. Here it should be considered that the theory of species transformation does not destroy the concept of species, it simply modifies it. Should we neglect the study of islands of a particular sea because we know that they are subject to uplifting and lowering, and that at some depth they are all connected? We must not forget that a species can remain unchanged for many thousands of generations, and that although the species may be in the process of transformation, this process takes place so slowly that people once believed organic forms unalterable.[40]

The Darwinian point of view on species transmutation, in other words, should not have led to conflict with the tradition of systematic zoology. Canestrini indicated the objective reasons that made such a dispute pointless: Darwinian transformations were produced so slowly that the description of present species could ignore them. With these remarks Canestrini was no doubt also defending the disciplinary tradition of his own training: still seeing things from within this tradition, he felt that "the ideas on species current among evolutionists" did not provide a satisfactory definition of the concept.[41] And this was a good reason for not casting out the old disciplinary tradition in the name of the new theory.

At first it was not at all clear in Italian scientific circles just how innovative Darwin's theory actually was. The early information that circulated was inadequate to reveal its originality. News of the publication of the *Origin* was promptly reported in Italy even by periodicals addressing a wide audience, such as the *Rivista contemporanea* in Turin, Carlo Cattaneo's *Politecnico* in Milan, and the Jesuits' *Civiltà cattolica*. The accounts published in these journals, however, were rather unreliable. Italian journals often relied on French or German periodicals for reviews of English books. The language barrier appears to have made itself acutely felt here. Additional confirmation is the fact that even the two most frequent Italian translators of Darwin's works, Canestrini and Lessona, carried on their correspondence with Darwin in German and in French respectively.[42]

The *Rivista contemporanea* gave a correct but extremely succinct notice of the *Origin*, probably written by De Filippi, who contributed regularly to the periodical.[43] The Jesuit geologist and naturalist Gian Battista Pianciani informed the readers of *Civiltà cattolica*, apparently borrowing his information from the *Bibliothèque universelle* of Geneva.[44] The brief review published in the *Politecnico*,[45] though it mentioned some key concepts of Darwin's theory, did so in language so obscure that doubts remain as to what sources had been used and what readers understood. As with Canestrini's professional reaction, when the new theory first appeared in these reviews aimed at less qualified audiences, it settled untraumatically into the tradition of previous natural history studies.

When news of the *Origin* arrived, De Filippi had just published an essay in the *Rivista contemporanea* reporting on the recent discovery of human fossils that conclusively disproved Cuvier's beliefs as to the recent origin of the human species.[46] In *Civiltà cattolica* Pianciani had for some time been keeping his readers informed on recent geological theories, and he was cautiously attempting to clear Lamarck of the old charge of pantheism.[47] He must have found it reassuring to read in the *Bibliothèque universelle* that Darwin had reproposed Lamarck's theory "in a more judicious and acceptable form."[48] In any event, he endorsed the appeal to creationism with which Pictet concluded his review of the *Origin* in the *Bibliothèque*. But in this early phase, the "creationism" that was contrasted with Darwin's theory did not offer clear-cut and obvious distinctions. When presenting the *Origin*, the "secular" journal *Politecnico* recalled that some time earlier Richard Owen had availed himself of paleontological evidence to establish "the axiom that creation is continuous."[49]

Readers of journals for the educated lay audience were thus informed that Darwin's theory could be traced back to a research tradition with firm roots in past natural history. Reporting in 1861 on a recent university course held by the electrophysiologist Carlo Matteucci, who would become minister of education a few months thence, the *Rivista italiana* wrote that

> our professor seems to be inclined to admit the progressive metamorphoses of many parts of plants and animals under various circumstances, but in the moderate form that the works of Goethe, de Candolle, Frank, and Carus have obliged us to recognize, a far cry from the excesses of Lamarck's system. . . . If we were to interpret our teacher's position, we would say that, while he does not greatly depart from the opinions of Geoffroy Saint-Hilaire and other learned naturalists, he is approaching the new theory of the developments and metamorphoses of living beings now proclaimed by Darwin.[50]

As we know, Matteucci had revealed his partiality to transformism twenty-five years earlier.[51] He could now look on Darwin's theory as an offshoot of a scientific tradition that, with its roots in Lamarck's views and the German philosophy of nature, by then spanned over half a century. This view was clearly not affected by the fact that a part of this tradition, Lamarck, continued to be regarded by some with particular distrust.

It has been seen that the first sign of Darwinian influence in Canestrini's works was his increased awareness of some conceptual uncertainties about the boundaries between species and varieties. The next step—one capable of provoking a real shift—led beyond the search for a natural classification carried out by progressively adjusting the classificatory groups on the basis of new observations on living organisms, and moved toward the search for a *genealogical* classification. Darwin had insisted that a classification of that sort would solve systematic zoologists' problems once and for all: present similarities and differences between organisms, as well as the features of fossils, would all be interpreted in terms of the degree of common descent between the organisms in the evolutionary process.[52] This promise of Darwin's was the one that most impressed systematic zoologists such as Canestrini. It should be pointed out, nevertheless, that the same promise could have been made in the name of any theory of biological evolution, and that it was not immediately clear how the evolutionary process and genealogy suggested by Darwin differed from those of other evolutionists.

A good example of the changes that the evolutionary perspective introduced into systematic zoology can be seen in Canestrini's studies on lophobranchians, a group of teleost fishes that includes the common sea horse.[53] Before Canestrini made his cautious shift toward evolutionism, e.g., in his critique of Müller's account of labyrinth fish, his search for a natural classification was based on the observation and the appropriate systematic use of particular features capable of discriminating between the various groups—for example, the labyrinth. Now what appeared *natural* to Canestrini was the classification which, besides taking into account new observations and the usual principles of systematics, was also consistent with the most reasonable hypothesis on the past history of those living forms. Thus the discriminating feature—e.g., in sea horses, whether or not there was a caudal fin—was investigated not only in adults but also in embryos and fossils. Fossils from Mount Bolca near Verona revealed that in the Eocene a fish similar to the sea horse had a fully developed rounded fin at the end of its tail, whereas in present-day sea horses traces of that fin were found only in the embryo (fig. 4). For this reason nonevolutionary systematists such as Louis Agassiz had considered the Eocene sea horse a species (*Calamostoma breviculum*) distinct from the present-day sea horse. The evolutionary perspective suggested instead that the presence of the caudal fin should be considered a difference in *degree*, not an absolute difference, and that the once well-developed fin had become first rudimentary in the adult and then visible only during the embryonic state. In the future it could be expected to disappear altogether even in the prenatal stages of life. Nevertheless, these facts did not invalidate the classificatory subdivisions: sea horses totally lacking a caudal fin were, Canestrini claimed, "a genus in the making."[54]

The new evolutionary systematics that was emerging did not utilize radically new means. Studies of fossils and embryos were already well developed in the work of systematists of the first half of the century, as we have seen in the Italian scientific community of that time. Still, an explicitly evolutionary point of view made the relationships between paleontology, embryology, and systematics particularly significant: in the search for features that were relevant for classification, the evolutionary perspective offered a new "Ariadne's thread" leading through the "labyrinth" of nature.

To the advantages brought to systematic zoology by the evolutionary viewpoint, Darwin's theory, or what went by that name, added further benefits. This perspective made it legitimate to explore certain questions perceived as "more profound"[55] than those ordinarily permitted by systematics. For example, *why* were sea horses in the process of losing the caudal fin they had in common with other fish? According to Canestrini, a likely explanation was that the earliest sea horses had inherited the fin from other fish genera in which the fin was still an important organ in locomotion. But given sea horses' distinctive vertical posture, an organ of locomotion located on the back became more effective than one on the tail. So the dorsal fin had gradually assumed the function of locomotion performed in other fish by the caudal fin, which was disappearing in more recent sea horses (fig. 4).

All this meant that the evolutionary perspective considered the characteristics of organisms from two standpoints: one focusing on the set of features that each organism inherited from its ancestor, the other on the usefulness of these features in the actual life of the single organism. Ca-

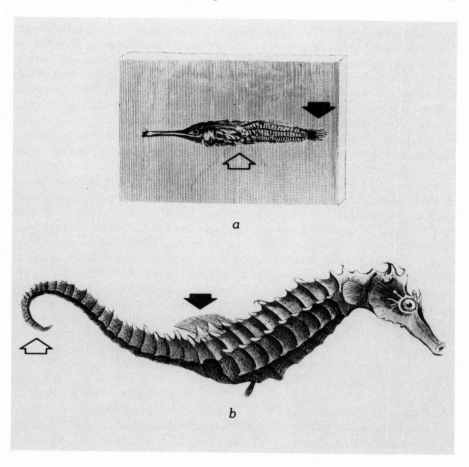

a

b

Fig. 4. Adopting an evolutionary perspective, Giovanni Canestrini argued that the sea horse of his day (*b*) had descended from an extinct fish (*a*) whose fossil remains had been found some time earlier on Mount Bolca, near Verona. Louis Agassiz (*Poissons fossiles* [Fossil fishes], 1833–43) had called the extinct fish *Calamostoma breviculum*. Subscribing to no evolutionary theory, Agassiz thought that the fossil fish should be considered a separate species from present-day sea horses, or that it might even represent a separate genus. In Canestrini's opinion, instead, it was the change in the sea horse's life habits that had made it assume its present nearly vertical posture, leading to the disappearance of *calamostoma*'s caudal fin and to the development of the dorsal fin, barely perceptible in the extinct fish. Fig. 4a comes from *Ittiolitologia veronese* (Veronese ichthyolithology) (1796); 4b from *Encyclopédie méthodique* (Systematic encyclopedia) (1788).

nestrini expressed the conviction that an organ which was useless in the organism's life would *necessarily* gradually disappear,[56] a hypothesis that Lamarck had formulated earlier and more insistently than Darwin. A strictly Darwinian explanation would have claimed that a "useless" organ might disappear only in the event that the species underwent a series of variations which—if they led to a reduction of the organ, and if this turned out to be advantageous in the struggle for existence—would be retained by natural selection until the organ disappeared. Like Lamarck, Canestrini tended to emphasize that the failure to use an organ would instead have immediate effects on the species' hereditary patrimony, and to this extent he disregarded Darwin's natural selection.

Despite his Lamarckian leanings, Canestrini did not prove to be a particularly inconsistent Darwinian. As Peter J. Vorzimmer has shown,[57] Charles Darwin himself, though desirous to affirm the primacy of "his own" natural selection, never wholly repudiated the Lamarckian factors of the use and disuse of organs. As we will see more fully below, it could be argued that the distinction between Lamarckian and Darwinian concepts, though crucial in later developments of evolutionary biology, did not appear so for a long while after 1859. Judging by the way Canestrini saw things from Italy, threats to the primacy of Darwinian evolutionism seemed, if anything, to come from hypotheses that denied that environment or use and disuse could have *any* effect on organisms. In the 1860s a hypothesis of that sort had been formulated by Rudolf Albert von Koelliker,[58] claiming that biological evolution was the product of a general law of development of organisms, implicit in their very "germs" and wholly independent of both Lamarckian "environment" and Darwinian "struggle for existence." Canestrini pondered Koelliker's hypothesis, eventually deeming it unacceptable but regarding it as the only serious alternative to what he meant by "Darwin's theory."

In sum, there is enough evidence to show that Darwin's theory—in spite of the novelty of its concepts and the hopes it raised for a new synthesis of recent work in biology—was viewed by Canestrini and many of his Italian colleagues as being profoundly grounded in the zoology of the first half of the century.

PREHISTORIC ITALIANS, NINETEENTH-CENTURY ITALIANS, AND ANTHROPOLOGY

Darwin is well known to have carefully avoided mentioning human beings in the *Origin of Species*. Apropos of the human species, he confined himself to predicting, at the end of the book, that in the near future his theory would throw light "on the origin of man and his history."[59] It is also known, however, that in the controversy raised by his theory in England and elsewhere, the question of the animal origins of human beings immediately impressed most as the crucial problem posed by that theory: news of the historic confrontation in Oxford in June 1860 between Bishop Samuel Wilberforce and Thomas H. Huxley on the issue of whether the human species might have had monkey ancestors quickly made the rounds of Europe.[60]

In Italian scientific circles there do not appear to have been special reasons why Darwinian evolutionism was discussed more often from the standpoint of anthropology than from other angles. As a matter of fact, physical anthropology had not recently been attracting particular attention among Italian naturalists. As has been seen,[61] they tended to lean toward systematic interests, in the broad sense that had become current before 1859, embracing research on embryology, physiology, paleontology, and geographical distribution. And yet in Italy, too, anthropological issues provoked the fiercest debates on evolutionism and Darwinism. At least three circumstances contributed to this: the broad diffusion of medical studies and related disciplines in the universities, the popularity of historical and archeological studies, and the impact the problem of human origins had on the lively controversies then in progress between the supporters of the religious tradition and the exponents of secular culture. We will return to this last point in chapter 6.

For the wider audiences the discussions on Darwinism began in Italy with Filippo De Filippi's famous lecture "Man and Monkeys," held the evening of January 11, 1864, in Turin.[62] Even before the publication of the *Origin*, De Filippi had shown interest in the problem of the antiquity of the human species. He had in fact dealt in his journalistic writing with the discovery of human fossils that—quite independently of the impact of Darwin's work—were revealing that humans' appearance on earth dated back to much more remote times than previously suspected.[63] He did not, however, treat anthropological subjects in his scientific publications: these revealed, if anything, a predilection for fish, as in Canestrini's case.[64] By deciding to publicize evolutionism in connection with the problem of the human species, De Filippi recognized that he was responding more to his inclinations as a lecturer and the wishes of the audience, rather than pursuing his own area of scientific expertise. "This evening I go on stage with 'man and monkeys.' I am going to play the blabbermouth in a big way," he wrote to his friend and colleague Emilio Cornalia of the Milan Museum of Natural History a few hours before the lecture.[65] Another colleague, Canestrini, would later express reservations about De Filippi's decision to introduce wider audiences to the new evolutionary theory in connection with the problem of human origins.[66] He evidently deemed the cautious strategy used by Darwin in the *Origin* more opportune. But even Canestrini would soon enter the fray, and with contributions of greater scientific significance than De Filippi's.

In the mid-1860s there were frequent opportunities for discussing the origins of human beings besides those offered by such human fossil finds as the celebrated discovery of the Neanderthal man toward the end of the previous decade. In 1863 alone, three important works on the subject had come out, all destined to be debated as vehemently as Darwin's book. At the beginning of the year a series of brilliant anthropological lectures by Thomas H. Huxley had been published under the stimulating title *Man's Place in Nature*.[67] A few months later came the ponderous *Antiquity of Man*, by Darwin's celebrated geologist friend Charles Lyell,[68] in which Lyell finally embraced evolutionism. The third work was Carl Vogt's *Vorlesungen über den Menschen* (Lectures on man).[69] The last two works were promptly translated into French, and they soon circulated in that form in Italy as well. The Italian translation of Huxley's book, begun shortly after the publication of the original in English, was completed in 1869 under the pressure of the impassioned debates on evolutionism in anthropology that reerupted that same year.[70]

All three of these works, it should be stressed, had rather odd relationships with Darwin's work. All agreed that the *Origin* had proved an extraordinary stimulus for the adoption of an evolutionary conception of living nature, and therefore also of the human species and its origins. But all three refrained from endorsing Darwin's theory of natural selection, a circumstance not to be forgotten when considering why the widespread success of evolutionism was not accompanied by an equally wide circulation of Darwinian concepts in anthropological debates in Italy in the 1860s.

For Canestrini, less tempted than others by the success that greeted popular lectures on anthropological subjects, the decision to take up the origins of humans, in spite of the fact that he was an ichthyologist, should be traced in part to the new environment in which he worked from November 1862. After having studied cabinet fish in the Vienna museum and living fish from the nearby sea in Genoa, Canestrini was transferred far inland to Modena. The obvious way to convert his research might have been to take up freshwater fish; but at that time in Emilia a new, more stimulating area of study was attracting the attention of historians, archeologists, and naturalists, and it attracted Canestrini as well. It was the discovery of "terramare," remains of huge settlements consisting of huts built on pilings, dating back according to some to Roman times, and according to others to prehistoric Italy. While the study of the terramare was mainly a task for historians, archeologists, and "paleoethnologists," the remains of living creatures found at those ancient sites also offered the naturalist interesting materials for research.[71] An examination of animals of the same age as the inhabitants of the settlements might provide evidence of the changes undergone by single species and possibly solve the problem of the uncertain dating of the terramare.

Canestrini's research in this field was carried out using a thoroughly Darwinian approach.[72] By comparing modifications undergone by some present-day domestic species with the animals used by the terramara inhabitants, he established that there had been a process of artificial selection.[73] Selection employed by breeders had been proposed by Darwin as a model with which to compare the selection that occurs in nature.[74] Occasionally the wild species found in the terramare revealed a process of extinction that also conformed in some ways to Darwin's hypothesis.

Although rich in animal remains, the terramare near Modena examined by Canestrini proved to be singularly poor in human remains. They did not offer new material for ascertaining the changes that the human species might have undergone like the other inhabitants of those ancient sites. The lack was partly made up for by the finds of other scholars, such as Pellegrino Strobel[75] and Luigi Pigorini, who had studied human remains found in terramare in other regions. In 1866 and 1867 Canestrini was therefore able to include the observations on ancient human remains found in Italy when dealing with the controversial theme of the origin of the human species. The *Origine dell'uomo* (Origin of man), which Canestrini published in 1866, offered a useful reappraisal of the controversial problem,[76] in spite of the dearth of new empirical evidence. Although the general terms of the question remained those delineated in the works of Lyell, Huxley, and Vogt, all of whom agreed at least on the principle of an animal origin of humans, Canestrini formulated a hypothesis of his own on the course and timing of that descent. Systematist that he was, he also connected the problem of origins with that of how most appropriately to classify the human species among present-day forms.

In this work on human beings, Canestrini took into account some objections leveled against the hypothesis of the animal origins of the human species by one of Darwin's best-qualified Italian adversaries, Giuseppe Bianconi,[77] a former student of the "Cuvierian" Ranzani.[78] Unlike Huxley,[79] and following Bianconi's lead, Canestrini felt it opportune to maintain the distinction introduced by Blumenbach and Cuvier between "four-handed" quadrumana, i.e., monkeys, which had limbs adapted for grasping, and "two-handed" bimana, human beings. Canestrini regarded the distinction as necessary, along with the recognition—previously noted by Bianconi[80]—of the importance for systematics of two features that differentiated human beings from apes: feet suitable for bearing the weight of the body, and a jaw and teeth lacking feral characteristics. Canestrini thought these two features justified classifying human beings as *a separate order* within the class of mammals,[81] a choice he deemed compatible with the hypothesis of the animal origin of human beings. Canestrini rejected, on the other hand, the proposal that De Filippi had advanced in order to reconcile the hypothesis of the animal origin of humans with religious tradition. De Filippi had concluded his famous 1864 lecture with the proposal that human beings, despite their animal origins, be placed in a special, fourth kingdom of nature.[82] De Filippi's proposal was clearly unsatisfactory from the standpoint of systematic zoology, the one Canestrini favored.

The adoption of a sharp distinction between quadrumana and bimana had clear-cut consequences for Canestrini's hypothesis on the descent of human beings. Known fossils indicated that both apes and human beings had made their appearance on earth during the same geological period, the Tertiary. Apes appeared first, followed by humans. The interval of time was thought to be too short for there to have been a transformation of some four-handed creatures into two-handed ones. Therefore, Canestrini argued, it had to be supposed that "man did not descend from apes, but rather from a common ancestral stock."[83] Apes' and humans' common ancestor must have been the "prototype" of all primates, in other words, of that group of forms to which Linnaeus had assigned both humans and apes. But what was this common ancestor of all primates like? According to Canestrini, it had undoubtedly become extinct subsequent to the success of the species derived from it, which, as Darwin's theory taught, had ended up by leaving it no room in which to exist. Nor should anyone think that its fossils would be easy to find, for the reasons that Darwin had already adopted to explain the incompleteness of the paleontological record. Canestrini thought, however, that some conjectures could be made on the features of that distant ancestor: "The ancestral Primate stock must have been quadrupeds. . . . While in monkeys the four feet were transformed into four hands that continued to be perfected, adapting their owners to life in trees, in man the rear limbs improved, becoming adapted to support the body alone. The anterior limbs, freed of their earlier tasks, assumed more delicate functions."[84] The transformation of the foot into a hand was explained as a result both of the laws of use and disuse of organs, according to what both Darwin and Lamarck had thought possible, and of the natural selection of variations produced in the muscles of the limbs, according to a more strictly Darwinian explanation.

The descent of the human species hypothesized by Canestrini illustrated another important Darwinian principle, that of the "divergence of characters."[85] According to this principle, forms derived from the same species tended to assume increasingly divergent features. This, Darwin argued, was because forms that have their own place in the "economy of nature," not directly contested by similar forms, are more successful. Something of the kind must have happened with the differentiation of quadrumana and bimana, starting with their quadruped ancestor, which evidently could neither live in trees like apes nor exploit the resources of erect posture like human beings. The "divergence" had thus permitted the descendants to occupy two places in the economy of nature instead of the single place occupied by their ancestor.

As Canestrini saw it, a further Darwinian element in this hypothesis on the descent of the human species was that it postulated "a progressive development, or perfectioning" of living forms.[86] Darwin was in fact very cautious on this point: he certainly admitted that natural selection tended to improve the adaptation of species to their physical environment and in their relationships with other organisms, but he held that this did not necessarily involve the realization of more complex organic structures. In any case, he pointed out that we have no objective criteria for judging such structures more advanced.[87] In accentuating the theme of progress in connection with Darwin's theory, Canestrini on the one hand reclaimed Lamarckian themes yet again, and on the other adhered to an interpretation of Darwinian evolutionism that was rather common in the second half of the nineteenth century.

With all this, Canestrini's *Origine dell'uomo* emerged in the mid-1860s as one of the most consistently Darwinian works to appear on the subject in European scientific literature.[88] It certainly lacked the lucidity and effective argumentation of Huxley's *Man's Place in Nature*, or the textbook completeness of Lyell's *Antiquity of Man* and Vogt's *Vorlesungen*. Canestrini's hypothesis on the descent of the human species depended in various ways on all these works, but it was—at least in the author's intentions and in spite of some concessions to the antievolutionists—the most Darwinian yet formulated. And Darwin did not express himself on the subject until five years later. But by 1871, when Darwin's *Descent of Man* was published,[89] many others, among them W. R. Greg, Alfred R. Wallace, Francis Galton, Ludwig Büchner, and Ernst Haeckel,[90] had tried to apply Darwinian principles to the study of the evolution of the human species.

For reasons that will soon be seen, in the *Descent*, Darwin mentioned not Canestrini's hypothesis on human genealogy but some observations Canestrini published in 1867 in a more specialized and much less ambitious paper in which he examined some anomalous and rudimentary characters that appear in present-day human beings as traces of older forms.[91] One such case consisted of occasional anomalies of the malar bone, a cranial bone in vertebrates. The malar is normally all in one piece, but according to Canestrini, observations revealed

that in some quadrumana and other mammals the malar is normally divided into two parts, as is observed in man in exceptional cases; that the malar in the human fetus develops with two distinct bone nuclei; that the above anomaly is found more frequently in the prognathous, less advanced races than in the orthognathous and more advanced races; and lastly, that the very few cases in which this anomaly has been found include an ancient cranium.[92]

The occasional division of the malar into two parts in human beings was thus interpretable as a "reversion to features of a remote stock."[93] This, Darwin claimed, confirmed that the most modern human races were formed by gradual differentiation from their older "semi-human progenitors."[94]

Darwin, in any event, was much more radical than Canestrini in his conclusions on the place of human beings in the classification of living forms. As we have seen, Canestrini had proposed that humans be assigned the rank of an order, wholly distinct from the order of monkeys. He was prompted to do so both by his scruples as a systematist and by his desire to attenuate the conflict between the evolutionists and the antievolutionist

Bianconi. Darwin, instead, thought that human beings could at the most be classified as a family or subfamily of the order of primates, including both human beings and monkeys, who were therefore seen as more closely related.[95] Apropos of human genealogy, Darwin suggested a *direct* descent from a suborder of apes, Catarrhines,[96] instead of from an ancestor common to both humans and apes, as Canestrini proposed. These were probably two good reasons why Darwin did not give as much weight in the *Descent* to Canestrini's theoretical contribution on human genealogy as he did to Canestrini's empirical studies on "reversion" phenomena.

Neither Darwin's work on the human species nor the many others that were subsequently published on the subject appear to have modified Canestrini's views. As late as 1894, with regard to what he described as the "none too rapid advances in paleontology," Canestrini was still inclined to give human beings a completely separate place in the classification of species.[97] And he continued to search for a compromise between the traditionalists, now represented by Giustiniano Nicolucci, and the most fervent evolutionists, now represented by Enrico Morselli:[98]

> As for man, we must return to the time when zoology identified the order of the *Bimana*, and simply change the name; because in my opinion in recent times our views have strayed out of excessive zeal. We fail to consider that human beings differ from apes not only in the morphological and anatomical features familiar to any naturalist, but also in their great intellectual and linguistic faculties that are corollaries of this, and in their broad geographical distribution, the result of their aptitude for acclimatization.[99]

When Canestrini was faced with the controversial problem of the human species, then, his solid training as a systematic zoologist eventually overcame his evolutionist's "zeal." Various circumstances in the 1890s may have made the systematist's concerns seem more urgent than before. Disappointment with paleontology may have contributed, when this field turned out to be less generous than hoped in providing evidence on the genealogy of the human species. The uncertainty of the fate of Darwin's theory in the 1890s may also have been partly responsible. What is clear is that Canestrini continued to go on record in defense of the "general theory of evolution" but no longer went beyond this to formulate hypotheses, Darwinian or otherwise, on human genealogy.

It is very likely that in the case of the human species, problems of an ethical and social nature also made themselves felt. Of all the Italian evolutionists, Canestrini was particularly cautious in applying biological theories to the study of human society. This was a stance that he felt Darwin, too, had always respected. "Anyone who applies the notions of natural history to human society lightly," Canestrini wrote in 1894, "comes to conclusions that can lead us to detest evolutionism."[100] He admitted that something like Darwin's struggle for existence was produced in human society. But concurring with the well-known French anthropologist Paul Broca, he preferred to ascribe to this battle the attributes and the name of "a civil struggle." It was a struggle, Canestrini explained,

> that is fought with weapons of a psychological nature, such as intelligence, rectitude of character, sympathy, fluent speech, quickness of spirit. . . . Physical features are of course useful in that struggle . . . , but a much more important part is played by intellectual and moral characteristics. . . . What natural election and artificial election achieve through the inheritance of characters, civil election obtains through tradition and history.[101]

But why did Canestrini in the 1890s ultimately comment on these controversial issues, relinquishing the Darwinian circumspection he had so faithfully observed? Canestrini's own answer to this question is one to which the historian might subscribe: "One scrutinizes the pages of the great masters to learn their views on the grave problems that torture the present age; and each party, interpreting what it finds in its own way, finds whatever it wishes to. Darwin was right not to deal with these subjects, because in his day it was not urgent to speak up on such issues."[102] What, then, were the "grave problems" that had become more urgent than ever before? Canestrini mentioned one, which must have summed up many:

> If socialism refrains from siding with those parties that attempt to drive civil society back toward conditions that have been successfully overcome, and if it desires the improvement of the means of existence of the neediest and tries to obtain it through evolution, . . . evolutionism, which in human society is inspired by the sentiments of sympathy and justice, cannot but cooperate, so that socialism may achieve its intent. Further suggestions are for statesmen to give, not evolutionists.[103]

Actually, it had not been unusual in Italy in the last three decades of the nineteenth century for "evolutionist" and "statesman" to be one and the same. Well-known evolutionists had occupied political positions ranging from secular conservatism to socialism. Although Canestrini never went beyond the Padua town council, other evolutionists, among them Carlo Matteucci (for a time minister of education), Paolo Mantegazza, and Enrico Ferri, were elected to the Italian parliament, where they brought the many and often divergent political messages that were drawn from evolutionism in the attempt to legitimize different political positions.

Thus in the 1890s concern for the social uses of evolutionism, along with some more solid scientific motivations, oriented Canestrini's position on the origin of human beings. He found new reasons for confirming the particular position that, first as a systematist and then as an evolutionist, he had assigned the human species in 1866. On the other hand, skepticism for the evolutionists' "excessive zeal" and the most recent developments

of the theories of evolution now cautioned him not to resume his original
hypothesis on the genealogy of human beings. Under these circumstances,
of the hypothesis that had asserted the animal origin of human beings,
Canestrini retained little but the principle.

THE EVOLUTION OF DARWIN'S THEORY

We occasionally noted that when Canestrini singled out the causes of particular segments of the evolutionary process, he appealed to Lamarckian
factors (use and disuse, inheritance of acquired characters) as often as to
Darwinian ones (natural selection, divergence of characters). It is well
known that Darwin himself had his doubts about the relative weight of
these factors, as shown in the subsequent editions of the *Origin of Species*
to which he attended.[104] But how and how much did the "Darwinian"
Canestrini puzzle over such questions? How did they affect his reactions
to the concepts that Darwin was developing, such as sexual selection, or
to the entirely new concepts, such as pangenesis, that he was introducing
to complete his theory? How did Canestrini react to the controversies between neo-Lamarckians and neo-Darwinians at the end of the century?

In view of Canestrini's training and the disciplinary tradition within
which he worked, an answer to these questions will cast light on the me-
dium-term effects of the Darwinian innovation. It will also help us to com-
prehend what sort of relations had been set up in the new scientific
tradition inaugurated by Darwin between Darwinian principles and preexisting concepts and beliefs. These are obviously important points to clarify
if we are to avoid oversimplifying the picture of the relationships between
preexisting scientific traditions and Darwinian innovation in the development of biological sciences.

Natural Selection, the Use and Disuse of Organs. In the *Origin*, Darwin defined
natural selection as "the preservation of favorable variations and the rejection of injurious variations" in the struggle for existence.[105] He repeatedly stated that natural selection should be regarded as the main cause of
the transformation of species, though not the only one. Nevertheless, his
ideas on the origin of variations, the raw material on which selection op-
erated, were such that they in fact limited the role of natural selection.[106]
What did Darwin think actually caused the appearance of what were called
variations—those differences, for the most part slight ones, in the features
of one or more individuals compared with the average of the species? If
these variations were conceived of as being produced in some way by the
organism's living conditions, then the natural selection of variations became
a *completion* of the evolutionary process and not its crucial step. Even in
1859, Darwin was leaning toward a conception of the causes of variations
that, as Peter J. Vorzimmer has pointed out, would later undermine his
attempts to claim first place for natural selection over other evolutionary

factors.[107] In spite of his new, original theory of natural selection, Darwin had not completely ruled out Lamarckian factors. He admitted, for example, that variations could be produced by the use and disuse of organs as a result of particular living conditions or, indirectly, by the action living conditions might exert on the organism's reproductive mechanism.[108] Darwin was convinced that these factors could not achieve major and lasting modifications of species without the intervention of natural selection. Many of his followers, however, proved to be less certain of this than Darwin was.

"A prolific source of variations is the use and disuse of the parts, use enlarging and reinforcing the organs, and disuse diminishing and weakening them." This was Canestrini's Lamarckian statement in his 1880 discussion of Darwin's theory.[109] Darwin would have agreed, since in the *Origin* he had stated that "habit, use and disuse have, in some cases, played a considerable part in the modification of the constitution, and of the structure of various organs."[110] Darwin had, however, added, "but that the effects of use and disuse have often been largely combined with, and sometimes overmastered by, the Natural Selection of innate differences."[111] By "innate" differences here Darwin meant the variations caused not by external factors, such as the action of the environment or use and disuse, but originating in the reproduction process in some way that was not yet understood. Canestrini was aware of Darwin's distinction between direct and indirect action of living conditions on variations, "indirect" meaning mediated by the reproductive system and its yet unknown laws. But Canestrini assigned first place unconditionally to the *direct* action of the environment: "in the final analysis, variations must be considered the product of external living conditions."[112]

It is appropriate here to emphasize that by holding such views, Canestrini, and to a lesser extent Darwin himself, subscribed to a preexisting tradition of biological thought. The effects of use and disuse were, of course, the main evolutionary factors according to Lamarck. More generally, the direct action of environmental conditions in producing individual variations had already been studied by Thomas A. Knight[113] and Prosper Lucas,[114] sources extensively used by Darwin. Teratologists, for their part, had emphasized the indirect reactions the reproductive system was capable of inducing under particular environmental conditions.[115] The tendency of certain modifications to be accompanied by alterations in some other part of the organism had been studied by such authors as Cuvier, Goethe, and Étienne and Isidore Geoffroy Saint-Hilaire as an aspect of the so-called law of the correlation of organs.[116]

The Inheritance of Acquired Characters. The effects of use and disuse appeared significant to Darwin and his followers such as Canestrini because of some widespread beliefs regarding the laws of inheritance. The individual that had undergone the effects of the use and disuse of an organ was commonly thought to be able to transmit them to offspring. Belief in the inheritance of acquired characters, as stated by Lamarck, permitted the conjecture that an individual's modifications could become part of the hereditary patrimony of the species. Darwin held that this was not enough to produce significant modifications in species, because of the general blending of organic features that occurred in breeding.[117] He did not, therefore, consider this "law" of inheritance a serious threat to natural selection's leading position. Nevertheless, in Darwinians such as Canestrini, belief in the inheritance of acquired characters detracted from the salience of natural selection. The principle that "all features, including individual ones, are inherited" seemed to Canestrini an essential condition for natural selection to work.[118] In other words, Canestrini reasoned that Darwin's theory of natural selection would not be valid without the notion of the inheritance of acquired characters.

In this case, too, Darwin's and his followers' adherence to an earlier scientific tradition imposed serious limits on the validity of the theory of selection. This was all the more evident in regard to the law of inheritance, since it dealt with a legacy of widespread notions and beliefs. It is known how much Darwin counted on the experience of domestic breeders in this area.[119] According to Canestrini, the belief in the inheritance of acquired characters was confirmed by the experience of physicians, breeders, and laymen. Not having personally carried out research on inheritance phenomena—unlike Darwin—Canestrini was particularly prone to accept unconfirmed reports of the most extraordinary "cases" that seemed to confirm the inheritance of acquired characters, such as the following, incidentally connected with a crucial episode in the process leading to Italy's unification:

> In the Battle of Solferino, that is, in 1859, Mr. Ottone Grueber received a triangular bayonet wound below the left shoulder blade, which eventually healed. The distinctively shaped scar, however, naturally persisted for a long time. . . . In 1864, Mr. Ottone Grueber married; and nine months and three days after the wedding a son was born who (in his father's words) "bore a mark identical to my scar, in the same spot and on the same side as my wound." This young man was fifteen years old in 1880, and according to his mother and another relative, that mark was still visible.[120]

Prone as he was to believe such dubious hearsay on the inheritance of acquired characters, Canestrini would naturally object to August Weismann's decision a few years later to eliminate that concept from the Darwinian theory of evolution.

Canestrini's espousal of pre-Darwinian concepts adopted by Darwin himself did not stem from loyalty to whatever ideas Darwin might endorse. The persuasive strength of such ideas lay, rather, in the earlier scientific tradition that also led Darwin to believe them. When support from that tradition was lacking, Canestrini was capable of severe criticism of Darwin's ideas, as he demonstrated in connection with the theories of sexual selection and pangenesis.

Sexual Selection. Canestrini was never fully won over by Darwin's theory of sexual selection. Darwin had formulated it summarily in the *Origin* and had then devoted the whole second part of the *Descent of Man* to it.[121] The theory originated from the observation that in some species the general characteristics of the male are very different from those of the female. Since natural selection accounted for the transformation of species as such, it was essential to introduce some further principle to explain the differences between the sexes in the same species. Sexual selection was meant to account for the evolution of features such as secondary sexual characteristics that did not have an immediate survival value and therefore did not seem to be traceable to the action of natural selection.

According to Darwin, sexual selection was the combined effect of two phenomena: struggle among males for the possession of females, and the choice that females make, through complex courting rituals, of males that not only are victors but also are better endowed with adornments for attracting females. Darwin argued that males with these advantages left more numerous descendants, other factors relevant to natural selection being equal. As a result, males of that species were gradually modified in ways independent of the phenomena of natural selection affecting the whole species.

Darwin enlisted Canestrini in the sort of data-gathering network he used to organize in order to collect information.[122] In particular, Darwin expected Italian naturalists and breeders to be able to produce reliable estimates of sexual distribution in the populations of two species well known in Mediterranean countries, silkworms and bees. The proportions between the sexes were clearly important, along with information on sexual habits, in order to verify Darwin's hypotheses on the struggle between males and the choice of females. The information that Canestrini was able to convey to Darwin was actually rather uncertain. In fact, there was a divergence of opinions between the Italian naturalists who had studied the subject, such as Cornalia, and the breeders.[123] In any case, Darwin was unable to obtain more reliable information on those two species from other sources.

Alfred Russel Wallace, who had formulated the theory of natural selection independently of Darwin, did not accept Darwin's subsequent hypothesis on sexual selection. He thought that at least some of the phenomena the theory purported to account for could be traced to natural selection.[124] As for Canestrini, after the publication of the *Descent* he did some studies on the subject in which, working once again in the spirit of the taxonomist, he meticulously described the secondary sexual characteristics of some fish and arachnids.[125] He was nevertheless reluctant to concede that sexual selection had the important role Darwin attributed to it; he preferred to heed the objections of Gustav Jäger (similar to those of

Wallace), according to whom "not all secondary sexual characteristics are the effect of a choice made by the female; many are produced by natural selection." In the case of the showy plumage that distinguishes many male birds from females of the same species, for instance, it could be supposed that it was initially present in both sexes, and that in the females it was gradually suppressed by natural selection, less conspicuous plumage making her less noticeable to enemies while brooding.[126]

What prevented Canestrini from espousing the hypothesis of sexual selection was apparently the capacity of "choice" attributed to the females of some species. The presence of such a capacity in organisms occupying a very low position in the usual hierarchy of living forms seemed highly unlikely to him: in such cases, he insisted in 1894, "no true choice is exercised at all."[127] What kept Canestrini from following Darwin and attributing to the peahen, for example, the particular "aesthetic taste" that had indirectly favored the male's development of his extraordinary tail, was the adhesion to a research program that aimed at reducing psychological phenomena to their biological substrate. The appeal of such a program had been fostered by the success of evolutionism, though in Darwin the reductionist program had underpinnings that were incomparably richer and more variegated[128] than those Canestrini was drawing on when, for instance, he wrote:

> the way a closed-circuit electric battery generates electricity is the way the brain produces thought. . . . Psychic faculties are in direct relation to the development of the animal's masses of ganglia, a fact that can be observed both by going up the zoological scale from the lowest animals to man, and by following an individual in its various phases from the onset of life up to death.[129]

What interested Darwin, instead, and led him to discuss sexual selection in insects and birds in his work on human beings, was precisely the possibility of identifying, even in living forms with very simple nervous systems, faculties of "choice" comparable to those of mammals or human beings. This signifies, too, that the evolutionary process as Darwin conceived it was more various and unpredictable than the rigid ascending line some of his followers envisioned.[130]

Pangenesis. With the hypothesis of pangenesis, Darwin tried to provide a comprehensive solution to the controversial issues of inheritance, a set of problems of critical importance for his theory. First published in 1868, in *The Variation of Animals and Plants under Domestication*,[131] the hypothesis asserted that invisible "gemmules" continually detach themselves from all parts of the organism, reaching the sexual organs by channels yet unknown, where they combine with the sex cells governing the formation of new creatures. Although of a highly speculative nature, as Darwin himself was well aware, the hypothesis made it possible to account for a great many phenomena. First of all, it could explain the inheritance of acquired characters: the "gemmules" faithfully transmitted modifications in an individual's organ to its descendants. Additional hypotheses permitted the use of pangenesis to explain phenomena such as hybridization, the existence of features that remain latent only to appear in subsequent generations, and of the regeneration of which the organs of some species are capable.

Darwin's hypothesis met with some skepticism in scientific circles. It encountered increasing opposition from Francis Galton, who had debated the issue firsthand with his cousin Charles Darwin.[132] Others advanced alternative hypotheses diverging from Darwin's to varying degrees. This was what Haeckel did in Germany,[133] Royer in France,[134] and Gustav Jäger in Austria.[135] In Italy Paolo Mantegazza and Gabriele Buccola came out in favor of pangenesis,[136] but Canestrini was less inclined than they to follow Darwin to the new, uncertain terrain of a general theory of inheritance.

In this case it was precisely the desire to generalize that Canestrini found inopportune. Although quite willing, as we saw, to accept the common beliefs of domestic breeders and laymen on inheritance, he was skeptical of the possibility of arriving rapidly at a general theory of inheritance. He expressed himself as follows in an 1879 letter to Buccola: "If I have not yet spoken out on pangenesis, this is because the hypothesis seems fallacious in its details. There is the germ of a great theory there (similar to the atomic theory in chemistry), but the fruit is not yet ripe."[137]

Such skepticism may well have been the result of the particular position in which Canestrini found himself with regard to recent research in biology. He was well enough informed on what was going on in the study of cell reproduction phenomena in the 1870s and 1880s, especially in Germany, to understand the close link that from then on would connect the theories of inheritance to that type of investigation.[138] On the other hand, he was and would remain extraneous to the research program that sought the answer to the questions of inheritance in cell phenomena. The new branch involved two possible research strategies, each in its own way inappropriate for Canestrini. One required the acceptance of bold speculations on hereditary mechanisms, just the sort of conjectures that Canestrini reproached both Galton and Weismann for,[139] and that he eschewed—despite his declared faith in the role of hypotheses in biology—because of his training as an empirical zoologist. The other strategy required experimental laboratory research which again was no easy step away from the disciplinary tradition to which he belonged.[140]

Darwinism and Bacteria. Canestrini's skepticism toward the theory of sexual selection and his diffidence toward a general theory of inheritance did not simply express an aversion to new ideas. When a new area of research opened fresh vistas to evolutionism and was compatible with his theoretical and disciplinary background, Canestrini still met it with interest in the 1880s. This is what happened with bacteriology. For the many physicians and naturalists who in Italy, too, were exploring it, the microscopic world of bacteria was proving to be an ideal environment in which to test Darwin's laws, from variation and the struggle for existence to natural selection and inheritance of characters.

Examination of Canestrini's writings on bacteriology, which came rather late in his career, suggests that a new area of phenomena can in itself instill new life in the theory used to study them.[141] This was all the more true because of the advantages, as Canestrini was well aware, of studying Darwinian principles in organisms that reproduced very rapidly and whose specific characters were very simple. Bacteriology also provided Canestrini with the chance, late in his career, to try his hand at laboratory biology, although in less sophisticated forms than those then developing around cell biology. In the late 1880s at the University of Padua, he set up a bacteriological laboratory that had "the necessary means for both teaching and original research."[142] Judging from Canestrini's writings on the subject, however, the research was aimed more at problems of "public hygiene" than at theoretical biology proper.

Biomechanics, Neo-Darwinism, Neo-Lamarckism. In any case, Canestrini's last collection of writings, published in 1894 and entitled *Per l'evoluzione* (For evolution),[143] confirms that for the Darwinian of the 1890s, not even the new areas of research were capable of dispelling the doubts and a certain disappointment. The doubts mainly concerned the principles of inheritance, as Canestrini felt that Weismann's decision to abandon the old principle of the inheritance of acquired characters had raised more questions than it answered.[144] And there was disappointment especially over the slow progress of paleontology, which did not permit reconstruction of the evolution of species as completely as had been hoped, particularly in the case of the human species.[145] Under these circumstances there was no room for the enthusiasm that in the 1860s and 1870s had surrounded the theory of evolution. Above all, it no longer seemed legitimate to identify evolutionism with Darwinism, as had been customary over the past thirty years. There were many signs that Darwin's theory had itself undergone and was yet to undergo a profound evolution, and rightly so. Indeed, Canestrini's last inaugural lecture, delivered on the threshold of the twentieth century, was entitled "L'evoluzione della teoria della discendenza" (Evolution of the theory of descendence).[146]

Canestrini declared there that his faith in the further development of the theory rested on two cornerstones. One was the Darwinian concept of natural selection, which he maintained should still be considered a major evolutionary factor, although by no means the only one. The second cornerstone did not, strictly speaking, originate with Darwin, but it fulfilled many of the requirements that Canestrini thought a theory of evolution should meet, specifications that expressed his conception of biology in general, as well as his conception of evolutionism. Canestrini now believed that a new cornerstone of the theory of evolution was represented by "biomechanics," or the "mechanics of development" (*Entwicklungsme-*

chanik). This was a recent research program that Wilhelm Roux had extended from embryology, where it had originated, to embrace a wider range of biological phenomena.[147] Canestrini shared with other late-nineteenth-century evolutionists the concern that natural selection, with its accent on the utility of variations in the struggle for existence, could not account for the more minute characteristics of organic structure, those features that, like the smallest variations, did not seem in any sense useful or harmful to the organism. Biomechanics seemed instead to explain such features: "Natural evolution takes care of the relationships between organs and between organisms; biomechanical factors take care of the detailed structure of the living being," Canestrini wrote.[148] The "mechanics of development," moreover, had the virtue in his eyes of preserving intact the belief in the inheritance of acquired characters, a concept that served in Roux's work to connect (and at times to confuse) phenomena of individual development with those of evolution.

Canestrini, furthermore, saw Roux as the champion of a "mechanistic" approach,[149] which he envisioned as a welcome alternative to the speculative tendencies emerging in neo-Darwinism, thanks to Weismann. For Canestrini, Roux had all the traits of the anti-Weismann he was convinced Darwinism greatly needed.

Some of Canestrini's statements seem to indicate, however, that the acceptance of Roux's work and "biomechanics" had potentially dangerous consequences for Canestrini's reception of recent developments in biology. Canestrini thought, for example, that Roux's studies demonstrated conclusively that the egg "was *not* that extremely complex cell described by biologists studying micromeres, and especially by Weismann, i.e., a cell equipped with millions of particles representative of [the organism's features], all bundled together and endowed with a mysterious aptitude for developing at a predetermined time and place."[150] Statements such as this confirm that the superiority of Roux's position in Canestrini's eyes was precisely what led Roux away from future developments in genetics.

It is also clear that Canestrini's preferences were shaped by a particular image of science rather than by adhesion to any specific theory. Mechanism itself, a respect for the "long experience of stock breeders and gardeners" on the inheritance of acquired characters, and the rejection of the "preformationism" of the individual in the egg all counted as points in favor of this image of science, and as points in favor of Roux, against Weismann. Canestrini himself, in any event, no longer would carry out research in either biomechanics or cell biology.

Thus, in spite of his firm adherence to the theory of natural selection, in 1897 Canestrini was not particularly desirous to side with Weismann and the neo-Darwinians; nor could he follow the lead of the neo-Lamarckians or of Herbert Spencer,[151] when they denied that natural selection had any influence. In a sense, the one he felt closest to was Ernst Haeckel, whom he called the "present representative of *classical* Darwinism."[152] Not being a paleontologist, however, he had no particular reason for devoting himself to Haeckel's program, aimed at demonstrating evolution primarily through the reconstruction of the history of living forms. Moreover, this program, Canestrini warned, was running into "very serious difficulties."

DISCIPLINARY TRADITIONS AND THE DARWINIAN REVOLUTION

The case of Canestrini suggests some general remarks on the introduction of Darwinism into biology in the second half of the nineteenth century and on its diffusion. Since Canestrini's activity falls almost entirely within the area of systematic zoology, these remarks focus mainly on the impact of Darwin's theory on systematic zoologists, but they extend to some aspects of the "Darwinian revolution" as a whole.

The shift that Darwinian evolutionism brought about in systematic zoology is very evident in Canestrini's writings of the 1860s. An enhanced awareness of the difficulties in drawing neat boundaries between species and varieties was one of the first signs of this shift, which was then accentuated by the adoption of a new "Ariadne's thread" in studies aimed at delineating the map of the living world. This thread was provided by the study of organisms' evolutionary tree, which entailed closer connections between systematics, paleontology, and embryology.

The kind of reactions examined at the beginning of this chapter seem to indicate that the impact of Darwin's *Origin* on systematic zoology was not traumatic. To judge from Canestrini's example, there were no headlong conversions, nor was an opposing front created forthwith. Various circumstances may have contributed to this fact. In the first place, prior to 1859 Italian scientists embraced no prevailing coherent theory of species that could be considered definitely antithetical to Darwin's. In fact, it would be inaccurate to describe the dominant tone of the Italian debate on species in the 1840s and 1850s as "fixist," or "creationist." Moreover, various theoretical traditions existed that were quite open to Darwin's ideas. As we saw in chapter 2, these included the "moderate" transformism inspired by Isidore Geoffroy Saint-Hilaire, the "radical" transformism traceable to Lamarck, and the kind of transformism cultivated by German natural philosophy. The ease with which Darwin's theory was likened to these earlier traditions was partly due to the fact that for some time in Italy, information on the theory remained derivative and imprecise, a circumstance that may have attenuated the *Origin*'s impact and the perception of its novelty. Historians of Darwinism now seem to agree, in any case, that Darwin himself might not have totally repudiated such links with earlier traditions, and that they expressed, to a different extent in the different cases, Darwin's own debt to the natural history of the first half of the century.

In the years immediately following the publication of the *Origin*, what might be said to have occurred in areas such as systematic zoology was not a confrontation between opposing theories but a confrontation of *a new theory*, Darwin's, with *a complex disciplinary tradition*.[153] This tradition encompassed different theories, as well as a range of different methods and styles of research accepted as adequate tools by those working in the field of systematic zoology.

It seems inappropriate to describe this confrontation between the new theory and the existing disciplinary tradition as conflictual. Canestrini's slow passage from the pre-Darwinian to the Darwinian period could better be described as a gradual adjustment of the two. It was only later, when the new theory so effectively expounded in the *Origin* had polarized the debate among naturalists, that those who did not adopt it began advancing alternative theories. Koelliker's hypothesis—it, too, evolutionary; it, too, carefully weighed by Canestrini—was one of the first examples of this kind.

The polarization thus produced in scientific circles—a rift for which there were at best only a few premises prior to 1859—then combined with the curiosity and interests of a wider audience, attracted by various aspects of Darwin's theory and evolutionism. At this point, all the necessary conditions were in place to turn the debate on Darwin's theory into a dispute involving not only differing theories but also different world-views, such as "evolutionism" and "creationism" and the many other isms that Darwinian science was capable of eliciting.[154]

This account of phases and protagonists may surprise those familiar with the rapid British response to Darwin's theory.[155] And yet it seems the most appropriate reconstruction in the light of the reactions to Darwinism that were produced, as if in slow motion, in the Italian scientific community of the early 1860s.

The persistent vitality of the disciplinary tradition displayed by pre-Darwinian systematic zoology was also revealed in Canestrini's writings on human beings. Although he wholly subscribed to the principle of the animal origins of human beings, he suggested classifying the human species in the way he found most reasonable from the traditional systematist's standpoint, rejecting what he considered the "excessive zeal" of some evolutionists. In this as in other respects, Canestrini can be said to have remained first of all a systematist, and only secondarily an evolutionist.

Where systematic zoology was less competent to judge a new theory or a new concept, Canestrini's opinions were shaped by various less reliable and less consistent presuppositions. His "Lamarckian" belief in the evolutionary efficacy of the use or disuse of organs and in the inheritance of acquired characters was bolstered, apparently, by his faith in the "practical wisdom" of domestic breeders, physicians, and laymen. These common-sense notions were severely shaken but not overthrown in Canestrini's mind by Darwin's theory of pangenesis. His rejection of sexual selection and of the capacity of "choice" that Darwin attributed to females of some lower species was affected by his belief in a rather rigid determinism as to

the relationship between the development of the nervous system and behavior. Methodological concerns and global images of science clearly affected these preferences of Canestrini's and his stance in the late-
nineteenth-century controversies on evolutionism.

Whatever the impact of these concerns and doubts, Canestrini recognized in the 1890s that the future of the theory of evolution would depend
on developments in cell biology, or as we would say, in genetics. It of
course would have been quite another matter for him to translate this awareness, rather late in his career, into a renewed research program.

When the Origin of Species was published in 1859, systematic zoology
was a cosmopolitan disciplinary tradition, already well established in a
number of countries. At that time a theory originating in England could
meet with consensus or resistance expressed in terms which, though by
no means identical, were comparable among systematists working in London, Vienna, or the Italian states. Could the same be said of cell biology
at the end of the century? More specifically, what were the relations within
the Italian universities between systematic zoology, pursued by naturalists,
and experimental biology, pursued mainly by physicians? Were these relations similar to those in German universities of the same period? How
much weight should be attributed to the fact that the proportion of writings
published in foreign languages by someone such as Canestrini was appreciably smaller than that typical of a leading Italian naturalist of the
previous generation?

This investigation must leave questions of this sort partly unanswered.
I can only remark that whereas in the 1860s and 1870s Canestrini could
still make significant contributions to evolutionary systematics, in the 1890s
he was merely an interested bystander pleading for an encounter between
evolutionary systematics and cell biology.[156]

It is well known that the encounter between systematics and cell biology
would eventually take the form of the "new synthesis" bridging the various
disciplinary traditions concerned with biological evolution, a development
which, in the 1930s, would relaunch Darwinian evolutionism.[157] Ernst
Mayr has remarked that in the last decades of the nineteenth century,
systematic zoology underwent a series of radical conceptual changes, pav-
ing the way for that new synthesis even independently of the strides made
in genetics.[158] The example of Canestrini confirms that the need for a
meeting with genetics was unquestionably felt by some systematists. It
also suggests, however, that some of them, in countries such as Italy, may
have lacked the conceptual and disciplinary tools to make such an encounter fruitful or even possible. The situation was apparently the consequence of both institutional and conceptual factors. It is plausible, after
all, that in order to arrive at the encounter with genetics and the "new
synthesis," systematic zoology had to undergo yet other shifts in addition
to the powerful intellectual shift enjoined by Darwin with his "old" synthesis.

FOUR

Darwin's Theory and Design

Innovation and Tradition
in Botany: F. Delpino

Three years after the *Origin of Species*, while the uproar it had created in England and other countries was still in full swing, Darwin published a new book having a very particular relationship to the *Origin*. In it he treated a limited question that did not appear to have much to do with the broad issues of the origin of species and their transformation by natural selection, a concept barely mentioned in the new book. This work, entitled *The Various Contrivances by Which Orchids Are Fertilised by Insects*, endeavored to demonstrate that "the contrivances by which Orchids are fertilised are as varied and almost as perfect as any of the most beautiful adaptations in the animal kingdom."[1] Darwin also showed that the main function of such contrivances was to facilitate the fertilization of flowers by means of pollen brought by insects from *other* plants of the same species. In this way, crossbreeding was made possible even in hermaphroditic species, in accordance with a law Darwin thought held good in nature generally.

While this was the specific objective of the new work, Darwin did not disguise the fact that it might also perform an important function in the general debate generated by the *Origin*. The description of the extraordinary adaptations observed in the relationships between insects and the flowers they fertilized might serve to temper the turbulent disputes in progress on his theory and the image of nature it proposed. Darwin suggested that the *Fertilisation of Orchids* afforded an opportunity of showing that "the study of organic beings may be as interesting to an observer who is fully convinced that the structure of each is due to secondary laws, as to one who views every trifling detail of structure as the result of the direct interposition of the Creator."[2] Darwin was referring here to the interpretation of natural phenomena traditionally proposed by natural theology, a school of thought in which many of his British readers and he himself had been raised.[3]

In the *Fertilisation of Orchids* Darwin never actually construed the phenomena of adaptation as the result of a plan imposed on nature by some external force, as it was natural theology's central aim to demonstrate. He appealed to functional and evolutionary factors that were wholly consistent with the theory of natural selection. But as a result of his discretion in dealing with that long-standing theological tradition, and possibly also reflecting his deliberate strategy, the new work provided an opening for those who were interested in reconciling evolutionary theory and natural theology rather than pitting the two views against each other.

The chance offered by Darwin's new book was immediately welcomed by America's most authoritative botanist, Asa Gray, assiduous correspondent of Darwin's and advocate of a religious interpretation of Darwin's theory of evolution. In reviewing the *Fertilisation of Orchids* for American readers, Gray remarked that

> had Mr. Darwin begun with this little book, and kept back a few theoretical inferences, it would have been a treasury of new illustrations for the natural theologians, and its author, perhaps, rather canonized than anathematized, even by many of those whom his treatise on the origin of species so seriously alarmed.[4]

Proceeding from views of this sort, Asa Gray vied tirelessly against a variety of adversaries in the United States to affirm the compatibility of evolutionary theory and religious tradition, and he eventually published a collection of essays with this very aim in 1876.[5]

The prolonged success of natural theology well into the nineteenth century has generally been regarded as a peculiarly British phenomenon, or as limited to English-speaking Protestant countries. This conviction has had consequences for interpretations of the relationships between Darwin's theory and a finalistic and religious conception of nature. This conception has too often been identified with the kind of natural theology represented in the late eighteenth and early nineteenth centuries by William Paley. This was fostered by Darwin's own remark in his autobiography that he had been educated according to Paley's tradition, and that the development of his scientific ideas went hand in hand with his gradual emancipation from Paley. Consequently, until very recently Darwin studies have tended to disregard other traditions of European philosophy and biology that kept a finalistic conception of nature alive. Until recently, there has been relatively little research into the relations between such continental traditions and Darwin's theory and its transmission, even though Peter Bowler pointed out the need a number of years ago.[6] According to Bowler, biological works linked to German idealism and Naturphilosophie deserve special attention in that regard. That tradition had, in fact, put down roots in England, thanks to Richard Owen, and, as we have seen, exerted a significant influence in Italy as well.[7]

Attributing importance almost exclusively to Paley and British natural theology has had another effect on Darwin studies. Investigation of the relations between Darwin's theory and the finalistic conception of nature has focused mainly on the phase of the theory's formation, neglecting to some extent the matter as it related to the reception of Darwinism subsequent to the publication of the *Origin*. And yet there are cogent reasons for arguing that the question continued to have considerable weight in the controversies over Darwinism up until the turn of the century, and that it involved many naturalists besides those most often mentioned in this connection, such as Asa Gray, Richard Owen, George Jackson Mivart, and Walter Benjamin Carpenter.

In this chapter, the focus will be on the relations between Darwin's theory and the finalistic conception of nature as they emerge from both the controversies and the cooperation between Charles Darwin and the Italian botanist Federico Delpino. Delpino was, in the 1870s, Darwin's most assiduous and certainly his most highly esteemed Italian interlocutor,[8] although the two differed on important theoretical issues. Darwin gave Delpino credit for having formulated the severest but most instructive critique of his theory of pangenesis. The most important interest they shared, however, was ecology, particularly in regard to the relations between insects and flowers in plant fertilization, an area of research that had been enlivened by Darwin's treatise on orchids and was enriched by Delpino's observations, which represented an impressive contribution to the field at the international level.

The relations between Darwin and Delpino offer a fascinating case study for the historian of science, a well-documented and as yet unexplored instance of cooperation between scientists of different cultures and theoretical inclinations. In addition to the abundant information contained in their published works, a variety of other sources are available to the historian: Darwin's comments written in the margins of the publications Delpino regularly sent him, a portion of their correspondence, and a number of interesting observations by Delpino in the margins of his copy of the *Origin*.[9] Altogether, there are grounds for new answers to a number of questions that are important for the history of Darwin's theory and its reception. What relations existed, during the crucial years of the debates on Darwinism, between Darwin's evolutionary theory—which many assumed had made finalism definitively obsolete—and the traditional but still vigorous finalistic conception of life? What strategies did Darwin adopt for dealing with those who, like Delpino and Asa Gray, admitted evolution but placed it in a finalistic perspective? What was the background of this finalism in scientists such as Delpino, who had not been exposed to the influence of British natural theology? How did finalistic positions fit into Darwinism within the Italian context, where, according to many, materialistic or monistic orientations prevailed?

INHERITANCE AND EVOLUTION: MONISTIC AND VITALISTIC PERSPECTIVES

Darwin and Delpino's exchanges in the 1870s focused, as has been noted, on the interpretation of adaptation phenomena observable in insects' fertilization of plants. The first significant contacts between the two scientists, however, came about at the end of the 1860s through the debate on the new hypothesis Darwin formulated to explain inheritance: pangenesis.

Darwin had advanced his hypothesis of pangenesis in 1868 in a chapter of his voluminous treatise on the variation in animals and plants under domestication.[10] Delpino felt that pangenesis offered an excellent chance to take stock of Darwin's theory of evolution from an explicitly vitalistic standpoint, an intention he had announced several years earlier.[11] Delpino's comments on pangenesis, which appeared early in 1869 in the prestigious *Rivista contemporanea*, so impressed Darwin that he immediately had them translated and reprinted in English.[12] Darwin followed the translation with his own answer, which Delpino then circulated in Italy along with further comments.[13] Several years later, in a new edition of *The Variation of Animals and Plants under Domestication*, Darwin declared that Delpino's appraisal of pangenesis was the best of the many that had appeared, while the criticisms in it had contributed constructively to his efforts to improve the hypothesis—something, he added, that could not be said for analogous criticisms advanced some time earlier by Mivart.[14]

With pangenesis—a "provisional hypothesis," as he cautiously called his new theory—Darwin undertook to advance a single explanation accounting for a wide range of phenomena, especially those of generation and inheritance.[15] Following a trend already well established in biology, Darwin hypothesized that cells, or the elementary units that make up all living beings, are renewed by reproducing continuously in the course of life. He furthermore speculated that before being converted into completed, passive organic material, each cell emitted "gemmules," these being tiny hypothetical particles which had never been observed, and on which Darwin's theory entirely rested. Gemmules were supposed to have particular properties such as being able to circulate freely throughout the body, because of their tiny size, to multiply by dividing when adequately nourished, like some elementary organisms, and to form new cells similar to the ones from which they originated.

Darwin claimed that gemmules emanating from all parts of the body were transmitted by reproduction to offspring and descendants, where they developed, duplicating the characteristics of the parents. Some of the gemmules, however, though transmitted, would remain latent; that is, they would develop only one or more generations later. This could account for phenomena of "atavism," i.e., the reappearance in descendants of characteristics found not in the parents but in earlier ancestors. Darwin chose the term *pangenesis* to signal that the hypothesis envisioned each organism not only as being the product of the elements directly involved in reproduction (eggs, buds, and so on) but also as acquiring through gemmules something from all the cells or elementary units of its parents or earlier ancestors.

These hypothetical gemmules were thus delegated the task of transmitting from one generation to another the basic, relatively constant characteristics of organisms. Within the domain of an evolutionary theory such as Darwin's, however, pangenesis also had to explain cases in which, instead of being transmitted unaltered, the characteristics underwent variation, that is, acquired those usually minor differences on which natural selection acts by preserving and accumulating them.

This was achieved, according to Darwin, by two types of processes, each involving the gemmules in a different way. In one, the gemmules themselves underwent no change. The emergence of an organism with partly new characteristics was explained by assuming that something had changed in the combination of the gemmules involved in its formation, as a result of some being oversupplied and others undersupplied, or of phenomena involving fusion or transposition of the gemmules, perhaps in concomitance with the development of gemmules that had been latent for some time. In the other type of process the gemmules themselves were modified, through changes in the organism's living conditions, or by the effects of use or disuse of their organs. Darwin assumed that by acting on the cells, modified conditions in turn modified the gemmules emitted by those cells; and as a result, modified gemmules would give rise to descendants with similarly altered aggregations. The effects of living conditions and the use or disuse of organs would thus be transmitted to descendants, as called for by the Lamarckian belief in the inheritance of acquired characters, which Darwin shared.[16]

With the hypothesis of pangenesis, Darwin clearly undertook not only to delineate a unitary explanation for a wide variety of phenomena but also to point to the probable existence of a substrate, the hypothetical gemmules, responsible for the still-little-understood phenomena of inheritance and variation. By doing so, he had no intention of playing down the complexity of organic phenomena. As he expressed it, "Each living creature must be looked at as a microcosm—a little universe, formed of a host of self-propagating organisms, inconceivably minute and as numerous as the stars in heaven."[17] But certainly with the hypothesis of pangenesis he was firmly stating—consistent with an outlook he had developed some time earlier— that there were no insurmountable obstacles along the route that sooner or later would lead to a satisfactory scientific explanation of inheritance. "Inheritance," he said, "must be looked at as merely a form of growth, like the self-division of a lowly-organized unicellular plant."[18]

John Hodge and David Kohn have shown that Darwin's theorizing on inheritance was strictly linked, in all its different phases, to his reflections on transformism.[19] Hodge has noted that in some ways pangenesis reproposed in the 1860s a monistic orientation already present in Darwin's early notebooks on species in the 1830s.[20] Accordingly, Delpino's decision in 1869 to take stock of Darwinism through a detailed analysis of the hypothesis of pangenesis was entirely appropriate and effective.

In his analysis of pangenesis, Delpino first of all stressed the importance of theories and hypotheses, even the most audacious ones.[21] He felt that this had not been adequately recognized in Italian scientific circles, because of what he regarded as "positivism" and an unfortunate prevalence among scientists of an "overcautious habit of mind." Hypotheses such as pangenesis were therefore welcome, as were wide-ranging syntheses such as Darwin's theory of evolution. This theory was, in Delpino's opinion, "the best theory hitherto produced with regard to the genesis of living forms," and he argued that although not everything about it could be accepted, the fact of evolution by then had to be considered proven beyond any doubt.[22] According to Delpino, then, Darwin's science stood out above all for its highly theoretical character, which Delpino was interested in interpreting as being against the kind of positivism he deplored in Italian cultural circles. But what was it that Delpino instead found unacceptable in Darwin's explanation of evolution, and in pangenesis in particular?

One of Delpino's chief criticisms of pangenesis, and certainly the one that best reveals his brand of evolutionism, pertains to an apparently limited point. In formulating his hypothesis, Darwin repeatedly had emphasized that there were many similarities between the asexual reproduction observed in simple organisms capable of reproducing by budding or division and the sexual reproduction typical of higher organisms. On the one hand, Darwin argued that phenomena considered exclusive to sexual reproduction, such as the emergence of variations, sometimes occur in organisms that reproduce asexually. On the other hand, he pointed out that in cases of parthenogenesis there was development of an egg cell without fertilization by the male even in organisms that reproduced sexually. In his three decades of reflections on inheritance, Darwin in fact repeatedly wavered in his estimation of resemblances and differences between the two main types of reproduction; but when he came to expound the hypothesis of pangenesis, strong theoretical reasons induced him to focus on the resemblances. Phenomena of asexual reproduction by budding or division of one organism into more had inspired him when hypothesizing the gemmules themselves, which were assumed to multiply by division. Moreover, he traced this type of reproduction to some basic phenomena that pangenesis was meant to explain. Among these were the regeneration of organs that various species are capable of, and the phenomena of growth and conservation typical of all organisms.

Likening sexual to asexual reproduction fulfilled the need for unification that was essential to Darwin's hypothesis of pangenesis. For Delpino, instead, likening them meant not only refusing to recognize the peculiarities of each type of reproduction but also underestimating the importance that the introduction of sexual reproduction must have had in the history of life. In fact, Delpino thought it imperative to explain what special function—or "final cause," as he preferred to call it—the introduction of sexual generation might have had in the evolutionary process: "Why should Nature, when the energetic means of agamic reproduction does not fail her in the vegetable kingdom and in the lower classes of animals, require and visibly prefer the complicated and apparently strange means of sexual reproduction?"[23]

Sustained by a firm faith in the oriented and progressive character of evolution, Delpino felt that the question left little room for doubt. Sexual reproduction must have been introduced at a certain stage of the evolutionary process, because, as some botanical observations seemed to indicate, it guaranteed the preservation of variations much better than agamic reproduction. The introduction of the sexes, in other words, made the "progress of organisms" more reliable and rapid and represented an important, necessary advancement in the evolutionary process. If, Delpino explained, Darwin seemed unready to adopt this progressive, finalistic interpretation of the sexes, it was because "although Darwin is a very acute teleologist (after his own fashion), as is proved by his beautiful researches upon the fecundation of the Orchideae and in general by all his publications, he does not here show himself to be sufficiently a teleologist."[24]

Statements of this kind recall similar declarations by Asa Gray. Delpino's criticisms on a particular point of the hypothesis of pangenesis, in any case, offer glimpses into how profoundly his conception of the evolutionary process differed from Darwin's. Eager to reconcile evolutionism and a finalistic conception of nature without leaving room for anyone who denied the transformation of species, Delpino would not have called attention in print to how distant he actually was from Darwin in the interpretation of the modes and timing of evolution. He was less guarded, however, in his notes in his copy of the *Origin*,[25] which he read in the French translation. There the differences emerge very clearly.

Nature proceeds gradually everywhere, Darwin stated repeatedly in the *Origin*; and Delpino commented in the margin, "Here is a principle I consider false."[26] Henri Milne-Edwards, Darwin reported, claimed that nature is prodigal in variety but niggard in innovations; "Another false principle," wrote Delpino.[27] Species, Darwin declared in the chapter on the difficulties of the theory of natural selection, are not subject to indefinite variability in any period; Delpino rejoined, "I think species *are* indefinitely variable."[28] It must be admitted, Darwin recalled more than once, that some variations emerge slowly in the course of thousands of generations; "And why not in a moment, as teratology shows," countered Delpino, who elsewhere specified that "teratology teaches that small differences spring up all of a sudden."[29] Darwin stressed that his theory did not require sudden geological transformations. Delpino did not reject such causes:

[Darwin] rules out the idea of cataclysms. But by admitting them we would obtain a more satisfactory explanation. Suppose that instantaneous variations of climate take place. Few living beings would survive. But in a very short time those few would develop, producing very different forms, and would quickly fill up vacant places. A new equilibrium would then be established.[30]

These examples suffice to show that though Darwin and Delpino shared a belief in evolution, they differed profoundly in their ways of construing it. For Darwin evolution was gradual and slow, with rare innovations; for Delpino it was a discontinuous process, marked by constant variability and sudden leaps forward.

Their interpretation of the causes of evolution also differed. Starting from a panpsychic conception of the living world, which attributed to all beings, plants included, a certain measure of "instinct," Delpino was not in the best of positions to appreciate Darwin's natural selection. In the chapter of the *Origin* on instinct, Darwin undertook to demonstrate that the evolution of animal behavior, too, depended on variations and natural selection. Unlike Lamarck, he ruled out the possibility that will or instincts could be considered causes of evolution. Delpino, in his marginal notes in the *Origin*, portrayed the relations between instinct, variation, and natural selection in terms that were diametrically opposed to Darwin's: "Instinct is common to all beings, even plants. Instinct causes variations, so what need is there for the chimera of natural selection?"[31] If Delpino indeed believed that instinct was the source of variations, it would have been difficult for him to consider them "accidental," as Darwin often reiterated. By calling variations accidental, Delpino commented, Darwin "denies the freedom of the molding principle. It is instinct, not the random production of new organs, that provides the basis for variations."[32] So, according to Delpino, evolution was determined in the final analysis by this "molding principle," responsible, as we will see, for the overall harmony of nature and present in each single organism, through a psychological faculty ranging in complexity from instinct to reason.

With such a conception he was certainly not likely to be interested in establishing, as Darwin tried to do with pangenesis, the material basis ("gemmules") of inheritance, variation, and, ultimately, evolution itself. There is no reason to doubt, however, that Delpino did have a genuine interest in the bold synthesis of knowledge on inheritance that Darwin attempted. Thus, while from the standpoint of contrasting world-views pangenesis seemed to Delpino a confirmation of the impotence of any scientific explanation not postulating a vital principle,[33] yet he saw very clearly that Darwin's hypothesis cast a preliminary glance at a vast new world of microscopic biological phenomena. Delpino's awe and a measure of incredulity toward this suggest how the new world must have appeared to many contemporaries. His reaction to this aspect of Darwin's hypothesis reveals that perhaps more than is ordinarily recognized, the hypothesis was projected toward the future of research on inheritance.

This emerges clearly from Delpino's discussion of how many gemmules it would take to perform the tasks Darwin attributed to them.[34] Darwin thought each cell of the organism emitted gemmules that were, under certain particular circumstances, capable of producing new cells identical to the ones that had produced them. According to Delpino, the hypothesis signified that each cell must emit new gemmules *at each stage* of its development. Besides this enormous number of gemmules, there were the ones that remained latent for generations, emerging later in phenomena of atavism, adding up to a total number of gemmules that "astounds the imagination," as Delpino attempted to show by means of laborious calculations:

Let us take, for example, an *Acropera*, a plant of the family Orchideae. Darwin has computed that it produces about 74,000,000 seeds. Now the gemmules do not collect only in the seeds, but they exist also in pretty nearly the same abundance and proportion in the pollen-grains. We are certainly within the truth if we assume for these grains a number five times as great as that of the seeds, that is to say, 370,000,000. Taking the sum of the pollen-grains and embryonal vesicles, we have 444,000,000 capsules which must be filled with gemmules. On the other hand, keeping always to the lowest calculations, let us suppose that the cells of the entire plant are 1,000 millions, and that in every pollen-grain, and in every embryonal vesicle, in order to satisfy the exigencies of atavism, and to represent all the vital stages of a cell, there enter 100 representatives of every cell, and we arrive at the enormous number of 44,400 thousands of millions of gemmules.

But this number is almost insignificant in comparison with others, which, according to Pangenesis, it is necessary to accept. For example, calculating at two billions the number of pollen-grains, and at two billions the number of living cells in a tree of the Cedar of Lebanon, we shall certainly not be far from the truth; and if we multiply one number by the other, we have at once the tremendous number of 4,000 millions of billions of gemmules. . . .

Pangenesis, considered from the point of view of the number and minuteness of the gemmules, becomes almost identified with the atomic theory, with the disadvantage, however, that its corpuscles cannot be atoms or molecules, but compound and organized corpuscles.[35]

In his copy of Delpino's essay, Darwin drew two thick vertical lines next to this last sentence, to stress that he found the observation "very good."[36] Delpino's remarks showed, in fact, that he had a good grasp of the level of generalization chosen by Darwin with his hypothesis of pangenesis, and that he lucidly perceived that the limited knowledge of the day made verification of the hypothesis hardly possible.

Just as lucidly, Delpino pointed to another difficulty that Darwin's gemmules would have to overcome. If these organized corpuscles encompassed all the complex characteristics so as to reproduce the cells they came from, how could it be imagined that they remained unaltered through the innumerable "chemical tempests" continually being generated within the organism?[37] Delpino returned to this last point in his rejoinder to Darwin's response, where, however, the subject had not been mentioned:

It is impossible to understand how the organization and composition of the gemmules . . . could have remained unimpaired after undergoing the action of innumerable chemical tempests and an incalculable number of decompositions and recompositions of the plastic materials [i.e., proteins, hydrocarbons, etc.]. In fact, if every chemical action has the effect of attacking even the last molecules, altering the position and numerical proportion of the atoms composing these molecules, it seems all the more evident that this must interfere with and destroy the organization of the gemmules.[38]

Darwin and Delpino's public exchange on pangenesis ended with Delpino's reply. But on his copy of Delpino's reply, Darwin noted a succinct counterobjection with which he still could have challenged Delpino. The "chemical tempest" criticism, Darwin noted, loses its force if we admit that gemmules are "alive,"[39] thus enjoying some kind of autonomy with respect to their environment. If this counterargument of Darwin's had been made explicitly and publicly, it would have represented a substantial concession to his adversary: attributing all the properties of life to gemmules in fact signified raising about them many of the same questions that gemmules had been introduced to solve. But not even granting that gemmules shared all the properties of "life" would have been enough for Delpino. His criticism would be answered, he himself declared, only if "Darwin's gemmules were converted into *incorporeal germs*, into *immaterial units*."[40] Darwin never would have gone so far, and Delpino's offer to write an "apologia of pangenesis from the standpoint of vitalism"[41] in such a case remained a generous but implausible declaration that he was still open to Darwin's further suggestions.

Delpino made no secret of the fact that his grounds for criticizing pangenesis included a basic philosophical and methodological divergence with Darwin. Pangenesis, he remarked, "accords very readily with monism, and reduces to a mere act of necessary germination all the phenomena of the evolution of living beings." And again, "by denying the intervention of a free principle in the formation of organisms, pangenesis arrays itself beneath the banners of monism."[42] It is likely that by such statements, juxtaposed to highly conciliatory comments calling Darwin a "very acute teleologist (after his own fashion)," Delpino hoped to elicit some statement from Darwin distinguishing his position from monism. Such an outcome would have considerably reinforced Delpino's strategy aimed at diminishing the prestige that monists gained by presenting themselves as the foremost interpreters of Darwin's theory. But in his response, Darwin carefully avoided addressing the general philosophical and methodological questions raised by Delpino.[43] He confined himself to conceding that Delpino was right when he emphasized that to be acceptable, the hypothesis of pangenesis required a long series of corollary hypotheses. Darwin did not mention finalism or teleology, much less the contrasting world-views that, according to Delpino, were called into question by the debate on pangenesis. Darwin focused instead on rejecting some objections regarding gemmules' ability to multiply by division, the phenomena of regeneration of amputated organs, and the supposed need to admit the emission of gemmules at every stage of cell development.

By circulating Delpino's criticisms in an English translation he himself had provided for, and by the tone of his response, Darwin achieved several objectives. He promoted the diffusion in England of a text that very effectively summed up the most important concepts of pangenesis. By a reply showing a thoughtful regard for some specific objections raised by Delpino, Darwin displayed his respect for criticisms coming from the vitalists' camp, even if these were represented by a scientist who was not well known in England and who came from the periphery of the scientific community. By not committing himself on the philosophical level, as Delpino instead did and urged him to do, Darwin once again could show publicly that he preferred facts and scientific theories above all else. By not commenting in any way on the charge that he was advancing the cause of monism, Darwin implied that he had no interest in publicly dissociating himself from his numerous supporters in the ranks of the monists.

For Delpino, the whole episode must have been gratifying, especially on the personal level. At that point he was thirty-five and had occupied the post of Filippo Parlatore's assistant at the Museum of Natural History in Florence for less than two years, and already he had succeeded in engaging one of the greatest scientific authorities of the day in a public confrontation on theoretical questions of great importance. If, as was predictable, he did not manage to wrest any concessions to vitalism from Darwin, he at least could show the Italian scientific community and a wider audience (as he wasted no time in doing in the pages of the *Rivista europea*) that the vitalist Delpino was Darwin's interlocutor, listened to and respected as much as and perhaps more than many monist followers of Darwinism.

INSECTS AND ORCHIDS: UTILITY VS. HARMONY?

In the chapter of the *Origin* illustrating natural selection, Darwin's examples included a very telling one involving some varieties of flowers and the insects that habitually visited them. Delpino saw in it some insuperable difficulties that he thought made it impossible for Darwin's theory to account for the relations between living organisms without recourse to the idea of a plan of preordained harmony in nature. Darwin wrote,

> Certain plants excrete a sweet juice, apparently for the sake of eliminating something injurious from their sap: this is effected by glands at the base of the stipules in some Leguminosae, and at the back of the leaf of the common laurel. This juice, though small in quantity, is greedily sought by insects. Let us now suppose a little sweet juice or nectar to be excreted by the inner bases of the petals of a flower. In this case insects in seeking the nectar would get

dusted with pollen, and would certainly often transport the pollen from one flower to the stigma of another flower. The flowers of two distinct individuals of the same species would thus get crossed; and the act of crossing, we have good reason to believe . . . , would produce very vigorous seedlings, which consequently would have the best chance of flourishing and surviving. Some of these seedlings would probably inherit the nectar-excreting power. Those individual flowers which had the largest glands or nectaries, and which excreted most nectar, would be oftenest visited by insects, and would be oftenest crossed; and so in the long run would gain the upper hand.[44]

Thus natural selection explained the evolution of some plant forms by connecting it to the behavior of the insects that visited them. And indeed Darwin went on,

> Let us now turn to the nectar-feeding insects in our imaginary case: we may suppose the plant of which we have been slowly increasing the nectary by continued selection, to be a common plant; and that certain insects depended in main part on its nectar for food. I could give many facts, showing how anxious bees are to save time; for instance, their habit of cutting holes and sucking the nectar at the bases of certain flowers, which they can, with a very little more trouble, enter by the mouth. Bearing such facts in mind, I can see no reason to doubt that *an accidental deviation* in the size and form of the body, or in the curvature and length of the proboscis, etc., far too slight to be appreciated by us, might profit a bee or other insect, so that an individual so characterized would be able to obtain its food more quickly, and so have a better chance of living and leaving descendants.[45]

For Darwin the evolution of plants and the evolution of the insects that fed on their nectar were therefore interrelated:

> Thus I can understand how a flower and a bee might slowly become, either simultaneously or one after the other, modified and adapted in the most perfect manner to each other, by the continued preservation of individuals presenting mutual and slightly favorable deviations of structure.[46]

Delpino wrote some various comments next to these passages in his copy of the *Origin*: "This paragraph is most essential. It is the refutation of Darwin's interpretation based on chance." And again, "It is odd that Darwin, who writes these lines, a few years afterwards published his fine research on the fertilization of orchids."[47]

What is it in these pages from the *Origin* that Delpino considered a refutation of the theory Darwin himself meant to defend? What sort of conflict did he discern between the *Origin* and the *Fertilisation of Orchids*? Here, as in the case of pangenesis, two different ways of interpreting biological phenomena were at issue. With pangenesis the disagreement turned on the interpretation of the laws of inheritance, and the stakes were, for

Delpino, the possibility of claiming that a certain number of phenomena concerning inheritance could not be accounted for by the material gemmules hypothesized by Darwin. The dispute was, according to Delpino, a conflict between monism and vitalism. And although Darwin refrained from admitting it, there can be little doubt that this is exactly what it was, besides, of course, being a confrontation over many specific questions raised by the still-vague cellular conception of organisms. In the case of phenomena of pollination by insects, the conflict was between an explanation that avoided appealing to any hypothesis of a preordained plan and an explanation, Delpino's, that saw those phenomena as the definite proof of design imposed on nature by an intelligent being. Pollination phenomena being easier to observe than inheritance phenomena, the divergence here, more clearly than in the case of pangenesis, took the form of a clash between different interpretations of precise "facts."

Darwin and Delpino's exchange on the ecology of plant fertilization began at about the same time as that on pangenesis, in the late 1860s. It lasted, however, until 1877, when, in a new edition of his work on the fertilization of orchids,[48] Darwin rejected more emphatically than ever before—though still cautiously—Delpino's arguments for a teleological interpretation of fertilization. Meanwhile, the confrontation between the two had developed on three questions, which, though very specific, offered good opportunities to test their respective theoretical views. The three questions can be summed up as follows:

1. How can one account for the fact that insects also visit flowers that apparently do not produce the nectar that normally attracts them?

2. What function can be assigned to the production of nectar in species where this takes place outside the flowers, and therefore cannot facilitate contact between the insects and the plant's reproductive organs?

3. How can one account for the existence of completely closed flowers, for which there can be no cross-pollination by either insects or the wind, though this seems to be so important for all species?

Insects and Nectarless Flowers: An Imposture of Nature? Darwin's idea that the evolution of some insects and that of the flowers they visit are linked, a thesis he had already formulated in the *Origin*, entailed some additional hypotheses in order to fit into his view of nature. It was implicit, for instance, that insects transported pollen from flower to flower wholly spontaneously, driven simply by the search for nectar. And yet Darwin was well aware and admitted in his work on orchids, "I have looked to all our common British species and could find no trace of nectar,"[49] a fact already noted by other naturalists in many different species of the same family. How, then, could one account for the fact that insects continued to look for nectar in flowers that apparently contained none?

The problem had already been posed by Christian Konrad Sprengel, the first naturalist to attempt a systematic treatment of the fertilization of

Fig. 5. The frontispiece-cover of Christian Konrad Sprengel's 1793 book *Das entdeckte Geheimnis der Natur im Bau und in der Befruchtung der Blumen* (The secret of nature in the construction and fertilization of flowers revealed), the first thorough description of insects' action in the fertilization of flowers, both represented here, combining illustration and decoration. The book had a fundamental role in orienting Darwin and Delpino in their researches, although they interpreted the phenomenon in the light of evolution theory. Unlike Darwin, Delpino subscribed to Sprengel's belief in the existence of a plan that regulated the relations between organisms.

flowers by insects. His work,[50] published in 1793 (see fig. 5), served both Darwin and Delpino as a valuable source of observations and hypotheses in a field in which Sprengel had not managed to attract the attention of many naturalists. Darwin deserves the credit for rescuing Sprengel's work from oblivion; he cited many of his observations, though he rejected Sprengel's undisguised penchant for marvelous adaptations and the harmony of nature.[51]

To designate the species that produce no nectar, Sprengel had coined the term *Scheinsaftblumen* (fig. 6), or "sham-nectar flowers," implying that the insects visiting them must have been attracted and deceived by the shape of the nectaries, which resembled those of flowers that did produce nectar.[52] Darwin found such an explanation rather absurd for a number of reasons. As he energetically stated, "we can hardly believe in so gigantic an imposture."[53] In the efficient Darwinian world of insects, some of which, such as bees, were anxious to save time and to exploit the advantages of the division of labor, it seemed implausible that some would continue to visit flowers that provided no nourishment.

The "organized system of deception," as Darwin called the stratagem hypothesized by Sprengel,[54] was incompatible with Darwin's conception of the relations between organisms. Darwin believed these relations to be controlled by chains of behavioral patterns ultimately governed by basic biological needs such as nourishment and reproduction. Sprengel's hypothesis, moreover, contradicted Darwin's conviction that behavior evolves, just as forms do, even in the simplest organisms. Sooner or later, Darwin assumed, insects would have "learned," in the course of evolution, to distinguish the flowers that never give nectar and would consequently avoid them. According to Darwin's theory of transformism, it might indeed be admitted that for some reason this evolution of behavior did not take place; but Sprengel's hypothesis was also in contrast with the distinctive "intelligence" that Darwin attributed to insects, particularly bees. "It appears to me incredible," Darwin declared, "that the same insect should go on visiting flower after flower of these Orchids, although it never obtains any nectar. Insects, or at least bees, are by no means destitute of intelligence."[55] Consequently, Darwin needed a different explanation, and he had suggested one in the first edition of his work on orchids.[56] In flowers that do not secrete nectar, insects suck a liquid located between the double walls or membranes forming orchids' nectary, or "spur." In flowers that regularly secrete nectar, those membranes are perfectly adherent and hold no liquid. In both cases insects visit the flowers because they are driven to do so by the search for food, which in one way or another they never fail to find.

These are the broad outlines of Darwin's account of nectarless flowers, which was also included in the second (1877) edition of the *Fertilisation of Orchids*, the last to be edited by him. The account was consistent with some major factors of evolution as specified by Darwin's theory: availability of

Fig. 6. A plate from Sprengel's book (see fig. 5) showing inter alia some "sham-nectar flowers" (*Orchis latifolia*, details 31 and 36–39), Sprengel's expression designating species with a nectary that produces no nectar. Sprengel thought these flowers attracted insects by their deceptive form, thereby fostering their own fertilization without "recompensing" the insects with nectar. Darwin, who had a high regard for insects' instincts and conceived of the relations between species in terms of utility, denied that an "imposture" of this sort could take place: if insects continued to visit those flowers, it could only be because they found some sort of food there. Delpino rejected this explanation, which was less consistent than Sprengel's with his own finalistic view of nature.

and access to food (for the insects), and advantages and disadvantages for reproduction (for the plants). Since these factors were assumed to have acted for the very long period of time that the plants and insects lived in the same regions, the evolution of the two groups of organisms was naturally interconnected: this was why they now displayed the observed reciprocal adaptation.

By 1877 Darwin's interpretation of the fertilization of nectarless flowers by insects had been endorsed by a number of scholars. Hermann Müller,[57] in particular, concurred with Darwin's nonteleological stance and rejected Sprengel's interpretation. By then, in fact, there was little chance Darwin would receive tributes like those of Gray or Delpino that had greeted his work on orchids when it first came out fifteen years earlier, praising him for being a "very acute teleologist." But what led Gray and Delpino to interpret fertilization teleologically and to consider their version congruous with Darwin's, in spite of Darwin's opinion to the contrary? How solid were their arguments, and to what extent did Darwin take them into account during the fifteen years separating the two editions of the *Fertilisation of Orchids*?

It is fairly obvious that from the standpoints of "aesthetic" or religious conceptions of nature, the coordinated evolution of plants and insects hypothesized by Darwin was no less "marvelous" and extraordinary than the stratagems conjectured by Sprengel to explain the fertilization of nectarless flowers. Gray and Delpino, in any event, were also good scientists and did more than simply assert their finalistic viewpoint. Delpino, in particular, tirelessly tracked down evidence to support his teleological conception of nature, and the store of "facts" he accumulated during the confrontation with Darwin on the subject of nectarless flowers is well worth perusal.

In his first scientific work, published in 1865, Delpino extended to the asclepiad family the kind of observations that Darwin had published three years earlier on orchids.[58] With new observations and simple experiments, Delpino demonstrated that insects have a key role in fertilization in that family of plants as well. He did not yet carry out a systematic comparison between his own interpretation—already explicitly inspired by the idea of "final causes"—and Darwin's. In some concluding comments he intimated, however, that his current research aimed at "the emendation of Charles Darwin's theory on the origin of species."[59] Delpino indeed devoted the better part of the next decade to the study of plant fertilization by insects and wind. Fertilization phenomena were central to the discipline that he suggested be called "plant biology."[60] By this expression he meant the study—to which Darwin had called naturalists' attention—of the relations established between organisms in their actual lives. The description of organisms' habits or behavior had a key role in the discipline, and Delpino suggested that the term *plant ethology* would have conveyed the object of the new field just as accurately.[61] The most significant results of Delpino's studies in this field were described in essays published between 1867 and 1874.[62] The broadest of these[63] traces his controversy with Darwin on nectarless flowers, as well as the developments in the confrontation between Darwinian ecology and the finalistic conception of nature as it unfolded within the international scientific community of Darwinian botanists interested in the fertilization of plants.

Darwin's book on orchids was in fact the starting point of a new international specialty. As soon as it appeared, it was hailed as opening a new field. Twenty-one years later a classic treatise on the fertilization of flowers could list around eight hundred articles by some thirty-five authors.[64] Apart from Darwin himself, only ten of these authors had ten or more publications listed, and all ten at least occasionally corresponded with Darwin. If we look more closely at the extant correspondence, we see that at least five of those botanists had a significant exchange of information with him on fertilization. They were the American Asa Gray, the Germans Fritz Müller, Hermann Müller, and Frederic Hildebrand, and the Italian Federico Delpino. We can consider them as belonging to an inner circle of botanists concerned with cross-fertilization and characterized by their close relationship with Darwin. Within this inner circle, views on teleology in relation to fertilization were—if we leave out Darwin himself—both explicit and divergent. Frederic Hildebrand and Hermann and Fritz Müller were to differing degrees all declared opponents of teleology. Gray and Delpino, on the other hand, fervently defended it.

We have seen that as early as 1862 Darwin had hypothesized that insects continued to visit the flowers of orchids that did not produce nectar because they were attracted and regularly satiated by the liquid contained in the walls of the flower. In the years that followed, Delpino, carrying out observations on *Ophris araneifera* in Tuscany and Liguria, had found, on the contrary, that insects rarely visited the flowers, and that few were fertilized. He concluded that the lack of nectar in the "illusory" nectary of the Ophris would sooner or later lead to the extinction of that species. It was therefore, he wrote in 1868, a "clear instance of imperfection, indeed, of organic degeneration."[65] Paradoxically, in this first phase of Darwin and Delpino's controversy on nectarless flowers, we find the antiteleological Darwin convinced of the perfect efficiency of orchids' system of fertilization, while Delpino, the champion of teleology and the perfect harmony of nature, has found flaws in the system.

In 1869 Darwin's interpretation received an early endorsement from Hermann Müller,[66] who confirmed the existence of a liquid, located inside the walls of nectarless orchids' spur, on which insects presumably fed. Delpino, commenting the next year on his own Italian translation of Müller's essay, recalled that in the observations he had carried out, he had never found a single trace of such a liquid. Not even microscopic examination of the spur, whose walls were sometimes found open or "blistered," ever revealed anything of the kind. Delpino concluded that although it might not be appropriate to speak of a "false nectary" as Sprengel had done, that was certainly an "illusory nectary," which perhaps had produced nectar in a remote past.[67]

Delpino's firm though implicit belief was that insects visit flowers expressly to gather pollen, that is, for the purpose of fertilizing them. This was precisely the finalistic link that Darwin and Müller rejected, and that a Darwinian conception of the relations between organisms ruled out: in this conception, each species can act only in its own interests. Still, at this stage Delpino exercised some caution: the preordained plan, the trick of the illusory nectaries, he argued, was not perfect. As he had observed in eastern Liguria,[68] orchids were for the most part neglected by insects, and few were fertilized by them: insects were not particularly eager, after all, to carry out gratis the action assigned them in nature's teleological plan!

In the meantime Darwin, too, had resumed his observations on the subject. In addenda published on the occasion of the French translation of his orchid book,[69] he mentioned new evidence to strengthen his earlier hypothesis on the liquid contained in the walls of "nectarless nectaries." In *Orchis maculata*, during the time it is visited by insects and at the points where they linger, Darwin had observed "very tiny dark spots" that might be traces of tiny perforations made by the insects. The hypothesis that the insects pierced the walls of the nectary and fed on the liquid found there seemed confirmed. At the same time Darwin emphasized that, on the basis of new observations, orchids lacking true nectar were regularly visited by insects, which—he had no doubts on this—found food there.

The new observations, which Darwin had communicated to Müller and which Müller reported to Delpino,[70] convinced Delpino for some time that matters must actually be as his two colleagues claimed. Or at least so Delpino wrote to Darwin in a letter of January 1871, shortly after receiving the news from Müller:

> Due to my bad memory I missed the very interesting information you give on pages 2 and 3 ("Notes on the Fertilisation of Orchids")[71] on *Orchis morio*, *O. maculata*, etc. and their pollinators. Now that I have gone over it again, *I find I am obliged to modify my opinion significantly*. It is true that I have never found liquid in blistered spurs; but what I have been unable to substantiate in Liguria and Tuscany might very well happen in other regions. All the more so, because I see that in England the Orchis mentioned are visited frequently by many insects—Empis, Bombus, Apis, Eucera . . . while in Liguria I have never been able to find insects there at all. . . .
>
> An observation I made a few months ago actually leads me to believe in the possibility of a subepidermal secretion of nectar or the like. This phenomenon is very frequent in Malpighiaceae. I also suspect that it takes place in some Primulae whose corolla I have found blistered on the inside in a way wholly analogous to the spur of our native orchids. I will rectify my over-hasty proposition the first chance I have.[72]

These firm statements may sound like an unconditional surrender, at least on the battlefront where Delpino fought for a finalistic conception of nature through nectarless flowers. In fact, they were no more than a temporary truce.

In the spring of 1873, Delpino was once again engaged in a series of observations on orchids. He may have been led to resume his research by Hermann Müller's new work, a classic treatise on the fertilization of flowers published that same year. Like Müller's other works, this one combined the Darwinian theory of flowers with harsh attacks on finalism. For one thing, Müller devoted four full pages to a refutation of Delpino's teleological views.[73] Although Darwin had never openly expressed his opinion of Delpino's views on finalism, he praised Müller's treatise highly to Delpino. Müller, for his part, in letters to Delpino repeatedly represented his anti-teleological convictions as being shared by both Darwin and Haeckel, whose attacks on finalism were well known. In his treatise, Müller declared that the question of nectarless flowers had by then been settled in favor of Darwin and against Delpino. But Delpino was not ready to give up. In fact, he now wielded Sprengel's hypothesis and some new observations energetically against both Müller and Darwin, after having espoused their interpretation only a year before.

Delpino's new observations were of two types.[74] Some concerned insects' visits and established that in the case of nectarless orchids, visits occurred only when the plant first began blooming, after which they virtually ceased. In other words, each year the false nectaries deceived a new generation of insects that then promptly detected the stratagem. This put the orchids' fertilization constantly at risk, but—Delpino now claimed— nature had "compensated" by providing them with a very large number of seeds for each fertilized capsule.

The second type of observation concerned the presence and the nature of the liquid that Darwin and Müller claimed was contained in the walls of false nectaries. Delpino now established that a "subcutaneous transudation" of lymph was sometimes produced in orchids, but only when it became exceptionally cold at night, and affecting all the walls of the flower, not just the nectary. It was therefore not, Delpino objected, a secretion of nectar "with a definite biological purpose,"[75] i.e., the attraction of insects, but an independent phenomenon. It goes without saying that by making such statements, Delpino took for granted what he had to demonstrate: that is, that every function of organisms coincides with preordained goals. On this occasion Delpino refrained from stating that his observations substantiated a teleological conception of nature, and we know that elsewhere he even had declared that nectarless flowers represented a case of degeneration. The reaffirmation of the finalistic ideal was, however, achieved indirectly by his accolades for Sprengel, whom he praised as a "very acute and very wise observer," and by supporting Sprengel's hypothesis that there actually exist "illusory nectaries and deceitful flowers."[76]

Using the same strategy but with the opposite objective, Darwin, in his reply to Delpino on the occasion of the second edition of the *Fertilisation of Orchids,*[77] explicitly attacked not the finalistic conception of nature but rather Sprengel's and Delpino's observations, and the idea of illusory nectaries. We have already examined the broad lines of Darwin's explanation in this definitive 1877 version. Now it can be seen how much—or indeed, how little—this owed to Delpino's resistance to Darwinian views.

Darwin must have been somewhat surprised at Delpino's resistance after his letter claiming to have been won over, but he nevertheless took the objections very seriously. Upon learning that Delpino "still believed in Sprengel's views," in 1875 Darwin decided to conduct a new set of observations on *Orchis maculata* and *O. pyramidalis.*[78] The new observations did not confirm Delpino's idea that insects stopped visiting nectarless flowers after doing so briefly and finding nothing to feed on: the walls of nectarless orchids really must contain a liquid that continued to attract them. So Darwin could emphatically repropose his own account and go on to illustrate what he already had described in the first edition of the *Fertilisation of Orchids* as "one of the most wonderful cases of adaptation which has ever been recorded."[79] Darwin aimed at showing, by this case, that there was no adaptation, however complex, that could not be traced to the kind of nonteleological explanation he proposed.

Why, Darwin wondered,[80] is nectar freely accessible in some species, while in others insects must repeatedly pierce the internal membrane of the flower in order to obtain anything? In the latter case the insects must stay inside the flower longer in order to obtain an adequate amount of food. Is there any connection between fertilization and the differing lengths of the insects' visits to orchids with easily accessible nectar and to those with the liquid contained in the walls? Darwin thought there had to be some connection, and he found it in differences in the characteristics of the viscid substance that fastened the pollen to the insects in the two types of orchids. In orchids with easily accessible nectar, where insects linger briefly, this "glue" fastens the pollen to the insects very effectively and remains sticky long enough and after exposure to air, that is, during the insects' flight to the next flower. In orchids with concealed "nectar," where insects are obliged to stay longer, the "glue" quickly dries in air, rapidly losing its effectiveness. A lengthy visit by the insect is indispensable in this case for the pollen to become securely attached. In both cases the pollen has to remain fastened firmly enough not to fall off in flight, so that it is located in an appropriate position to fertilize the next flower when the insect deposits it there (fig. 7).

Darwin found this "wonderful case of adaptation"—combining the accessibility of nectar, the duration of insects' visit, and the characteristics of the "glue"—explicable quite naturally by evolution through natural selection in insects and orchids that had lived together for a long time in the same region. From many standpoints it was more "wonderful" a case of adaptation than the one hypothesized by Delpino when he claimed that species visited less often by insects were given a proportionally larger num-

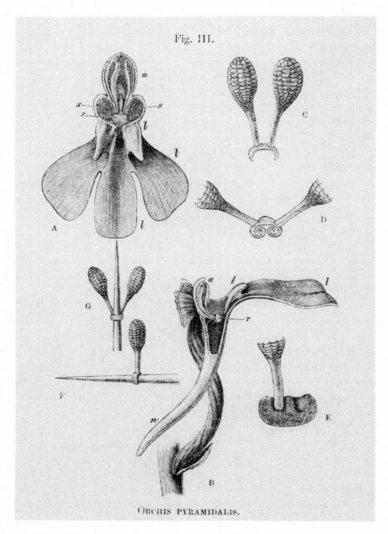

Fig. III.

ORCHIS PYRAMIDALIS.

Fig. 7. A front view (*A*, with sepals and all petals except the labellum removed) and details (*B-E*) of *Orchis pyramidalis*. This is one of the nectarless flowers which required an explanation of why insects visited them. Darwin showed that in these flowers insects repeatedly perforated the walls of the nectary (*B*, *n*), drawing out a nectarlike juice. The operation prolonged the insects' visits, and this, he maintained, was in keeping with the features of the apparatus (the sticky double disk in *E*) by which the pollen masses (*C*, *D*) adhered to the insect that then transported them to another flower, fertilizing it. *F* and *G* show the position subsequently assumed by the pollen masses—placed on a needle by Darwin to simulate the insect's proboscis—as the sticky disk dried.

The figure is from C. Darwin, *The Various Contrivances by Which Orchids Are Fertilised by Insects* (1862).

ber of seeds per fertilized flower as a "compensation." Darwin could have argued that when it came to wonderful adaptations, the reality of evolution by natural selection exceeded the imagination of those who believed in a preordained plan of nature. Yet Darwin apparently had no interest in pushing his quarrel with teleologists to the limit. He chose to contradict the teleological view of nature in general by contradicting Sprengel and Delpino on nectarless flowers. It should be noted, moreover, that in the English translation of Müller's treatise, which Darwin promoted, the section attacking Delpino's teleological views was dropped. The case of the nectarless flowers helps clarify, I think, both Darwin's attitude toward teleology and his strategy for the Darwinians. Apparently he did not want to forfeit the support the theory of evolution received from some highly qualified naturalists such as Gray or Delpino, who believed in both evolution and finalism.

Flowerless Nectar: To What End? Darwin's strategy required, nevertheless, that each new attempt to create room for finalism be cautiously but firmly rejected. This emerges clearly from the way he responded to some new observations conducted by Delpino, aimed at relaunching the cause of teleology after it had failed as far as nectarless flowers were concerned.

Delpino had devoted particular attention to a phenomenon previously noted by Darwin,[81] the ecological significance of which had not yet been thoroughly investigated by Darwin or anyone else. The secretion of nectar, which in many plants normally occurs within the flower, in others takes place outside the flower and cannot, therefore,be connected with fertilization. The species producing "extranuptual" nectar, to use the term coined by Delpino,[82] included some very common and easily observable species, such as the acacia, the castor-oil plant, and the hibiscus. What function could this secretion perform?

Delpino held that this particular nectar, too, must have a precise function, which he confidently traced to his favored principle of "final causes."[83] He definitely ruled out the possibility that it might be an excremental secretion, as Darwin suggested,[84] because the liquid contained sweet substances too precious to the plant for it to be merely a waste product. He also noted that this type of secretion was not universally present in plants, but only in those that were more complex and frequently visited by ants. Delpino concluded—Darwinianly, but in his own way:

> If in so many local and foreign plants nature was able to preform and replicate physiologically identical organs that secrete a sweet substance extremely attractive to ants, ants must perform some service for the plants, and a very important one at that. Otherwise these organs would have no reason for being reproduced and perpetuated generation after generation. This service . . . must be none other than that of freeing the plants of mortal enemies, especially the caterpillars of certain butterflies.[85]

Delpino thus used Darwin's struggle for existence to account for the secretion of "extranuptual" nectar in a way that was consistent with his
finalistic view of nature. By his explanation, Delpino was once again able
to maintain that the relations between insects and plants were not accidental but designed to serve the plants' welfare, through the complex relations of the struggle for existence.

Darwin challenged Delpino's hypothesis with firmness and his usual
tact in his new botanical treatise, *The Effects of Cross- and Self-fertilisation in
the Vegetable Kingdom*, published in 1876.[86] In the first place, Darwin maintained, there was every reason to think that the secretion of that liquid
depended on accidental factors; in some species it occurred only when the
plants were exposed to the sun. He then conceded that in some rare cases
the secretion might have assumed the special function of attracting enemies
of the plants' enemies, as Delpino claimed. But so few plants were at mortal
risk from caterpillars and insects that the power of secreting a sweet fluid
outside the flowers was unlikely to have been "specially gained"[87] to attract
ants and wasps as defenders of the plant. Although formulated by Delpino
with recourse to such Darwinian concepts as the struggle for existence,
this was a teleological explanation that Darwin had no intention of accepting.

Closed Flowers and the Origin of Sexes: Foresight or Parsimony of Nature? In
1877 Darwin published, in addition to the second edition of the *Fertilisation
of Orchids*, a new botanical treatise in which he undertook to explain why
different forms of flowers sometimes appeared in the same species.[88] The
voluminous work was dedicated to Asa Gray, "as a small tribute of respect
and affection." The subjects Darwin treated included plants that have another flowering before or after the normal one, with the extra blooming
characterized by closed flowers (cleistogamy).[89] These flowers, of course,
must reproduce by self-fertilization alone, since neither insects nor the
wind can bring about fertilization between different plants. And this, despite the advantages that Darwin firmly believed cross-fertilization had for
the plant, judging from the vigor of descendants. How, then, to account
for this patent exception to the law of cross-fertilization?

Delpino had addressed the problem of cleistogamic flowers ten years
earlier in some published notes that Darwin had carefully read and commented on.[90] As usual, Delpino had been guided in his interpretation of
cleistogamic flowers by the teleological conception of nature:

> We maintain that the key to these phenomena is to be found in teleological
> explanations.
> This closed flowering—accessory, secondary, and subordinated to the nor-
> mal one—is in our opinion an ingenious expedient devised by nature to assure
> the posterity of a given species by anticipating external conditions of low
> temperatures or other climactic causes that in some years might jeopardize or
> indeed destroy the products of normal fertilization.[91]

In this case, too, Darwin challenged Delpino's explanation cautiously but firmly.[92] He admitted that in some circumstances closed flowers did perform the function identified by Delpino, but this was not the same as claiming that they had developed precisely for this purpose, thus attributing a peculiar foresight to nature. As usual, Darwin refrained from debating the philosophical or methodological aspects of the finalistic explanation proposed by Delpino. This time, however, Darwin's account showed not only the contrast between his approach and Delpino's but also some significant points on which they agreed.

Darwin suggested considering the production of closed flowers as an example of the observable tendency in nature to produce more while consuming less: "The whole [cleistogamic] flower is much reduced in size; but what is much more important, an extremely small quantity of pollen has to be formed, as none is lost through the action of insects or the weather. . . . "[93] So, in Darwin's account closed flowers owed their existence not to the provident stratagem of nature hypothesized by Delpino but to the fact that they permitted "the production of a large supply of seeds with little consumption of nutrient matter or expenditure of vital force."[94] Such circumstances obviously improved the chances of the plant in the struggle for existence.

Thus while Delpino stressed the "foresight" of nature, Darwin insisted on its "parsimony." The two perspectives, however, had something in common: it was quite easy, ultimately, for Delpino to consider parsimony a *result* of nature's foresight. Like Darwin, Delpino was highly receptive to the theme of the "economical" efficiency of nature. In Delpino's essay on cleistogamic flowers, well known to Darwin, there were interesting remarks on the subject. Describing the flowering of a red valerian (*Centranthus ruber*), Delpino called attention to the fact that the flowers had only one anther and one stigma, and that they were projected alternately in a coordinated manner. He described all this as "a beautiful confirmation of the great law of economy and parsimony, so widespread in nature." Delpino, in fact, went beyond this and formulated a broad generalization: "It can be deduced from this that greater savings in materials and homologous organs correspond to a greater perfection in the organism. . . . This provides a good criterion for measuring the scale of organic perfection."[95]

In his customary annotated index of this 1867 paper of Delpino's, Darwin noted that Delpino's were "very good remarks."[96] Darwin, in fact, used both the example of cleistogamic flowers and the principle of "less consumption" in what was probably the most important theoretical conclusion of his 1877 treatise on the forms of flowers, namely, his hypothesis on the origin of the separation of sexes.[97] Examining the hypothesis of pangenesis, we saw that according to Darwin, sexual reproduction represented the exception rather than the rule in the organic world, and must have originated from the more widespread asexual type of reproduction. Darwin's hypothesis, at any rate, attenuated the difference between the two types of reproduction. We have also seen that in criticizing pangenesis, Delpino expressed the opinion that the introduction of sexual reproduction, with its more complex mechanisms, represented an important step forward in the progressive evolution of organisms. Now Darwin proposed to account for this important step in the evolutionary process as a consequence of the same criteria of "economy" displayed by cleistogamic flowers and effectively pointed out by Delpino. Darwin wrote,

> The sole motive for the separation of the sexes which occurs to me, is that the production of a great number of seeds might become superfluous to a plant under changed conditions of life; and it might then be highly beneficial to it that the same flower or the same individual should not have its vital power taxed, under the struggle for life to which all organisms are subjected, by producing both pollen and seeds.[98]

At this Delpino might have remarked that through "greater saving in materials," sexual reproduction had realized a greater degree of "organic perfection." Darwin, however, was less inclined than some of his followers to underscore "progress" in evolution.

From our standpoint here, an interesting aspect of the hypotheses on the origin of sexes is that while Darwin may have been aided in formulating his hypothesis by some of Delpino's reflections on the "economy" of nature, Delpino preferred a different explanation, perhaps even more typically Darwinian, and it, too, inspired by an analogy from economics. In an essay on the evolution of plants fertilized by wind,[99] Delpino suggested that the separation of sexes might have been a consequence of a law drawn from economics and with a long history of applications to biology, of which Darwin was an authoritative supporter.[100] In the process of plant fertilization, according to Delpino, the separation of sexes could ensure "the benefit of a more perfect division of labor."[101] This was a principle that Darwin had appealed to more than once, though in this case he did not find it apt. The marginalia in his copy of Delpino's essay include the comment: "I do not think sexes have departed & developed from advantage of division of labor . . . but for ensuring a cross between 2 distinct individuals."[102] In the treatise on the forms of flowers, Darwin ultimately abandoned the hypothesis mentioned in this brief comment and adopted the one we saw, based on the "savings" in vital forces.

In this chapter I have dwelt on some issues on which Darwin and Delpino compared notes, stimulated each other, and in many cases found each other in profound disagreement. This account includes new testimonies on the relationship between Darwin's conception of the living world and the traditional, finalistic view of nature. The sources available on these issues cover the whole spectrum of evidence ranging from "public science" to "private science," to use Martin Rudwick's expression:[103] the writings that both men published, available to other naturalists as well; their correspondence, accessible only to the two of them; and the comments and notes that each wrote in the margins of the publications of the other, probably the most "private" of the texts now available to the historian. The issues and sources discussed in this chapter allow some reflections on the relations between Darwin's theory, the finalistic view of nature, and Darwin's own role in the international community of Darwinian botanists.

The first remark is that, whatever Darwin's attitude toward finalism may have been during the years of the formation of his theory of evolution, in the period considered here—the decade from 1867 to 1877, roughly—the campaign he waged against finalism was wholly consistent.[104] True, Darwin did his utmost to keep his campaign from taking the form of a philosophical or methodological attack, which might have alienated the sympathies of figures such as Gray or Delpino. Yet Darwin's relationship with Delpino proves beyond any doubt that Darwin fought to disprove each new move by the teleologist with new empirical evidence.

On the other hand—and this is my second remark—Darwin's relationships with botanists such as Delpino, Gray,and Müller show that only to his friend Gray did he completely reveal his philosophical opposition to finalism.[105] Judging from the extant correspondence, he kept silent on this point with all the others, including those such as Hermann Müller who shared his orientation. Evidently, Darwin was convinced that it was possible and opportune that both adversaries and supporters of teleology should call themselves "Darwinians." Indeed, even Delpino never stopped considering himself one of them. A peculiar combination of ambition and tolerance would seem to be the personal factor that led Darwin in this direction. But of course the particular situation of the British scientific community must have played a part as well. It would be interesting to investigate why Darwin was both willing and able to follow this policy, whereas many of his fellow botanists in Germany, the United States, and Italy could not or would not do the same.

A third remark is that there was a limited but not negligible area of phenomena to explain which both Darwin and the teleologist appealed to concepts that, strictly speaking, belonged neither to the tradition of natural theology nor to a consistent, antiteleological explanation like that toward which Darwin generally leaned. The phenomena in question were those—recurrent in the ecological studies launched by Darwin and very important in an evolutionary perspective—in which the principles of utility, conservation of resources, and efficiency seemed to manifest themselves in nature. Darwin and the teleologist concurred that it was advantageous to account for these phenomena by using concepts and analogies drawn from economics, a discipline that boasted of a long history of compromises between an "atomistic" view of society and various forms of teleological explanation. Delpino clearly perceived this convergence between biology and economics. Apparently he regarded it as an interesting circumstance: "Great signs of perfection [in biological phenomena] are unquestionably the economy of resources and time, and the increase of the usable product. This coincidence with the basic percepts of social and economic science is singular in nature."[106] In fact, adhering as he did to a philosophical tradition that pointed to the "dominion of intelligence in the order of cosmic phenomena," Delpino must have found the concurrence between biology and economics less surprising than Darwin did.

As for Darwin, it did not escape the notice of his contemporaries that his works on fertilization abounded in teleological expressions. Alphonse de Candolle brought this to Darwin's attention. He urged Darwin to adjust his language to the antiteleological spirit of his theories.[107] Darwin's reply, however, was inspired by a pragmatic attitude. He admitted there was "much justice" in de Candolle's criticism. He acknowledged that he had found it very difficult to avoid the terms *object*, *end*, and *purpose*. Ultimately he claimed the right to use those terms freely, a claim which may have had something to do with his flexible strategy toward finalism.[108] His difficulty in avoiding the terms *object*, *end*, and *purpose*, however, was indicative of yet another issue. As we have seen, to contradict the teleologist, Darwin often resorted to arguments assuming that nature displayed utility, efficiency, and economy of resources; but this was a side to Darwin's theory of selection to which a teleologist could willingly subscribe. It is doubtful, at any rate, that Darwin himself would have wanted or known how to do without such arguments. We can imagine that he would have found even more difficulty avoiding them than the terms *object*, *end*, *purpose*. In this connection it seems appropriate to suggest that in the 1860s and 1870s, teleology was something more than the dogmatic philosophy of some and the ideological target of others. It was both those things, to be sure. But it was also a habit of thought with deep roots in the language of many.

Another issue deserves mention in these concluding remarks: the question of the historical roots of teleology in biology as displayed in Delpino's works and in the lively debates on Darwinism which took place in late-nineteenth-century Italy. Not a great deal is known of Delpino's early education and scientific background. Self-taught, he published his first essay at thirty-two, beginning his academic career only two years later.[109] The door to this career was opened by Filippo Parlatore, whose profound interest in Romantic German philosophy of nature we have already seen.[110] This circumstance, along with Delpino's many explicit declarations, confirms the importance of that tradition for his biological work.

In particular, in his most far-reaching philosophical and methodological essay, *Pensieri sulla biologia vegetale* (Thoughts on plant biology), Delpino recognized a special affinity for "the ideas of life, intelligence, instinct, and reason in Nature" propounded by Gottfried Reinhold Treviranus, an adherent of the Kantian branch of German philosophy of nature.[111] Delpino's conception of nature was profoundly influenced by this scientific and philosophical tradition. He had every reason to protest against critics who glibly equated his meticulous empirical studies with "the ridiculous theorizing of the so-called philosophy of Nature founded by Hegel, Schelling, and company."[112] But he would not have denied that his language, his theoretical achievements, and his view of nature owed much to the works of the more empirically oriented adherents of that tradition such as Treviranus. Delpino's writings, on the other hand, suggest that this idiosyncratic interpretation of Darwin's was based more on philosophical than on religious grounds. Only rarely did he resort to arguments of a theological nature, and these did not express adherence to any specific credo. This circumstance, and the absence of any references to British natural theology, reveal that the roots of Delpino's teleology were unlike those of Asa Gray.[113]

A definition of nature that Delpino proposed in 1874 reveals his philosophical position clearly, along with his unshakable intention to reconcile Darwinism with the heritage of the Romantic philosophy of nature:

> We use the word *nature* as Darwin and other followers of his often used it. By this word we mean the complex network of all the effective and preceding causes that have determined a given organism in all its intrinsic and extrinsic features. . . . And if to this complex of causes we add the attributes of intelligence, foresight, and preformation, it is because we have long been convinced that, among these preceding and effective causes, a leading position is occupied by an intelligent and farseeing principle that pervades every organism.[114]

Delpino failed to add that Darwin had repeatedly warned his readers against interpreting certain expressions in the *Origin* in the sense that Delpino advocated.[115] The misrepresentation of Darwin's thought that Delpino arrived at was one price he had to pay for the demanding strategy he adopted in the heated debates on Darwinism, monism, and materialism in progress in the 1870s in Italy. And this brings me to the last of my concluding remarks.

In spite of Darwin's firm dismissal of all Delpino's attempts to make room for teleology within Darwinian ecology, Delpino did not relinquish the idea of a reconciliation between finalism and Darwinism. Again in 1880, in a lecture entitled "Il materialismo nella scienza" (Materialism in science),[116] in which he harshly attacked that school of thought, which he believed dominated Italian scientific and intellectual circles,[117] he eschewed any criticism of Darwin's theory of transformism. Here as elsewhere, Delpino avoided emphasizing the profound differences that separated him from Darwin. The adversaries to overthrow were Ernst Haeckel and the Italian disciples of monism, who Delpino thought constituted a substantial and menacing group. He saw in them signs of a moral degeneration that he feared affected the world of science as it did ethics, politics, and art. Delpino had never disguised his conviction that a teleological interpretation of evolution was indispensable for ethical and social as well as scientific reasons. In his 1868 critique of Darwin's pangenesis, he had stated emphatically:

> Dualism believes in *liberty* and *thought*, and therefore carries with it the popular sentiment and consciousness and, transfusing itself into the social and moral sciences, explains *duty, justice and the progress of humanity*. Monism, or materialism, denies *liberty* and *intelligence*; and with these it denies *duty, justice and the progress of humanity*.[118]

At the time of his 1880 lecture, he perceived the same problems in an even more accentuated form. Given his by then long and stimulating correspondence with Darwin, Delpino certainly had a point when he contended that materialists and monists were not the only accredited interpreters of Darwin[119] and that "vitalism extended a hand to Darwinism." But he went too far when he said that "the two doctrines uphold each other reciprocally, illustrating and completing each other."[120]

Darwin had chosen not to comment on similar views when Delpino expressed them eleven years earlier. In 1880—given the apparent success of antiteleological explanations within the international community of Darwinian botanists—Darwin would have had even less reason for doing so. And yet, positions such as Delpino's were the result not only of the scientist's personal convictions and the strictures of the Italian controversy over Darwinism but also of the adroit strategy used by Darwin for over twenty years in dealing with finalism—a strategy which did not explicitly rule out that evolution and teleology could be reconciled. Such a reconciliation, Darwin knew, contradicted his own biology on many points. Yet there was a place for it, too, in the strategy contrived by Darwin to ensure that the theory of evolution would triumph in the end.

PART III
Darwinism

Man's Ancestors and Criminology

C. Lombroso and Social Darwinism

In a work that has become a classic on the history of the relations between evolutionism and social theory, James Burrow warned that the idea that "Darwin's theory represented a turning-point in social thought" should be regarded as little more than a myth.[1] The myth was created in the late Victorian period, when the success of Darwinian and Spencerian ideas obscured the roots that connected late-nineteenth-century social sciences with social thought prior to the publication of the *Origin of Species*. From the critical revision of that myth, Burrow drew a radical conclusion: "The history of Darwin's influence on social theory belongs, except in the case of the theory of natural selection, to the history of the diffusion of ideas rather than of their development."[2] By this he meant that although social Darwinism (though "Spencerianism," according to Burrow, would also be appropriate) was unquestionably a relevant phenomenon in the transmission of the images of nature and science among a lay audience, it had little to tell the historian interested in the growth of knowledge. In other words, according to Burrow the adoption of Darwinian concepts and explanatory models did not contribute significantly to the development of the social sciences.

Burrow's views were formulated over twenty years ago. Since then there have been no definitive new contributions to the history of "social Darwinism." Little has been done, at any rate, comparable to what has been accomplished over the same period by historians studying the formation of Darwin's theory and its early developments. The disparity between the success of Darwin's theory and that of social Darwinism in attracting the attention of historians is not difficult to account for, given the recent impressive development of the history of biology as a subfield within the history of science. Studies on the formation of Darwin's theory, however, have themselves demonstrated that this disparity of treatment must not continue. Studies on the formation of Darwin's theory have revealed that the avenues of communication between the natural sciences and the social sciences were in fact open and accessible in the early Victorian age. Moreover, they were well traveled in both directions, and not just from the natural sciences to the social sciences, as late-nineteenth-century Darwinists assumed.[3]

During the 1830s and 1840s, biology frequently borrowed concepts from the social sciences, and as is shown by recent studies on the relations between Darwin's theory and Malthus's theory of population, such borrowings—while clearly encouraged by ideological factors—entailed more than mere ideology. Powerful ideological, contextual factors, of course, helped draw the attention of naturalists such as Darwin and Wallace to the theory of Malthus, a leading exponent of British political economy in the period between the French Revolution and the Restoration. The same is true for those physiologists of the same period who appealed to the concept of the division of labor borrowed from classical political economy.[4] Few historians of biology today, however, would deny that along with its debatable ideological messages, Malthus's work gave Darwin information— for example, demographic and statistical information on the human species—that was not yet available for other species. It also gave Darwin the concept of a tendency to imbalance between populations and means of survival, a trend that naturalists had not yet perceived to the same extent. Malthus, in any case, being committed to a static view of society, could not admit that imbalance might be an agent of change. Darwin, on the contrary, who assimilated Malthus's theory after reaching an evolutionary view of nature, saw in the imbalance between populations and means of survival, if extended to all species, a major factor in the transformation of organisms. Thus, in the 1830s the avenues of communication between the natural sciences and the social sciences permitted the work of the "antievolutionary" economist Malthus to furnish one of the key elements that went into the building of Darwin's evolutionary synthesis.

This story is familiar to historians of biology. Its most detailed reconstruction, and its suitable place along the path that led Darwin to the theory of natural selection, is probably still the one in David Kohn's essay of 1980.[5] While the story has now been substantiated, refined, and circulated, not all the implications have yet been assembled for the study of social Darwinism.

As I view it, the Malthus-Darwin episode reveals that in the first half of the nineteenth century, the transmission of concepts and ideas from the social sciences to natural science was, in fact, accompanied by a real growth in knowledge. If this is so, it is then legitimate to ask whether it is really true—as Burrow has claimed—that the flow of ideas in the opposite direction, from Darwinian evolutionism to the social sciences, produced no real development of those fields in the second half of the nineteenth century. And if so, why did the "repayment" of the social sciences' earlier conceptual loan to biology fail to contribute to their prosperity? And then, exactly what role did Darwin's theory play in these events, besides the images passed down by late-nineteenth-century and early twentieth-century interpreters?

Trying to answer these questions with yet another review of the literature produced by what was rightly or wrongly labeled social Darwinism is definitely pointless. If recent studies agree on anything, it is that the maps used up to now to give us our bearings in social Darwinism are unreliable.

Greta Jones,[6] for instance, has proposed extending the boundaries of social Darwinism to include a good portion of radical English liberalism of the second half of the nineteenth century. Darwinism admittedly most often has been seen as supporting a conservative laissez-faire ideology. But it is also true, Jones maintains, that the founder of eugenics, Francis Galton, and Manchester economists such as William Greg saw their brand of social Darwinism as an attack on the privileges of the aristocracy and landed gentry. From Darwin's *Descent of Man* they gleaned mainly his insistence that human nature was not immutable, and that models of behavior and moral inclinations had natural origins. This philosophy of human nature closely matched that subscribed to by John Stuart Mill in *On Liberty*, published the same year as the *Origin of Species*.

Other scholars have proposed even more radical revisions of the traditional map of social Darwinism. Robert C. Bannister has tried to demonstrate that as a rule the term *social Darwinist* was used only for adversaries: none of the many to whom the term is applied today would willingly have applied it to themselves.[7] Arguing on a different basis, John Durant has suggested that the many attempts to apply the findings of evolutionary biology to the human species and to society can be traced to what he terms nineteenth-century "scientific naturalism."[8] This naturalism had more extensive and more ramified roots than those attributed to the social doctrine whose date of birth is supposed to coincide with the works of Darwin or Spencer. According to Durant, moreover, the difficulty of identifying a coherent body of doctrine constituting social Darwinism is nothing other than a result of the fact that debates on the social implications of evolutionism were normally influenced by the ideological context, which obviously differed depending on the country and the historical moment.[9]

Analogous problems enter into any attempt to explore social Darwinism in the context of nineteenth-century Italy.[10] Apart, perhaps, from a comparatively limited appeal of the notion of "struggle for life," the range and disparity of the social uses of evolutionism were as broad in Italy as in other European countries. In this chapter I will deal with only one case— in fact, the most controversial one—of the application of evolutionism to the social sciences in nineteenth-century Italy, namely, Cesare Lombroso's criminal anthropology. A general survey of the uses of Darwinism in the Italian context is reserved for the next chapter.

LOMBROSO'S "ATAVISM" AND NINETEENTH-CENTURY BIOLOGY

Beyond their sometimes divergent opinions on the bulk of Lombroso's work, historians seem to agree that Darwinism was one source of his criminal anthropology. The theory of atavism, in particular, which provided an early basis of Lombroso's anthropology, is often traced to Darwinian evolutionism. In fact, the relations between Lombroso's atavism and evolutionism turn out to be revealing for a better understanding of the relations between pre-Darwinian evolutionary biology, Darwinism, and social Darwinism.

Lombroso[11] maintained that many criminals were characterized by anthropometrically identifiable physical and mental features that set them apart as a group. He thought the criminal's particular biological characteristics depended most often on the reappearance of features typical of remote ancestors of the human species, representing a step backward in evolutionary history. Criminals therefore merely acted in conformity with these biological characteristics. Their behavior was the "criminal" behavior (if the expression has any meaning at all in this context) that Lombroso thought typical of the human species' ancestors and of all lower organisms: later editions of Lombroso's work on criminal man began with a description of the behavior of carnivorous plants. Of course, Lombroso's theory had enormous consequences for prevailing conceptions of free will, the law, and the prison system. It may be unnecessary to recall here that Lombroso appreciably reduced the role of biological factors in the later versions of his criminal anthropology.

Lombroso's theory of atavism first circulated in 1876 and became widely known from 1878 on, with the second edition of *L'uomo delinquente* (Criminal man).[12] A number of years earlier, Lombroso had observed some phenomena that he described as "atavic." He himself traced his "discovery" to late 1870,[13] and he reported his later best-known case of atavism to the Lombard Institute of Sciences in January 1871.[14] That same month Darwin's friends were perusing early copies of the work in which Darwin first dealt with the problem of the human species' origins.[15] It is unlikely, of course, that Lombroso had seen Darwin's *Descent of Man* when he delivered his first paper on atavism. These dates, in any case, do not clear up the problem of the relations between Darwin and Lombroso. While Darwin made no mention of the human species in the *Origin*, after 1859 his evolutionary theory was at the center of anthropologists' debates in many countries.

At the beginning of the 1870s, Huxley's and Lyell's important works on the origins of the human species came out, supporting an evolutionary approach.[16] These two successful books were also well known in Italy.[17]

It is important to remember, however, that although they appeared at the beginning of what is considered the age of Darwinian biology, Huxley's and Lyell's books did not declare unconditional adherence to the theory expounded in the *Origin*. They certainly drew sustenance from and were in turn nourished by Darwin's evolutionism, but they were rather luke-warm toward the theory of natural selection. Even Huxley, for all his friend-ship with Darwin, defended an evolutionism that, as has been noted,[18] departed from Darwin's on a number of important points. In fact, historians of biology are coming to a fuller appreciation of just how many varieties of evolutionism besides Darwin's were circulating in European scientific circles both before and after 1859.[19]

In order to establish what links, if any, existed between Lombroso's theory and Darwinism, we need to look in more detail at Lombroso's writ-ings and those of the authors that he drew on in formulating his theory of atavism. Such an examination raises further doubts as to the existence of any special relations between Darwin's work and Lombroso's theory of atavism.

In his report to the Lombard Institute of Sciences in 1871,[20] Lombroso illustrated an anomaly he had observed in the skull of the "brigand" Vil-lella,[21] i.e., the presence of a "median occipital fossa." This median fossa, not normally present in the occipital bone of the human skull, is highly developed in lemurs, a family of prosimians then classified toward the bottom of the order of primates, and in some rodents (fig. 8). Lombroso got his information on lemur skulls from Henri de Blainville's classic treatise published over thirty years earlier,[22] and his information on the embryonic development of the nervous system in humans and other primates from a work of 1857 by Louis Pierre Gratiolet.[23] Lombroso maintained that the median fossa observed in Villella's occipital bone corresponded to a highly developed median lobe of the cerebellum. In Gratiolet he looked for some clue that would help him interpret this development, abnormal in the adult human species, as a case of arrested development at the fetal state.[24]

That Lombroso so facilely deduced the shape of Villella's brain or cer-ebellum (which he had not been able to observe directly) from the shape of the skull betrays his at least partial adherence to the old tenets of phren-ology.[25] In fact, new knowledge on the anatomy of the nervous system already had cast doubts on the possibility of proceeding confidently to the sort of deductions of which phrenologists were fond:[26] the correspondence between the skull and the brain was not as direct as assumed when models of the brain were obtained by filling an empty skull with wax, as Lombroso did.[27] Another belief derived from phrenology was, of course, that the development of a certain area of the cerebellum definitely corresponded to certain attitudes, in this case Villella's criminal tendencies.

Incidentally, Lombroso did maintain that Villella ran counter to at least one of phrenology's hypotheses. Phrenologists believed that "the organ of venereal appetite" was located in the median lobe. After consulting the

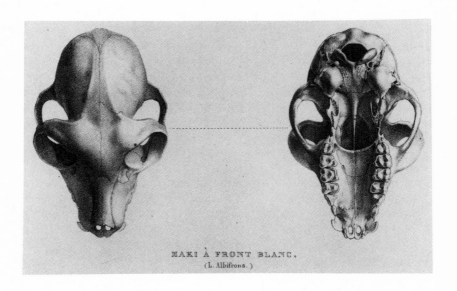

MAKI À FRONT BLANC.
(L. Albifrons.)

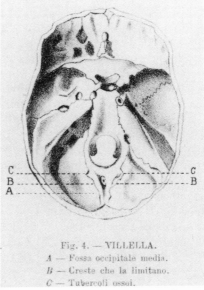

Fig. 4. — VILLELLA.

A — Fossa occipitale media.

B — Creste che la limitano.

C — Tubercoli ossei.

Fig. 8. According to Lombroso, criminals had biological characters typical of remote ancestors of the human species, a phenomenon called "atavism." In the brigand Villella's skull (*bottom*) Lombroso noted the presence of a "median occipital fossa" (*A*), normally not found in the human skull. Such a fossa was known in lower primates such as *Lemur albifrons* (*top*), as well as in some rodents. Lombroso argued that the fossa revealed a similarity between the cerebellum of the criminal and that of lemurs.

The figure at the top is from H. de Blainville, *Ostéographie* (1834–41); the other from C. Lombroso, *L'uomo delinquente*, (4th ed., 1889).

outlaw's prison mates and the records of his trials, however, Lombroso was convinced that in spite of his large median occipital fossa, Villella had shown no sign of an "excessive" sexual appetite.

It is by now clear that the kind of knowledge Lombroso used in his reflections on the Villella case belonged to the legacy of pre-Darwinian comparative anatomy, and in other respects to the phrenological tradition. In his formulation of the theory of atavism, in any case, Lombroso put all this together within a strictly evolutionary perspective. As Stephen Jay Gould has remarked, Lombroso's theory was "a specific *evolutionary* theory based upon anthropometric data,"[28] whereas anatomists, when they noted certain similarities in the development of the nervous system in the human fetus and in lower primates, did not necessarily adhere to an evolutionary hypothesis on the origin of the human species. Indeed, in the work to which Lombroso referred, Gratiolet devoted many pages to *rejecting* the evolutionary conclusions that might have been drawn from the similarities found between the human brain and that of monkeys.[29] What, then, were the roots of Lombroso's evolutionism?

The evolutionists Lombroso mentioned in his report to the Lombard Institute of Sciences did not include Darwin, Huxley, or Lyell, though Giovanni Canestrini, whom he quoted, had referred to all of them. As will be recalled,[30] Canestrini was himself the author of a hypothesis on the origin of man published a few years before Darwin's. According to Lombroso, the reappearance in criminals of a median occipital fossa not found in higher apes but observable in lower primates such as lemurs was a confirmation of Canestrini's hypothesis. Canestrini stated that humans had descended not from anthropomorphic apes but rather from a more distant common ancestor of both "bimana" and "quadrumana," to use the old terminology, which had been criticized by Huxley and Lyell but was still employed by Canestrini and Lombroso. Canestrini had presented his hypothesis as consistent with the theory expounded in the *Origin of Species*. Darwin, we know, did not agree: he did not mention Canestrini's hypothesis in the *Descent of Man* and proposed a *more direct* descent of the human species from apes. Moreover, as was shown in chapter 3 above, when formulating his own hypothesis, Canestrini had taken into careful consideration the objections raised by the "creationist" Bianconi against the idea that the human species had descended directly from apes. So, in formulating the theory of atavism, Lombroso adopted the genealogy of the human species proposed by Canestrini, which weakened the links between humans and other primates, locating them much earlier. And yet *at the same time* he hypothesized that even today the enormous step backward needed to reach those distant ancestors might occur in the criminal.

Just how rash Lombroso's hypothesis was, in view of the information available in the 1860s, is easy to show. In the *Origin* Darwin referred to the "reversion to ancestral characters" as a "well-known principle." He also maintained that the tendency of old characters to return in descendants could "be transmitted undiminished for an indefinite number of genera-tions," and this in the case of a breed which has not been crossed with a distinct breed. He appealed to this delayed reversion, for instance, to ac-count for the reappearance, in various breeds of domestic pigeons, of some features of the rock dove, from which he held that all the others had de-scended. In general, however, Darwin remarked that no facts were known supporting the belief that "the child ever reverts to some one ancestor" removed by more than a dozen or at most twenty generations. Years later, in the *Decent of Man* Darwin declared that in the human species "some of the worst dispositions, which occasionally without any assignable cause make their appearance in families, may perhaps be reversions to a savage state, from which we are not removed by very many generations."[31] Thus the reversions admitted by Darwin hypothesized far more limited backward leaps in evolution than that hypothesized by Lombroso when he compared the criminal's skull to the lemur's.

As for the history of primates, evolutionists such as Huxley maintained that greater differences separated the lemur's brain from that of the ape, compared with those separating the ape's brain from the human brain. It was precisely that first move that Huxley pointed to as the most amazing leap in the evolution of simians:

As if to demonstrate, by a striking example, the impossibility of erecting any cerebral barrier between man and the apes, Nature has provided us, in the latter animals, with an almost complete series of gradations from brains little higher than that of a Rodent, to brains little lower than that of Man. And it is a remarkable circumstance, that though, so far as our present knowledge extends, there *is* one true structural break in the series of forms of Simian brains, this hiatus does not lie between Man and the man-like apes, but be-tween the lower and the lowest Simians; or, in other words, between the old and new world apes and monkeys, and the Lemurs. Every Lemur which has yet been examined, in fact, has its cerebellum partially visible from above, and its posterior lobe, with the contained posterior cornu and hippocampus minor, more or less rudimentary. Every Marmoset, American monkey, old world monkey, Baboon, or Man-like ape, on the contrary, has its cerebellum entirely hidden, posteriorly, by the cerebral lobes, and possesses a large posterior cornu, with a well-developed hippocampus minor.[32]

Lombroso thus built his hypothesis of atavism in criminals by extrapolating on notions that around 1870 evolutionists themselves considered among the shakiest in their repertoire.

LOMBROSO AND DARWINISM

To explain the speculative character of Lombroso's evolutionism compared with Darwinian and Huxleyan evolutionisms, it should be recalled that Lombroso's was framed before the publication of the *Origin of Species*. An entomological paper he published when he was only eighteen and a medical student at the University of Pavia is good evidence of his familiarity even then with the whole range of pre-Darwinian evolutionism.[33]

In this 1853 paper—which also predated B. A. Morel's treatise on degeneration, sometimes regarded as having inspired Lombroso—he elaborated on the notion of the "unity of nature," a motif dear to German Romantic naturalists and to Étienne Geoffroy Saint-Hilaire. He displayed an interest in the study of "anomalies" in animal organization, viewed as an important tool for understanding the general laws of the organic world, as exemplified by Isidore Geoffroy Saint-Hilaire and other teratologists. Lombroso considered the notion, taken primarily from Carl G. Carus, of an animal series displaying a complete, gradual unfolding of apparatuses and functions, and the idea, borrowed from embryology, that the whole animal series is somehow summed up in the human being.[34] This conviction had nourished the first formulations of the law of recapitulation, according to which the development of the individual of a higher species retraces the evolutionary history of the lower ones.[35]

Some such convictions—circulating in Italian universities as early as the 1820s and 1830s through Meckel's anatomy textbook—were evidently at work in Lombroso's hypothesis that arrested development at the fetal stage must have been responsible for the presence of lemurlike features in Villella's brain.[36] That early essay of Lombroso's also cited Lamarck's idea that the use of organs and psychological functions could influence their development, which Lombroso utilized to explain why social insects performing different tasks had acquired different characteristics. Apropos of this, Lombroso referred to the "successive progress and concurrence of circumstances that has brought social insects to their surprising present condition."[37] All this does *not* signify that Lombroso adopted a general evolutionary perspective as early as 1853, but it is evidence that he already had at his disposal many evolutionary concepts he later used in formulating his atavism hypothesis.

Lombroso's writings on psychiatry published between 1855 and 1859 show his continuing interest in the application of teratological and embryological concepts to psychological phenomena. In his essay "Su la pazzia di Cardano" (On Cardano's madness) he proposed a "moral teratology" that would investigate the "uniformity of thought" in normal and pathological states, and in different countries and different historical periods. He identified an important aspect of madness as being its "regressive metamorphosis" to primitive times.[38] In a contemporaneous essay, the same perspective was proposed by Lombroso to account for cases of lycanthropy, which he regarded as "the most barbarous form that madness can take, where the regressive metamorphosis leaves behind even the earliest stages of savages; there are men and women who believe they have been changed into wolves or bears. . . . "[39] Cretinism, too, which Lombroso studied as an endemic phenomenon in the populations of certain valleys of Lombardy, seemed to him to be a form of "arrested development."[40] Consistent with his penchant for recapitulation theory, in 1860 Lombroso took an interest in some of Johannes Müller's hypotheses on "animal cretinism."[41]

Recapitulation theory and teratology were thus the areas of pre-Darwinian biology that most influenced Lombroso in the formulation of the theory of atavism; but they were not the only ideas to inspire him. His writings of the 1850s reveal that, alongside those biological models, Lombroso kept some concepts of Giambattista Vico's philosophy of human history firmly in mind. An interest in Vico's thought had been instilled in him especially by Paolo Marzolo, the proponent of a "natural history of languages" as the key to understanding the history of peoples, and a powerful influence on the young Lombroso.[42] The role of Vico's conception of the history of civilization in Lombroso's reflections has been emphasized by Hans Kurella and, more recently, by Luigi Bulferetti.[43] This is not the place to try to establish which was more influential—Vico's philosophy of history, anatomy, or natural history—in leading Lombroso to formulate the theory of atavism:[44] as I said, in the mid-nineteenth century the avenues of communication between natural sciences and social or human sciences were open in both directions.

What is certain is that in Lombroso's writings of the 1850s, the idea of studying insanity with the tools offered by anatomy and natural history was accompanied by a precise conception of human history and civilization. In these early writings of Lombroso's, the idea that "physical causes contribute much more than moral ones to the genesis of alienation" was coupled with the notion that, contrary to the claims of some, civilization was *not* responsible for the proliferation of madness. "All social progress," Lombroso protested, challenging those whom he considered belated followers of Rousseau's myth of the good savage, "is marked by the victory of reason over passion."[45] And if, he continued, "civilization increases the number of needs [that might cause psychological troubles], it also increases the means for satisfying them with new inventions and more convenient means of communication."[46] Side by side with his training in medicine and anatomy, faith in progress and civilization encouraged Lombroso to search for the causes of madness, and subsequently of criminality, in the occasional regression to the condition of the human species' animal ancestors. Races with biological features resembling those ancestors' could, by the same line of thinking, be considered "inferior."[47]

That all these pre- and non-Darwinian elements had a secure place in Lombroso's evolutionism, even after the diffusion of Darwin's works, is confirmed by the no more than occasional references he made to Darwin in his foremost treatise, *L'uomo delinquente*. In the first edition of the book, the rare mentions of Darwin give Darwin's theory of evolution no credit for being one of the bases of criminal anthropology.[48] The only slightly more frequent references to Darwin in the later editions do not modify this line of conduct: Lombroso used Darwin's works as one of the many sources with which he appeased his obsessive search for "facts."[49]

It would seem that Lombroso's familiarity with pre-Darwinian evolutionism actually hindered him from recognizing the originality of Darwin's work. In this regard it is interesting to see what he perceived in 1869 as Darwin's place in the history of biology and anthropology:

> In the study of natural history, Darwin brought to completion that concept of the unity of origin of organic beings that chemistry, embryology, and the discovery of the cell had begun to suggest long before. . . . His observations, along with those supplied by anthropologists through cranial measurements and the study of the brain in humans and primates, provided us with the explanation of the origin of human beings, which eluded us in the mists of a sacred mythology. . . . "[50]

Clearly, Darwin is presented here more as the culminator of an earlier tradition than as the initiator of a new research program in biology.

Lombroso's essays toward the end of the century confirm that his evolutionism remained essentially impermeable to Darwin's theory of natural selection. In them Lombroso showed that he preferred theories based on the *direct* action of the environment or on the (uncertain) knowledge available on inheritance. In one of his last articles on atavism,[51] for instance, he appealed to the environment to explain why, when a new race immigrated to a region and replaced a preexisting race, some basic characteristics of the earlier inhabitants could recur in the newcomers, even long afterward. Doubts and reservations as to natural selection's capacity to significantly modify organisms were from time to time expressed throughout these pages, where Lamarckian concepts prevailed.

As late as the 1890s, when it came to adopting models from natural history—to repropose, for example, the concept of the criminal "type," a concept so crucial for Lombroso and so marginal in Darwin—he referred to Goethe, Gratiolet, and above all Isidore Geoffroy Saint-Hilaire, rather than to Darwin and the Darwinists.[52]

In the preface to one of the last (1896–97) editions of *Criminal Man*, Lombroso proposed his own reconstruction of the relations between criminal anthropology and Darwinism:

> Not as a naturalist, but as an alienist who, having brought the clinical and anthropological method to psychiatry in place of the prevailing abstract and psychological studies based on individual case histories, I simply applied the same method to the study of the criminal, who accounts for such a large part of psychiatry and penal law.
> If after having harvested the fruits of this I became aware that they smacked of Darwinism, I was by no means unhappy, and later I indeed availed myself of this to corroborate or check my old and new observations, e.g., of the median

occipital fossa, of the crimes of animals, children, savages. However, so far was I from slavishly following Darwin that in the first editions I do not think I ever mentioned him. Even in the last edition, along with atavism I introduced *disease* as a key to crime, which has no relation to Darwin's theories.[53]

Granted, autobiographical statements such as this should be taken with qualification. Besides, being made at the turn of the century, they were probably influenced by the circumstance that Darwinism was going through a momentary slump. On the basis of what has been said up to now, in any case, there is reason to argue that Lombroso's own reconstruction of the relations between criminal anthropology and Darwinism was substantially correct.

A curious sidelight is that in this last phase Lombroso, interested as he was in connecting "disease," especially epilepsy, with genius—which had fascinated him ever since his earliest studies—also considered the case of Darwin in this light. Elaborating on biographical evidence published by his son Francis, Lombroso deemed Darwin a perfect neuropath, with symptoms of epilepsy, many obsessive manias, and accentuated misoneism, a poor genetic background as far as mental health was concerned, and with some clearly "degenerative" somatic features, such as a short snub nose and large, elongated ears, though Darwin shared these traits with Socrates and some scientific geniuses such as Josef Škoda and Karl Rokitansky.[54]

If the reconstruction offered in this chapter is reliable, there are good reasons for claiming that Lombroso's theory of atavism owed more to the pre-Darwinian tradition of natural history and medicine than to Darwin. The relationship between Lombroso's theory of atavism and Darwin's theory must therefore be set much earlier than generally admitted in the historical development of biology. The link lies in the array of ideas on evolution pervading European scientific culture during the first half of the nineteenth century, the weight of which in the formation of Darwin's theory, too, is only now beginning to be fully appreciated by historians of science.

The existence of this common ancestry for Lombroso and Darwin, on the other hand, makes it difficult to claim, apropos of the relations between them, what historians of Darwinism now rightly consider an inadmissible maneuver, namely, that of considering the entire body of Darwin's thought part of the domain of "true science," while considering the particular "Darwinist" in question a predestined victim of the ideology of his time.[55] However great the disparity in their expertise and their originality, both Darwin and Lombroso drew on the same fragmentary, uncertain, biased, but promising reserves of nineteenth-century "scientific naturalism."[56] A sizable group of naturalists, physicians, anthropologists, and philosophers in a number of countries had contributed to this store of knowledge and ideas. The fact that Lombroso's criminology was one of the few products of Italian evolutionism to be exported with any success, and to countries very different as to political-economic system and culture,[57] seems also to indicate that it was not, after all, the most aberrant and provincial of the many expressions of that naturalism.[58] However adversely Lombroso's criminology may be judged today, it cannot be liquidated simply as the product of the ideological transposition of evolutionary ideas from the natural sciences to the social sciences. Like Darwin's Malthusian views, Lombroso's criminal anthropology was grounded in a cultural tradition where conceptual borrowings between the natural and the social sciences were the order of the day.

Returning to and qualifying James Burrow's distinction mentioned at the beginning of this chapter, I would suggest that it is hard, and perhaps misleading, for the historian to try to establish to what extent these conceptual borrowings pertain to the diffusion of ideas, and to what extent they pertain to processes leading to the growth of knowledge. In fact, historians of Darwinism have paid too little attention so far to how ideological factors fostering the diffusion of ideas interacted with everyday fieldwork, with scientific creativity itself. To my mind, this interaction between ideology and scientific creativity is the more challenging and promising frontier for studies on ideology in science, and on Darwinism in particular.

The Popular Reception

Secularization, Radicalism, and the Church

Addressing the Italian parliament in 1881, one MP remarked that the names of Darwin and Spencer had become so well known in Italy that mentioning them in conversation would not qualify one as intellectually sophisticated. Even the English expression "struggle for life," he said, would have failed to impress Italian audiences as esoteric, being by then quite common in Italian political discourse. The same MP observed, on the other hand, that if all those who mentioned Darwin and Spencer in conversation had actually read their books, these books would have been best-sellers like *Nana*, Emile Zola's latest successful novel; and everybody knew that this was not the case.[1]

The paradox of the popularity of Darwin and Spencer in spite of the limited circulation of their books was a small matter compared with the daunting problems facing Italian cultural life. To illustrate some of these problems, the first part of this chapter deals with a few general features of Italian society in the second half of the nineteenth century. These features can be assumed to be relevant to an understanding of the popular reception of what at the time was called Darwinism, along with the motives inspiring its advocates and adversaries. Episodes and personalities will then be considered that illustrate the many different uses of Darwinism and the characteristics of its more frequent users in nineteenth- and early twentieth-century Italy. The exposition will focus on the issue of secularization, which was crucial in orienting supporters and adversaries of evolutionism in the Italian context. In fact, the peak moments in the popular diffusion of evolutionary naturalism coincided with the successive waves of a secularizing movement that ran intermittently through the peninsula during the nineteenth century. Secularization was in turn fostered by the intellectual ferment of the Napoleonic age, the initiatives toward national unification in the 1830s and 1840s, liberalism in the 1860s and 1870s, and socialism at the turn of the century.

Two preliminary provisos are needed. First, I have chosen not to introduce a consistent definition of Darwinism. The authors I deal with in this chapter often ignored or in any case avoided such a definition in their efforts at popularizing evolutionism. It would be arbitrary for the historian to impose a definition on them. The second proviso is that throughout the chapter, the word *popular* and its derivatives are used. The equivalent Italian words *popolare* and *popolo* were used very extensively and quite loosely in the period in question. As will become clear, the word referred to the middle classes more often than to workers in industry or agriculture. The expression "popular reception" in the title of this chapter should be interpreted accordingly.

EVOLUTIONISM AND THE NEW NATION

In 1861, at the time of national unification, Italy had one of the highest rates of illiteracy in Europe, but also the highest percentage of university students. In 1861 illiteracy was as high as 74.7 percent, and it was still 48.5 percent in 1901.[2] On the other hand, during the last two decades of the century, the number of university students was proportionately higher than in Germany, France, and the Netherlands.[3] By 1890, there were seventeen public and four private Italian universities, inherited by the new nation from the dozen states that had made up preunification Italy. The large number of university students was matched by a correspondingly large number of students in secondary schools. A law passed in Piedmont in 1859, and extended to the rest of Italy at the time of unification, kept access to secondary schools relatively open. The law nurtured unrealistically high expectations for the educational system among the middle classes. As a result of lagging economic and industrial development, education was long regarded as the only plausible—if often ineffective—instrument of social mobility. These circumstances had peculiar consequences. The percentage of unemployed or underemployed intellectuals remained singularly high, and the contrast between a person's level of education and the degree of social and economic status attained was often sharp. As contemporaries saw it, the situation favored social unrest and the widespread appeal of radical political positions.

Whatever the difficulties and the potential dangers of the situation, they were accompanied by a considerable liveliness in intellectual activities, as is shown by the production of printed books and the periodical press. The number of books published tripled in forty years.[4] The press, while clearly addressing a very limited portion of the entire population, comprised a remarkably large number of periodicals. Indeed, in this respect, at least, Italy in 1873 ranked just behind France and Great Britain.[5] The dynamism suggested by the statistics was linked to the intellectual and political unrest that characterized the decades just after national unification.

The period was perceived by its protagonists as being devoted to the "foundation" of the new country, all the more so since, according to many, most Italians still lacked any clear sense of national and cultural identity.

In the eyes of the elites who controlled national life,[6] the work of founding
and consolidating the new country implied, among other things, a systematic educational mission involving its citizens. The goals and priorities assigned to this educational mission also affected the popularization of
science. The basic motives inspiring the ruling classes led them, quite naturally, to pay special attention to those branches of science that had a direct
impact on general world-views. In such circumstances evolutionary ideas
were to exert a considerable appeal for the educated classes. The appeal
was stronger for those who thought it urgent for the new state to reinforce
its independence from the Catholic church. In order to counteract the traditional influence of the Church over Italian cultural, political, and economic life, many felt that a thoroughly secular and scientific education was
a powerful tool, perhaps the most powerful tool the new state could wield.[7]

The relationship between the new state and the Church was troubled
during the 1860s and 1870s, as the new country was still engaged in completing national unification. Bringing the capital to Rome was part of this
effort. Rome was finally annexed in 1870 through military force, against
the will of the pope, thereby bringing the temporal power of the Church
abruptly to an end. This was perceived by some as the culmination of the
young nation's historical mission, but it naturally caused resentment in
Catholic circles throughout the peninsula and in Europe.

Some of the protagonists of the popularization of science were themselves scientists, or had been trained as physicians. Indeed, many scientists,
including most of those quoted in previous chapters of this book, felt implicated in the educational mission the new nation demanded. This commitment, in fact, deflected considerable energy away from research.
However, another category of intellectuals was even more assiduous in
popularization. This included philosophers, historians, humanists, soci-
ologists, lawyers, and teachers in general. These intellectuals trained in the
liberal arts were the largest and most representative product of the educational system alluded to above. Judging from the limited circulation of
Darwin's books, they seldom bothered to read the *Origin of Species* thoroughly, even when, from 1864 onward, it was available in Italian translation. Yet they often and enthusiastically engaged in the popularization of
science, and of Darwinism in particular.

THE USES OF DARWINISM: THE
MODERATES AND THE LIBERALS

Having sketched the general context and some characteristics of those engaged in the popularization of science, I will now illustrate the uses of
Darwinism itself, organizing my account according to the main groups of
users that successively appeared on the Italian cultural scene. As will
emerge, the users of Darwinism in Italy often had deep and sometimes
explicit political leanings. I will first discuss the moderates and the liberals,

with their manifold commitments to education, philosophy, and journalism. I will then turn to the radicals, and finally to the Catholics themselves. The classification and the order, however, are largely conventional: thematic and chronological overlapping will become evident in the course of this overview.

For the reasons I have mentioned, secularization was a leading aim of the elites who had achieved unification and guided the country in its first steps as an independent nation. These elites were often politically moderate, monarchist, and constitutional. A British historian has characterized their commitments as Victorian: "Only too conscious of the enormity of the tasks that lay ahead, but truly Victorian in their confidence in their own capacities . . . , these followers of Cavour [i.e., the Italian moderates] saw their duties in an enlightened liberal manner as guiding an immature nation towards an ultimately tranquil, but ever distant future."[8]

The motives and the latent ambiguities of secularization as pursued by Italian moderates are well exemplified in a debate on education that took place in Parliament in 1866. Representing the clash of two world-views, on one side was a baron from Sicily, distinguished by his deep, Franciscan religious spirit, and on the other was a lay intellectual from the North, an anthropologist known for his evolutionary inclinations, and above all for his popular books on sex education, contraception, and divorce. The Sicilian baron, Vito d'Ondes Reggio,[9] had complained that a new generation of teachers was spreading materialist doctrines among Italian youth. The intellectual from the North, Paolo Mantegazza,[10] chose to answer in the following terms, recorded in the parliamentary proceedings:

> If materialism is taught in our schools, this is the doctrine that Galileo taught us (shouts from the floor: *Bene!*), this is experimental science (from the left: *Bravo!*). . . . We cannot and should not interfere with the teachers' consciences. Science must become our religion, the religion of the future (*Bravo!* from the left). D'Ondes Reggio made fun of us by saying that we teach that we are descended from monkeys. This is a most unfortunate thing for him to say. In my own view, if it could be proved that present-day, civilized man is descended from a monkey, this would show that endless progress is a law written into nature.[11]

The rhetoric expressed rather simplistic historical conceptions, of course. It proved very effective, however, when repeated in public lectures or circulated in the press. Mantegazza's message, in essence, articulated three main points that were to become popular. First came the idea that human beings' animal origins could be interpreted as implying that they were "self-made" beings, and that "progress" was a natural law, supporting a thoroughly secular and optimistic view of human history. Second, Mantegazza asserted the right of the exponents of evolutionary naturalism to proclaim themselves heirs to a glorious national tradition going back to

Galileo. Other Italian philosophers of the past, including Giordano Bruno and Tommaso Campanella, were duly recalled later in Mantegazza's speech. Mention of this noble ascendancy opened the way to his third bold and surprising claim: that science itself should become a religion, the "religion of the future."

Although not everybody in the audience would have endorsed Mantegazza's rhetoric, many shared the same basic tenets, often regardless of political inclination. Mantegazza himself sat on the right in Parliament, but he liked to call himself a liberal; and support for his exploits on behalf of evolution, as we have seen, also came from the left.

Declarations of similar ideals, permeated with naturalism, a faith in progress, and a liberal view of society, are found in other representatives of Italian evolutionism. I will mention only one, Tito Vignoli. In a book that also appeared in an English translation in a series including works by John Tyndall, Thomas Huxley, Herbert Spencer, Walter Bagehot, J.-L.-A. Quatrefages, and John William Draper, Vignoli asserted that the "social order is derived from and is based upon the order of nature."[12] He further maintained that

Science and freedom are the great factors of civilization, or of progress in every kind of conception, sentiment and social condition. Science dissolved and destroyed the matrix of myth that originally enveloped intelligence; and liberty, which was wholly due to science, guaranteed steady progress. So, it may be said that the whole web of human history, insofar as it consists in civilization or the progress of all good things, the arts, and every intellectual and material achievement, was the conflict of science, and her offspring freedom, against ignorance and the despotism that results from ignorance, under all the social forms in which they are manifested.[13]

Writing at the end of the 1870s, Vignoli felt compelled to adopt a more defensive stance than the one assumed by Mantegazza in the previous decade. Vignoli admitted that "science and freedom have been held responsible for sectarian intemperance, the disturbances of the lower orders, the inevitable disasters, the social and intellectual aberrations of both the learned and the common people. . . . "[14] Yet he did not budge an inch from his secular view of the conflict between science and ignorance, between science and religion.

But what was the concrete impact on the nation of the secularizing campaign carried out by intellectuals and politicians inside and outside Parliament? For an answer we can look first at the schools and the universities and then at the press.

SCHOOLS AND UNIVERSITIES

The few surveys carried out to date on textbooks used in primary and secondary schools after unification fail to confirm a dramatic shift toward secularization.[15] Granted, a number of textbooks were written or revised to comply with the new spirit and with the renewed system of primary and secondary education run by the state and local governments. The enlarged national market for schoolbooks was flooded by books printed in the North, by publishers often using new steam-powered printing presses, usually imported from abroad. Still, alongside the new content and the new products, a plethora of old books and old ideas remained on the market. The hope expressed by the Italian minister for education in 1864 that the new, secularized textbooks would prevail through a Darwinian process of natural selection did not turn out to be realistic.[16]

The disappointing results were often blamed on the influence of Catholic schools and seminaries, which continued to attract students beyond those headed for a career in the Church, and which could boast of a long experience in educational matters. However, complaints about the secularizers themselves were occasionally lodged. In 1872 a well-known literary critic interested in Darwinism condemned what he thought was an inclination among lay intellectuals to preach quite traditional sermons to the lower classes, ones they never would have delivered when addressing their peers.[17]

Within universities—the overwhelming majority of them state-run—secularization proceeded at a steadier pace. Of the university professors already in place before unification, some of the most conservative refused to swear loyalty to the new state and lost their jobs. Such was the case with the otherwise respected anatomist Giovanni Bianconi, author in 1864 of a thorough attack on Darwinian evolutionism as applied to the problem of human origins.[18] His place was taken by a professor sent by the Piedmontese, who led unification. They selected Giovanni Capellini, a well-traveled geologist and paleontologist, an admirer of Charles Lyell soon converted to evolutionism, which he taught in his courses at the University of Bologna.[19]

Where native scholars were not available to carry out the secularizing campaign, foreign scholars were called in. The "Darwinizing" literary critic mentioned above, while minister for education in 1861, appointed a Dutch physiologist, Jacob Moleschott, well known for his materialistic doctrines, to the University of Turin. The following year another minister, Carlo Matteucci—an early adept of Lamarckian and later Darwinian evolutionism[20]—appointed an evolutionist convert, the German Moritz Schiff, to a chair in Florence. Matteucci also attracted the Russian physiologist Aleksandr Herzen, son of the radical Proudhonian agitator of the same name. In 1869 Herzen delivered in Florence what was perceived to be the most shocking public lecture in Italian history on the animal origins of man.[21]

Strict adhesion to Darwinian concepts was the exception rather than the rule among these native or naturalized Italian followers of evolutionary naturalism. Actually, they subscribed to a broad range of pre-Darwinian and non-Darwinian evolutionary ideas, which had a wide circulation in Italy during the first half of the nineteenth century. As far as secularization and Darwin's symbolic role in it were concerned, however, all these adepts of evolutionary naturalism joined forces.

POPULAR LITERATURE AND LECTURES

Whatever the secularizers' successes or frustrations in the universities and in the schools, respectively, they also invested considerable energy in another, related activity: popularization, both written and oral. No detailed statistics are available yet on the proliferation of books, pamphlets, translations, reviews, newspaper articles, public lectures, and debates that touched on the issue of evolutionism in Italy in the second half of the nineteenth century. To give an idea of it, I will concentrate on a single, representative author, Michele Lessona.[22]

Lessona translated three of Darwin's books,[23] and his own writings are a good example of the amount and variety of the popular literature with evolutionary leanings that circulated in Italy. Trained as a physician and later becoming a naturalist, Lessona taught first in secondary schools and then at the universities of Genoa, Bologna, and Turin; but throughout his life he devoted most of his energy to popularization and journalism. As a naturalist and a scholar, he contributed only a few dozen articles to academic journals. But in the meantime (with the help of his wife, as he once confessed), he contributed many hundreds of articles to about fifty different periodicals with national or local circulation. In 1864 he started a series called Science at Ten Cents, producing twenty-two issues in the course of one year. He also compiled no fewer than seven textbooks for the teaching of physical and biological sciences in secondary schools. He published some twenty separate books and pamphlets, including a book modeled on Samuel Smiles's Self-help, entitled Volere è potere (Will is power).[24] This book alone sold twenty thousand copies between 1869 and 1883, as many copies as were sold in those same years of the memoirs of one of the national heroes of unification, Massimo d'Azeglio. As a translator, Lessona was responsible for or cooperated on the Italian editions of twenty-three foreign books. Besides Darwin's books, his translations included Goethe's Zoological Philosophy, Michael Foster's Treatise of Physiology, and John Lubbock's Prehistoric Times. He also wrote a preface to the Italian translation of Ernst Haeckel's Natural History of Creation.

Lessona's own views on evolution were far from orthodoxly Darwinian. There were profound Lamarckian echoes in his biological work.[25] His popular writings expressed adherence to evolutionism and naturalism, primarily as sweeping, general world-views. These were given prominence over any detailed account of the different explanations then current on the causes of evolution. On the other hand, as his book in the self-help tradition shows, Lessona was *not* interested in applying biological concepts directly to social issues; much less was he advocating some sort of social Darwinism. The chief ideological use to which Lessona put evolutionism was as a tool in the resolute anticlerical battle in which he had joined forces with many other Italian moderates and liberals of the time. Accordingly, the high point of Lessona's popular book on Darwin—a sort of "instant book" that he published on the occasion of Darwin's death, and that sold three thousand copies in a few months—was his harsh rebuttal of any attempt at reconciling Darwin and religion.[26] Lessona rejected these attempts with all the vigor, and some of the stereotypes, of the anticlerical literature disseminated by freethinkers and freemasons in Italy during the Risorgimento and later.

PHILOSOPHERS

The popularization of Darwinism pursued by moderates and liberals interacted with the diffusion of two philosophical currents also advocating secularization: positivism and Hegelianism. Both philosophies had a wide circulation and influence in unified Italy, often through the same press that engaged in discussions on evolutionism.

Earlier in the century the philosophy of Saint-Simon had exerted a notable influence in intellectual circles in northern Italy, attracting the attention of the Republican leader Giuseppe Mazzini, among others. Around mid-century a few representatives of the same circles had taken up Auguste Comte's philosophy, which, however, was destined to have a quite limited circulation south of the Alps in its orthodox form.[27] In the 1860s a positivistic current in philosophy developed in Italy quite independently of any strict allegiance to the ideas of Comte, John Stuart Mill, or Herbert Spencer. The representatives of this philosophical current—some with a background in the natural sciences or in medicine—professed to have been inspired above all by recent developments in biology, anthropology, and historiography, all of which, they maintained, had a decisive import for philosophy. Exponents of this position enjoyed a considerable popularity. They proclaimed themselves and were alluded to by others as "positivists."

An early manifesto of Italian positivism, published in 1866 and entitled *Modern Naturalism*, was in fact the work of a physician with a background in philosophy, Salvatore Tommasi.[28] An entire section of the manifesto was devoted to a discussion of transformism, including a detailed analysis of Darwin's theory of evolution. Deference for Darwin and his theory, viewed as supporting naturalism and positivism, did not prevent the author from expressing skepticism about natural selection as a causal explanation. Like many others in Italy and abroad, Tommasi preferred Lamarckian factors. Besides, he was eager to stress what he thought were the close links between evolutionary doctrines in biology and recent developments in anthropology and historiography. Emphasis on the human species and history was to give a strong historicist orientation to Italian positivism, affecting in turn its interpretation of Darwinism. As expounded by Italian positivists, Darwin's theory was above all a theory of descent, offering a genealogy of living forms rather than an explanation of evolutionary change. Italian positivists, in fact, inclined toward cosmology on the one hand, and toward a very general philosophy of history on the other.[29] In these circumstances, departures from and disillusion with Darwin were inevitable.

Equally attracted by Darwinism, but even more impatient with it, were the Italian followers of Hegel, for a long while a very influential group in cultural and political life south of the Alps. In the 1860s and 1870s the Hegelians, too, contributed to the literature on evolutionism. As the Hegelians saw it, Darwin's dynamic view of nature was reintroducing finalism into science; and this, they thought, was bringing modern science closer to Romantic, idealistic philosophy.[30] The evolutionists' emphasis on *descent* was also perceived as shifting biology toward the historicist orientation of Hegelian philosophy.[31]

Thus both the positivists and the Hegelians appropriated Darwinism while helping diffuse it in academic, cultural, and political circles. The images of Darwin they circulated were, accordingly, highly idiosyncratic. This was one more reason why the general public probably perceived only one major thread in the attempts to popularize Darwinism: that is, once again, its use as a weapon in the battle for secularization.

What unified the ranks of the secularizers was the struggle for supremacy that the young state was fighting against the Catholic church, often perceived as a menacing internal enemy. From the late 1870s, however, other factors acquired prominence on the Italian political scene. Increasing social and political unrest, the echoes of the Paris Commune, the growth of socialist and anarchist groups: all were destined to revive the differences between moderates and liberals temporarily set aside for the sake of national unification. In the new context, the struggle for secularization seemed to some less urgent, and the support of moderate Catholics welcome.[32] Concomitantly, Darwinism was put to new uses in the political arena.

Some of the same intellectuals who had contributed to the popularization of Darwinism in the 1860s now warned against the diffusion of science among the "proletariat." This was the case of Paolo Lioy, a frequent user of Darwinian metaphors in his political speeches, and a keen observer of their changing fortunes and meanings. By the 1880s Lioy had come to advocate what a contemporary called a new brand of Catholic positivism.[33] As he now viewed things, in the hands of extremists science was spreading "atheism, anarchism, and communism" among the lower classes. Lioy, in any case, did not refrain from using Darwinism to his own advantage in the new context. Declaring his opposition to the extension of suffrage rights, in 1881 he invoked modern biology as supporting an "aristocratic" view of society and stressed the need to let "elimination and repression" take their course.[34] The new, aristocratic view of evolution won followers in other quarters. The *Rivista di filosofia scientifica*—a new organ of the Italian positivists, who now often called themselves "monists," à la Haeckel—in

1889 published an article in which evolution was credited with a natural tendency toward the production of "superior men." Nature, it was proclaimed, is against socialism, and against democracy as well.[35]

Actually, in the course of the 1880s Italian positivists found themselves in a peculiar position. By then they had secured a number of important positions in universities, government service, publishing houses, and the press. Natural scientists and physicians with positivistic and evolutionary leanings were popular figures in the universities of northern Italy, and in fashionable novels as well. The so-called positive school of law had acquired considerable influence in a number of law schools. Younger scholars who had trained under the positivists of the former generation were trying to apply evolutionary positivism to the social sciences and economics. Somewhat surprisingly, the positivists had fared less well, by comparison, in philosophy departments.[36] Whatever their chosen field of interest and their academic success, they still felt a strong attraction toward the popularizing mission in which their teachers of a previous generation had joined. Yet the goals of the mission now seemed uncertain. Adversaries and allies distributed themselves along new, unfamiliar lines. Above all, while some now felt an urgent need to rally under the wing of the moderates or the conservatives, or even the reactionaries, others adhered to radical groups, including the growing socialist movement. By the mid-1890s, the political schism among the positivists was plain to everybody.[37]

RADICALS

Within socialist groups, the positivists found themselves side by side with party members of Marxist orientation, who sometimes regarded positivism as the perfect example of bourgeois philosophy. Two episodes will help portray the situation.

In 1892 an authoritative socialist journal, *Critica sociale*, attracted attention to what was presented as a (posthumous) duel between Charles Darwin and Karl Marx. The title read: "Karl Marx killed by Charles Darwin, says one of our Darwinians."[38] The Darwinian in question was a well-known positivist and popular writer, Guglielmo Ferrero. According to him, socialists should abandon Marxism and adopt evolutionary social science instead. For him, Auguste Comte, Charles Darwin, Herbert Spencer, Thomas Buckle, and Cesare Lombroso had definitely surpassed Marx. The invitation must have sounded like a provocation, but the leader of the socialists, Filippo Turati, thought it worth a reply, and in quite conciliatory terms. He played down the attempt to pit Darwin against Marx. Indeed, he asserted that Marxism was "the doctrine of social and historical transformism added to biological transformism." At the same time, he stressed what he considered Marx's superiority over Darwin. As he put it, Marx had not just shown that social systems change over time; he had also shown that they follow different laws at different stages of their development. For Turati this meant that biological laws could be applied to social systems only with qualification. Turati, in other words, was trying to dispose of social Darwinism while retaining Darwin. The issue remained unsettled among the socialists and led to the second of our episodes.

In 1894 the Socialist party decided to celebrate Labor Day by arranging, among other activities, a public lecture on "Science and Socialism" in Milan. Milan was a leading center of the then-emerging Italian industrialization. The more than one thousand people attending had to stand in the small room approved for the meeting by the police. The speaker was Enrico Ferri, a pupil of the founder of "criminal anthropology," Lombroso, and himself a well-known representative of the "positive school of law." He startled his audience with the declaration: "I am a socialist precisely because I am a Darwinian and a positivist."[39] In defending this claim, Ferri set forth his entire world-view. According to it, biological and social evolution was a necessary, natural law, leading society toward socialism regardless of the bourgeoisie's "unscientific" resistance to it. Inevitable progress toward socialism was the message with which some now credited biology.

Not everybody in the audience was convinced. Somebody from the floor called out, "How can you be a positivist *and* a socialist? You must be betraying one of your two masters." A report on the lecture published in the socialist newspaper the following day also displayed skepticism. Still, the journalist applauded the fact that in this Labor Day lecture science and socialism had been treated together, while all too often, he complained, science was used against socialism.

The substance of the popular lecture was published in book form,[40] with a subtitle specifying that it discussed "Darwin-Spencer-Marx." The book crossed the Alps. An English translation appeared in 1905,[41] chosen by Ramsay MacDonald to inaugurate the Socialist Library series he was editor of as secretary of the "labor representation committee," the forerunner of the British Labour party established the following year.

Other Italian socialists paid considerable attention to Darwinism, even those who had been trained in the Hegelian and Marxist traditions. This was the case, for example, of Antonio Labriola, probably the most lucid of the Italian socialist intellectuals. Labriola disliked the abstract evolutionary orientation of positivistic sociology. The artificial environment built by human societies, he protested, should not be regarded as a mere "prolongation of nature."[42] Hence there are "no reasons for tracing that work of human beings that is history back to the simple struggle for existence." In this sense, he maintained, historical materialism "must not be confused with Darwinism."[43]

Yet Labriola was interested in preserving some parts of the lesson he attributed to Darwin, and he found in it something analogous to Marx's doctrines, namely, an important methodological dimension, which he detected in both Darwinism and Marxism. As he put it:

> [Historical materialism] does not pretend to be the intellectual vision of a great plan or design; it is merely a method of research. That is why Marx spoke of his discovery as a guiding thread; and it is precisely in this respect that Marxism is analogous to Darwinism, which is also a method, and it is not a repetition of the old, speculative *Naturphilosophie*.[44]

Labriola's perceptive interpretation of the methodological dimension of Marxism and Darwinism shows that, while dismissing evolutionary sociology, he was not prepared to discard Darwin altogether.

Labriola's essays also had a considerable impact outside socialist circles, and they were read abroad. A French translation appeared in 1897, with an introduction by Georges Sorel. The English translation I quote from was first published in Chicago in 1903.[45] A high regard for Darwin was in fact common among socialists at the turn of the century. In Italy as elsewhere, this sentiment was no doubt linked to the enduring commitment to secularization which the socialists had inherited from the liberals of an earlier generation.

As committed to secularization as the socialists, but somewhat more skeptical about Darwinism, were the Italian anarchists. Despite systematic persecution, they had a considerable popular following in the last decades of the century. In their pamphlets and journals, they too manifested an interest in comparing notes with Darwinism. Nevertheless, following Petr Kropotkin, they had trouble reconciling Darwinian notions such as the struggle for life with their preferred ideal of cooperation. This was how the matter was perceived by Errico Malatesta, an Italian anarchist who spent much of his life in exile in London. As he put it, "every struggle aimed at gaining advantages independently of or at the expense of others is contrary to the social nature of modern Man and tends to drive him back towards the animal state." Cooperation itself, in any case, was presented as the outcome of a natural development: "as a result of the very struggle for existence waged against the natural environment and against individuals of the same species, a social feeling has developed in Man that has completely transformed the conditions of his life. . . ."[46]

CATHOLICS

We can now deal with the main target of the secularizing campaign. In Italy the target was, of course, Catholicism. To discuss the Catholic reaction to Darwinism after first having looked at the secularizers makes sense. For, as Catholic historians admit,[47] in the period we are interested in, and as far as scientific culture was concerned, Catholics rarely took the initiative.

However, we should not infer from this defensive stance that Catholics had lost their powerful influence on Italian culture. It seems appropriate to say, rather, that because of the political vicissitudes mentioned above, Catholic influence in this period was more indirect and more discreet than in perhaps any other period of modern Italian history. It must also be stated at the outset that there was no "Darwin affair" in the same sense that there had been a Galileo affair two and a half centuries earlier.

Indeed, going through the official documents of the Catholic church in the nineteenth century, one finds no explicit mention of Charles Darwin and his doctrines. The name of Charles Darwin is absent from the 1,359 new items added to the Index of prohibited books in the nineteenth century.[48] Curiously enough, one Darwin is listed in the Index: Charles's grandfather Erasmus, with his book *Zoonomia*.[49] The Italian translation was, apparently prohibited as a consequence of the merits, or demerits, of the translator, Giovanni Rasori, a physician and politician with notorious French Revolutionary inclinations. As we know, Erasmus Darwin's books had enjoyed considerable popularity in Napoleonic Italy.[50] The success of Erasmus Darwin's works, the controversial Rasori, and the reaction they sparked can in fact be regarded as indicative of the first wave of secularization Italy experienced at the beginning of the nineteenth century.

Lamarck is also missing from the Index of prohibited books. Instead one finds there little-known followers of Lamarck or Darwin, especially those who were eager to draw lessons for philosophy and morals from biology.[51] This seems indeed to have been the main criterion for inclusion. In other words, the Catholic church was by then apparently more worried by the threat of secularizing philosophies than by science itself. This seems confirmed by the fact that the Index, while excluding Lamarck and Darwin, included a number of the works of philosophers such as Jeremy Bentham, Auguste Comte, and John Stuart Mill, as well as occasional essays by authors such as John Tyndall, Emil Du Bois-Reymond, and John Lubbock.

More open to assessment are the day-to-day reactions to Darwinism documented in the Catholic press. A survey indicates that contingencies were no less influential than any supposed general strategy in shaping Catholic attitudes. As already mentioned,[52] when Charles Darwin's *Origin of Species* first appeared, the influential journal of the Jesuits in Rome, *Civiltà cattolica*, was publishing a long series of articles on geology and cosmogony. The journalist was himself a geologist of some repute. He of course condemned the traces of atheism associated with nineteenth-century natural history. But he was ready to exempt even Lamarck from the charge, being inclined to regard him as a deist. The series of articles had arrived at this delicate point when rumors of Darwin's *Origin of Species* reached the author. The nature of the rumors convinced the author that it was advisable to set aside the conciliatory line he had been pursuing up to then. He concluded his series of articles by endorsing the severe criticism of Darwin launched by François Jules Pictet in the name of orthodox Christianity.

Criticism of Darwin, in any case, was not formally incorporated into official statements issued by the Church. A document published in 1864, the Syllabus of Errors, regarded by many as the most unfortunate manifesto of the Catholic church's conservatism in the nineteenth century, condemned almost everything cherished by the liberals, including faith in progress and in science, but made no explicit mention of Darwinism.[53]

Thus, for Catholics the issue remained open to debate. In the following years a number of them were inclined to admit that some kind of conciliation between evolutionism and religious tradition was possible and advisable. They would argue, typically, that the entire evolutionary process could be viewed as one of continuous creation. The conciliatory approach tended to favor a wide range of non-Darwinian views of evolution. Nevertheless, some also attempted a religious interpretation of Darwin's own concepts. This was the goal pursued for over twenty years by Charles Darwin's most assiduous and esteemed Italian correspondent, the botanist Federico Delpino. Delpino, in any case, did not express adherence to any specific credo.[54]

At the turn of the century, further attempts were made to reconcile evolutionism and religion. One such effort earned considerable popularity thanks to the talents of its author, Antonio Fogazzaro, a successful novelist and a protagonist of the so-called modernist movement within the Catholic church. According to Fogazzaro, biological evolution was just another expression of God's existence. The entire evolutionary process could be viewed as a progressive triumph of mind and intelligence over matter and instinct. Fogazzaro tried to trace what he called "Christian evolutionism" as far back as St. Augustine. But he primarily followed English-speaking authors such as Joseph LeConte and St. George Jackson Mivart.[55]

Fogazzaro's "Christian evolutionism" won him support among liberal Catholics and harsh criticism from the Jesuits. The "modernist movement," which Fogazzaro had supported, was formally condemned in 1907. Again, biological evolutionism did not figure among the errors being attacked; but evolutionary views of human history and of Christianity were explicitly and severely condemned.[56] The oscillating attitude of Catholics toward evolutionism had entered a new, negative phase.

This was to be reversed again to some extent by a later encyclical letter, published in 1951.[57] In this document, evolutionism is mentioned twice. The first time, it is presented, and condemned, as an all-embracing, cosmic world-view, leading naturally toward pantheism, materialism, and communism. On its second mention in the document, evolutionism is presented, and cautiously admitted, as a working hypothesis that Catholic biologists are allowed to maintain while investigating the origins of the human body (souls being created directly by God), provided they are ultimately willing to subscribe to the Church's pronouncements on the matter. This section of the document was interpreted by an authoritative Italian Catholic observer of the time as implying that, on evolutionism, the pope was "ready to accept the conclusions of biologists, provided they are supported by a real, scientific demonstration."[58]

RACE

Having participated in the socialist and the Catholic controversies, at the turn of the century Italian evolutionists became involved in two other hotly debated political issues: the nation's perception of its own position within the European context, and its role in the international competition for colonial power. As contemporaries saw it, it seemed legitimate to enlist evolutionary anthropology in the task of shedding light on both issues.

The first debate was provoked by the attempt on the part of some late-nineteenth-century German anthropologists to rewrite the history of Europe as a history dominated by northern, Aryan stock. According to these German anthropologists,[59] even the achievements of Greek and Roman civilizations had to be credited to Aryans. The German anthropologists had taken pains to show that the celebrated heroes of Greek and Roman history and legends stood out as tall and blond amid the general population of short, dark common men and women. Italian anthropologists apparently felt compelled to adopt equally patriotic arguments.

In 1895 a leading Italian anthropologist, Giuseppe Sergi of the University of Rome, published a book entitled *The Mediterranean Race*.[60] It was aimed at overthrowing the pan-Germanist view and sought to replace it with a thoroughly pan-Mediterranean outlook. Sergi maintained that the bulk of European populations had descended from the human species he called Eurafrican. According to Sergi, this species had originated in Africa, whence it had migrated north, being transformed into Mediterranean and Nordic varieties. Within this perspective the Mediterranean race was older and nobler than the other human races, to which it had brought a superior civilization, exemplified in the Roman Empire. As for the Aryans, according to Sergi "they were savages when they invaded Europe."[61]

The African origin of the Mediterranean race postulated by Sergi offered a highly effective, if unexpected, rationale for another battle in which Italians were then engaged. Sergi's notion of an African origin for the Mediterranean race and, through it, for most European populations had developed while he was studying a rich collection of African skulls. Unastonishingly, these skulls had reached Rome at the time of Italy's otherwise modest African conquests. In the course of conducting the ritual measurements of the skulls, Sergi arrived at a startling conclusion: the origin of the European races lay not simply in Africa but in the very African regions that Italy was trying to conquer.[62] Sergi's readers must have read his story along the following lines: just as evolutionary anthropologists were rediscovering the origins of the human species, so the Italian troops were rediscovering, and reappropriating, their own origins in Africa. Furthermore, given the supposed role of the Mediterranean race in populating the rest of Europe, Italy could claim to be reappropriating its African origins in the name of Europe itself. This must have seemed an irresistible argument when used to counteract the resentment aroused among the great European powers by the annoying, late arrival of Italian imperialism on the scene.[63]

While evolutionism figured prominently in Sergi's speculations, a strictly Darwinian view of evolution was absent. For one thing, Sergi supported polygenesis in regard to the origin of the human species, and he had difficulty reconciling his views with Darwin's monogenism.[64] Even so, Sergi's speculations clearly exploited the prestige Darwin's name had come to lend evolutionary anthropology. Nor were Sergi's speculations an isolated phenomenon. In those same years at the turn of the century, another Darwinian—otherwise sound and honest—Enrico Morselli, addressed popular audiences in Genoa announcing the advent of a superior human species, finding in anthropology and in recent history signs of a resurgent Latin supremacy.[65]

At the popular level, such speculations by evolutionary anthropologists merged quite easily with ideas advanced in those same years by Friedrich Nietzsche, whose works were being translated into Italian in the same series as Sergi's book. Together, they are symptomatic of the potentially devastating heritage in regard to racial issues that late-nineteenth-century science and philosophy handed down to the century that followed.

It is now possible to attempt an overall assessment of the many uses to which evolutionary naturalism and Darwinism were put in nineteenth-century Italy, and to add a few concluding remarks. Judging from the extent of the popular literature that continued to be published, the considerable success of Darwinism lasted in Italy well into the twentieth century.[66] Yet if we look at the opinions circulated by a few leading intellectuals with considerable influence at the popular level, a reaction against evolutionism is discernible. Quite naturally, it was a reaction against Darwinism in the forms in which it had been appropriated by so many different parties in previous decades. Indeed, many of the notions that were now being opposed as "Darwinian" hardly deserved the adjective at all. Apparently this was a consequence of the very popularity Darwinism had enjoyed. A few examples will suffice.

The most influential Italian philosopher of the time, Benedetto Croce, rejected Darwinism and positivism together: he made very little effort to distinguish between them.[67] The usually perceptive Italian sociologist Vilfredo Pareto rejected Darwinism on the sophisticated but controversial grounds that Darwinism regarded adaptation—of both species and social institutions—as perfect,[68] although that clearly had never been a Darwinian concept.[69] In 1912 a former schoolteacher, provincial journalist, and ex-socialist, Benito Mussolini, rejected Darwinism together with another idol he had revered for a while: positivism.[70] Only three years earlier Mussolini had celebrated the first centennial of Charles Darwin's birth with enthusiasm and had proclaimed Darwin and Marx the greatest scientists of the nineteenth century.[71]

Evidently the reasons for rejecting evolutionary naturalism and Darwinism at this stage were just as complex and confused as those that had prompted many to appropriate Darwinism earlier. However, blurred interpretation and diversity of motives were not the only distinguishing features of the popular reception of Darwinism in Italy. One major pattern can be detected in the successive fortunes of Darwinism, and this might usefully be compared with what happened in other countries.

In Italy, the successful phases in the popularization of evolutionary naturalism clearly overlapped with the successive waves of what might be called—for lack of a better expression—the secularizing spirit. These waves of secularization were promoted by different groups at different times. As noted in previous chapters, in the first half of the century a number of Italian scientists had embraced pre-Darwinian evolutionary views, connecting them more or less explicitly to a secularizing perspective. This happened at the time of the Napoleonic wars, and again in the 1830s and 1840s. After national unification in 1861, many circumstances called for an acceleration of the secularizing trend, and the diffusion of Darwinism clearly benefited from it. In this new campaign the moderates and the liberals joined first, followed by the socialists, and finally by "modernist" Catholics. Each one of these groups, of course, had markedly different views on secularization and on the role of Darwinism in it. That clearly contributed to the variety and even the inconsistency of the images of Darwinism in circulation.

One may ask, however, why Darwinism—of the many secularizing isms circulating in the second half of the century—should have been so often accorded priority and appropriated by different groups. The answer, I think, is twofold. First, Darwin's prestige as a scientist made him a particularly powerful ally when addressing popular audiences already made sensitive to the well-advertised achievements of nineteenth-century science. Second, and more intriguing, it was Darwin's own proclaimed neutrality—philosophical, religious, and political—that appealed to the popularizers looking for supposedly objective, indisputable support for their own convictions.

Be that as it may, the views of secularization held in the nineteenth century seem remote from our own. To us, the religious overtones with which nineteenth-century secularizers endowed science—by presenting the theory of evolution as a sort of secular Genesis—make their attitudes seem hardly secular at all. In fact, this recourse to religious imagery may indicate how tightly nineteenth-century secularizers were locked inside the very tradition they were trying to overthrow. As noted in the preceding pages, the religious overtones and the consequent ambiguities were augmented in Italy by the commitments of the educational mission in which the secularizers saw themselves as being engaged.

By pointing to these nineteenth-century ambiguities attendant on conveying Darwinism to the masses, I am not implying that late-twentieth-century historians of science are themselves uniquely free from similar ambiguities. On the contrary, I think that the success of Darwin studies among historians of science in recent decades might itself profitably be regarded as—among many other things—yet another in the successive waves of the secularizing spirit we have inherited from the nineteenth century. In other words, in this as in other cases, the historian is partly implicated in the very story he or she is telling, and no legitimate claim to superior objectivity is possible, except that which comes from recognizing involvement.

Another concluding remark seems appropriate. We usually assume that whenever science is popularized, ideological factors come into play, thereby compromising science and understanding as such. I feel, on the contrary, that we should regard the interaction between science and ideology in popularization as reciprocal, and not necessarily negative in its effects. Even in the troubled Italian setting described above, a few perceptive interpretations of Darwinism found their way through the clash of opposing ideologies. I am thinking, for example, of Turati's and Labriola's reflections on the *methodological* dimension they pointed out in both Darwinism and Marxism. I am also thinking of some persistent residues of finalism that interpreters such as Delpino pointed out in Darwin, despite Darwin's own consistent campaign against the old teleological view of nature. Although clearly prompted by ideological concerns, these were and are discerning interpretations: they remain stimulating for the historian to explore when assessing Darwin's theory of evolution and its impact. It makes little sense to say that these interpretations were arrived at despite the din of ideological conflicts. It seems fairer to say that these insights were themselves part of the difficult but at times perceptive negotiation in which the popularizers of Darwinism engaged.

Notes

INTRODUCTION

1. See some illuminating remarks in I. B. Cohen, *Revolution in Science* (Cambridge: Belknap Press of Harvard University Press, 1985), 47, 291–92.

ONE. A HISTORY OF LIFE WITHOUT EVOLUTION

1. G. B. Brocchi, *Conchiologia fossile subappennina con osservazioni geologiche sugli Appennini e sul suolo adiacente* (Subapennine fossil conchology with geological observations on the Apennines and the adjacent terrain), 2 vols. [hereafter *Conchiologia*] (Milan: Stamperia Reale, 1814), 1: 219. Works on the life and writings of Giambattista Brocchi (1772–1826) include G. Larber, *Elogio storico di G. B. Brocchi* (Historical tribute to G. B. Brocchi) (Padua: Crescini, 1828); D. Sacchi, "Necrologio di G. B. Brocchi" (Obituary of G. B. Brocchi), *Annali universali di statistica* 15 (1828): 132–53; *Atti della festa commemorativa per il primo centenario della nascita di G. B. Brocchi celebratosi in Bassano il 15 ottobre 1872* (Proceedings of the commemoration for the first centennial of the birth of G. B. Brocchi held in Bassano 15 October 1872) (Bassano, 1873); V. Giacomini, in *Dizionario Biografico degli Italiani*, s.v. "G. B. Brocchi" (Rome: Istituto della Enciclopedia Italiana, 1960–); J. T. Gregory, in *Dictionary of Scientific Biography*, s.v. "G. B. Brocchi" (New York: Scribner, 1970–78); *L'opera scientifica di G. B. Brocchi* (The scientific writings of G. B. Brocchi) (Vicenza: Rumor, 1987); G. Berti, *Un naturalista dall'ancien régime alla Restaurazione. G. B. Brocchi (1772–1826)* (A naturalist from the *ancien régime* to the Restoration) (Bassano: Verci, 1988).

2. *Conchiologia* 1: 7, 30.

3. J. B. Lamarck, *Mémoires sur les fossiles des environs de Paris*, a series of articles in *Annales du Muséum d'histoire naturelle*, vols. 1–7 (1802–1806); see *Conchiologia* 1, Introduzione: 3. On Lamarck, see P. Corsi's major monograph, *The Age of Lamarck* (Berkeley and Los Angeles: University of California Press, 1988).

4. G. Cuvier and A. Brongniart, "Essai sur la géographie minéralogique des environs de Paris" (Essay on the mineralogical geography of the area surrounding Paris), *Journal des mines* 23 (1808): 421–58; see *Conchiologia* 1: 91.

5. J. Parkinson, "Observations on Some of the Strata in the Neighbourhood of London and on the Fossil Remains Contained in Them," *Transactions of the Geological Society of London* 1 (1811): 324–54; see *Conchiologia* 1: 91–92. On Parkinson, see J. C. Thackray, "James Parkinson's *Organic Remains of a Former World (1804–1811)*," *Journal of the Society for the Bibliography of Natural History* 7 (1976): 451–66.

6. *Conchiologia* 1: 11.

7. For a treatment of the different approaches to the problem of extinction during the eighteenth and nineteenth centuries, see B. Balan, *L'ordre et le temps: L'anatomie comparée et l'histoire des vivants au XIXe siècle* (Order and time: Comparative anatomy and the history of living organisms in the nineteenth century) (Paris: Vrin, 1979), especially 105–47.

8. "Discours préliminaire" to the *Recherches sur les ossemens fossiles des quadrupèdes* (Researches on the fossil bones of quadrupeds) (1812), repeatedly reprinted separately in French and various translations. On the extinction problem in Cuvier, see M. J. S. Rudwick, *The Meaning of Fossils: Episodes in the History of Paleontology*, 2d ed. (New York: Science History Publications, 1976), chap. 3.

9. On the key position of extinction in the origins of Lamarck's theory of trans-

formism, see R. W. Burkhardt, Jr., *The Spirit of System: Lamarck and Evolutionary Biology* (Cambridge: Harvard University Press, 1977), chap. 5.

10. *Conchiologia* 1, Introduzione: 11.

11. Ibid., 219–20.

12. Ibid.

13. Ibid., 221–23.

14. Ibid., 224–25.

15. Brocchi's manuscripts and letters are kept in the Biblioteca Civica of Bassano del Grappa (hereafter BCB).

16. MS 31.A.20, BCB, which Brocchi entitled *Giornale del viaggio mineralogico per vari paesi dell'Italia. An. 1811–1812* (Journal of the mineralogical trip through various Italian countries: Years 1811–1812). The pages of this voluminous handwritten diary being unnumbered, reference is made to the date of each passage, of which Brocchi took careful note.

17. See Larber, *Elogio storico di G. B. Brocchi*, 29; and R. Vergani, "Brocchi funzionario alle miniere: dal Regno Italico alla dominazione austriaca" (Brocchi the mine functionary: From the Kingdom of Italy to Austrian rule), in *L'opera scientifica di G. B. Brocchi*, 67–77.

18. This information comes from an extract of the "Incombenze degli Ispettori delle Miniere" (Duties of Mine Inspectors), approved in October 1808 by the minister of the interior of the Kingdom of Italy and kept among Brocchi's papers (Epistolario Brocchi, VI, BCB).

19. From 1801 to 1808 Brocchi taught natural history in Brescia at the Gymnasium of the Department of Mella, one of the administrative regions into which the Kingdom of Italy was divided (see n. 17). The job included the recently established position of curator of the botanical garden and the task of organizing a natural history museum at the Gymnasium (see Larber, *Elogio storico di G. B. Brocchi*, 22–29).

20. See G. B. Brocchi, *Ricerche sopra la scultura presso gli Egizi* (Researches on Egyptian sculpture) (Venice: Gatti, 1792). The passages on Roman scientific institutions are from *Giornale del viaggio mineralogico* [hereafter *Giornale*], MS 31.A.20, BCB, Oct. 1 and 3, 1811. Like *Conchiologia*, the *Giornale* repeatedly shows that Brocchi's interests in history and erudition were interwoven with those in mineralogy and natural history, not unusual in geologists of the time, as has been pointed out by, e.g., D. R. Oldroyd, "Historicism and the Rise of Historical Geology," *History of Science* 18 (1979): 191–213, 227–57.

21. *Giornale*, MS 31.A.20, BCB, Jan. 10, 1812.

22. Ibid., Mar. 5, 1812. On Maclure and Brocchi see J. Doskey, ed., *The European Journals of William Maclure*, vol. 171 of Memoirs of the American Philosophical Society (Philadelphia, 1988), ad indicem.

23. *Giornale*, MS 31.A.20, BCB, Jan. 10, 1812.

24. Ibid., May 25 and 27, 1812.

25. Regarding the 1813 trip see Larber, *Elogio storico di G. B. Brocchi*, 41–42.

26. On Andrea Bonelli and his course of lectures, see L. Camerano, "Contributo alla storia delle teorie lamarckiane in Italia: Il corso di zoologia di Franco Andrea Bonelli" (Contribution to the history of Lamarckian theories in Italy: Franco Andrea Bonelli's zoology course), *Atti della R. Accademia delle Scienze di Torino* 37 (1902): 3–12; and by the same author, "Materiali per la storia della zoologia in Italia nella prima metà del secolo XIX: I manoscritti di Franco Andrea Bonelli" (Materials for the history of zoology in Italy in the first half of the nineteenth century: The manuscripts of Franco Andrea Bonelli), *Bollettino dei Musei di Zoologia ed Anatomia comparata della R. Università di Torino* 21 (1906), nos. 535, 536; 23 (1908), nos. 579, 586, 591; 24 (1909), nos. 601, 606. See also B. Baccetti and P. Omodeo, in *Dizionario Biografico degli Italiani*, s.v. "F. A. Bonelli" (Rome: Istituto dell'Enciclopedia Italiana, 1960–);

and P. Corsi, " 'Lamarckiens' et 'darwiniens' à Turin (1812–1894)" ("Lamarckians" and "Darwinians" in Turin), in *De Darwin au Darwinisme: Science et idéologie*, ed. Y. Conry (Paris: Vrin, 1983), 49–67.

27. *Giornale*, MS 31.A.20, BCB, Sept. 27, 1811.

28. The extensive literature on the history of geology in the eighteenth and early nineteenth centuries includes C. J. Schneer, *Toward a History of Geology* (Cambridge: MIT Press, 1969); Rudwick, *Meaning of Fossils*; R. Porter, *The Making of Geology* (Cambridge: Cambridge University Press, 1977); M. Greene, *Geology in the Nineteenth Century* (Ithaca, N.Y.: Cornell University Press, 1983), chaps. 1, 2; R. Laudan, *From Mineralogy to Geology* (Chicago: University of Chicago Press, 1987). For Italian developments during the same period, the outline of the history of geology in Italy introducing *Conchiologia* is very helpful. See also L. Pilla, *Discorso accademico intorno ai principali progressi della geologia ed allo stato presente di questa scienza* (Academic discourse on the main advances in geology and the present state of this science) (Naples: Plantina, 1849), and the recent account by L. Ciancio, "La difesa dell'ipotesi nettunistica" (The defense of the neptunist hypothesis), in *L'opera scientifica di G. B. Brocchi*, 55–65.

29. Scipione Breislak was "administrator and inspector of nitres and gunpowders" of the Kingdom of Italy. His most important geological work, *Introduzione alla geologia* (Introduction to geology) (Milan: Stamperia Reale, 1811), appeared a few years before *Conchiologia* and was published, like Brocchi's book, with the help of a government subsidy: see M. Bernengo, *Intellettuali e librai nella Milano della Restaurazione* (Intellectuals and booksellers in Restoration Milan) (Turin: Einaudi, 1980), 29. In *Introduzione alla geologia* (2: 433–34), Breislak called Brocchi "the most eloquent orator" and "the fiercest defender" of neptunism yet at the same time rebutted his views. Brocchi's propensity for neptunism subsequently abated, following further research on the origin of basalt; see G. B. Brocchi, "Sulle geognostiche relazioni delle rocce calcaree e vulcaniche in Val di Noto nella Sicilia" (On the geognostic relations of limestones and volcanic rock in the Noto Valley of Sicily), *Biblioteca Italiana* 27 (1822): 56–67, particularly 63–67. On Breislak see L. Gennari, in *Dizionario Biografico degli Italiani*, s.v. "S. Breislak," and V. Francani, *Dictionary of Scientific Biography*, s.v. "S. Breislak."

30. *Giornale*, MS 31.A.20, BCB, Sept. 13, 1811.

31. Ibid., Jan. 23 and 25, 1812.

32. Ibid., Feb. 27, 1812.

33. See text corresponding to n. 141 below.

34. *Conchiologia* 1: ii.

35. Ibid.

36. Leibniz's ideas on the subject were made public in *Acta Eruditorum*, Leipzig, in 1693, and in *Histoire de l'Académie des Sciences de Paris* (History of the Paris Academy of Sciences) for the year 1706; cf. G. W. Leibniz, *Opera Omnia* (Geneva: De Tournes, 1768), 2: 178–79.

37. Brocchi had already endorsed the idea in *Trattato mineralogico e chimico sulle miniere di ferro del dipartimento del Mella* (Mineralogical and chemical treatise on the Mella iron mines) (Brescia: Bettoni, 1807–1808) 2: 336–37.

38. This emerges from a passage in G. B. Brocchi, *Zibaldone di Storia Naturale* (Miscellany of natural history) [hereafter *Zibaldone*] (MS 34.C.16, BCB, s.v. "Petrificati"), a collection of notes, given this title by Brocchi himself, in which he recorded significant passages from his readings in natural history, organized by subject.

39. A. Vallisneri, *De' corpi marini, che su' monti si trovano; della loro origine, e dello stato del mondo avanti il diluvio, nel diluvio, e dopo il diluvio, Lettere critiche* (On marine bodies found on mountains; on their origin, the state of the world before the flood, and after the flood: Critical letters), 2d ed. (Venice: Domenico Lovisa, 1728), 19, 47.

40. *Conchiologia* 1: 53ff.

41. Even in the case of the most surprising geological phenomena, Brocchi insisted that everything must have been produced "in a uniform and tranquil manner,
and in the most common ways; however extraordinary the effects may seem, the
causes were very simple." G. B. Brocchi, "Sulla Lignite bruna di Valgandino" (On
Valgandino brown lignite), *Giornale della Società d'incoraggiamento delle scienze e delle
arti stabilita in Milano* 6 (1809): 33–91, especially 73.
As we are about to see, however, some hypotheses which admit to geological
"revolutions" appear even in Brocchi's work. The inadvisability of seeing "unifor-
mists" and "catastrophists" as diametrically opposed in the history of early nineteenth-century geology has been pointed out by M. Bartholomew, "The Singularity
of Lyell," *History of Science* 17 (1979): 276–93, particularly 277. On related questions
see R. Rappaport, "Borrowed Words: Problems of Vocabulary in Eighteenth Century
Geology," *British Journal for the History of Science* 15 (1982): 27–44, especially 31–38;
and S. J. Gould, *Time's Arrow, Time's Cycle* (Cambridge: Harvard University Press,
1987), chap. 4. For the history of uniformitarianism see R. Hooykaas, *Natural Law
and Divine Miracle: The Principle of Uniformity in Geology, Biology and Theology*, 2d ed.
(Leiden: Brill, 1963).

42. See *Conchiologia* 2: 607ff.

43. Ibid., 617.

44. Ibid., 618. See also 1: 89.

45. Ibid. 2: 617.

46. Ibid. 1: 149–50: "These revolutions unquestionably took place. . . . [T]he
world of today is not as it once was."

47. Ibid. 2: 618.

48. C. Linnaeus, *De Telluris habitabilis incremento* (Leiden: Haak, 1744), § 27ff. On
the subject see T. Frängsmyr, "Linnaeus as a Geologist," in *Linnaeus: The Man and
His Work*, ed. T. Frängsmyr (Berkeley and Los Angeles: University of California
Press, 1983), 110–55.

49. *Conchiologia* 1: 125ff.

50. Brocchi discusses various hypotheses in *Conchiologia* 1: 206ff.

51. J. A. De Luc, *Lettres physiques et morales, sur les montagnes et sur l'histoire de la
terre et de l'homme* (Physical and moral letters, on mountains and on the history of
the earth and of man) (La Haye: Detune, 1778).

52. See *Conchiologia* 1: iv.

53. Ibid., 209ff.

54. Ibid., 89.

55. Ibid. 1, Introduzione: 21–22.

56. Ibid., iii; he will make the same methodological choice in G. B. Brocchi, *Dello
stato fisico del suolo di Roma* (On the physical state of the Roman soil) (Rome: De
Romanis, 1820), 205.

57. For instance, by William Smith in England. On Smith see J. M. Eyles, "William
Smith: Some Aspects of His Life and Work," in *Toward a History of Geology*, ed.
Schneer, 142–58; J. M. Edmonds, "The Geological Lecture-Courses Given in York-
shire by William Smith and John Phillips, 1824–1825," *Proceedings of the Yorkshire
Geological Society* 4 (1975): 373–412; and R. Laudan, "W. Smith: Stratigraphy without
Palaeontology," *Centaurus* 20 (1976): 210–26.

58. For this theory of rocks see *Conchiologia* 1, chaps. 1, 2.

59. See *Conchiologia* 1: 89, where the declarations on the uniformity of the laws
of nature in different ages are found.

60. Ibid., 84. This idea remained a fixed point in Brocchi's geological reflections.
He took it up again in G. B. Brocchi, "Osservazioni naturali sulle spelonche di
Adelsberg in Carniola" (Natural observations on the Adelsberg caves in Carniola),
Biblioteca Italiana 25 (1822): 275–91, particularly 280. On this subject in the history
of geology, see Laudan, *From Mineralogy to Geology*, chaps. 3, 5.

61. *Conchiologia* 1: 13.

62. Ibid., Introduzione: 29.

63. Ibid., 19.

64. G. B. Brocchi, "Saggio di osservazioni microscopiche sugli animaletti infusorj dell'acqua marina" (Essay on microscopic observations of marine infusorians), *Giornale della Società d'incoraggiamento delle scienze e delle arti stabilita in Milano* 8 (1809): 177–201 and 271–85.

Other works belonging to the same tradition are *Trattato anatomico sugli occhi degli insetti* (Anatomical treatise on insect eyes), submitted to the Academy of the Department of Mella in 1802 (MS 29.A. I. 12, BCB), and the researches on the action exerted by various physical agents on plants, recorded in MS 35.A. I. 12, BCB, and possibly dating back to the end of the eighteenth century. On Brocchi's education see Giacomini, in *Dizionario Biografico degli Italiani*, 396–97, and especially Berti, *Un naturalista dall'ancien régime alla Restaurazione*, chaps. 1, 2.

65. *Conchiologia* 1, Introduzione: 16–17.

66. Brocchi, *Trattato mineralogico e chimico sulle miniere di ferro del dipartimento del Mella*.

67. Ibid. 2: 256–57.

68. Ibid. 2: 262. Here Brocchi argued that certain tiny nautiluses found by Bianchi were the last descendants, now close to extinction, of the large fossil ammonites; see J. Plancus [G. Bianchi], *De conchis minus notis*, 2d ed. (Rome: Minerva, 1760). Later Brocchi maintained that this example was untenable, but not to the extent that it cast doubt on his general hypothesis (*Conchiologia* 1: 230–31): even if microscopic fossil nautiluses should be found, and plausibly belonged to species distinct from the ancient ammonites, there were plenty of other, slightly larger nautiluses which could be considered the ammonites' descendants in the process of becoming extinct.

69. See Sacchi, "Necrologio di G. B. Brocchi," 132ff.

70. *Conchiologia* 1, Introduzione: 30.

71. Ibid. 1: 213, 217.

72. Ibid., 60ff.

73. Ibid., 213.

74. Ibid., 229.

75. Ibid., 227–29.

76. Ibid., xxix.

77. Ibid., 240.

78. Ibid., 235.

79. Ibid., 227.

80. See G. L. L. de Buffon, *Les époques de la nature* (1774), critical edition edited by J. Roger (Paris: Editions du Muséum, 1962), 27, 241 (17, 18, 213 in the critical edition).

81. See J. F. Blumenbach, *Manuel d' histoire naturelle* (Manual of natural history) (Metz: Collignon, 1803), 1: 40. This edition was Brocchi's source of Blumenbach's reflections on life span reported in *Zibaldone*, MS 34.C.16, BCB, s.v. "Uomo" (Man).

82. *Conchiologia* 1: 228.

83. R. Hooke, *Posthumous Works*, ed. R. Waller (London, 1705) 435–56. The passage, pointed out by J. C. Greene in *The Death of Adam* (Ames: Iowa State University Press, 1959), is from "Discourse on Earthquakes." On Hooke and earthquakes see R. Rappaport, "Hooke on Earthquakes: Lectures, Strategy and Audience," *British Journal for the History of Science* 19 (1986): 129–46. On earth history and human history in Hooke see P. Rossi, *The Dark Abyss of Time* (Chicago: University of Chicago Press, 1985), chap. 1.

84. *Conchiologia* 1: 227.

85. "Saggio sopra il flogisto," MS 29.C.8.17, BCB, in fine, and "Dissertazione sul Principio Vitale di Sthal [*sic*] e sul Moto Tonico," MS 33.B.22.6, BCB.

86. See, e.g., *Conchiologia* 1: xvii.

87. "Dissertazione sul Principio Vitale di Sthal," MS 33.B.22.6, BCB.

88. G. E. Stahl, *Positiones, de aestu marij microcosmici, seu fluxu et refluxu sanguinis* . . . (Halle: Henkeling, 1716), especially 48.

89. MS 29.C.8.17, BCB.

90. Ibid.

91. *Conchiologia* 1: 228.

92. D. Diderot, "Pensées sur l'interpretation de la nature" (1753), in *Oeuvres complètes* (Paris: Hermann, 1975–) 9: 94–95.

93. B.-G.-E. de la Ville, compte de Lacépède, *Histoire naturelle des poissons* (Natural history of fishes) (Paris, 1800), 2: xxiii–xliv. On Lacépède see Corsi, *Age of Lamarck*, 85–87.

94. G. Gautieri, *Slancio sulla genealogia della terra e sulla costruzione dinamica della organizzazione seguito da una ricerca sull'origine dei vermi abitanti le interiora degli animali* (Outpouring on the genealogy of the earth and on the dynamics of the organization followed by a study on the origin of worms living in the entrails of animals) (Jena, 1805). On this work see Camerano, "Materiali per la storia della zoologia in Italia nella prima metà del secolo XIX," part 2, no. 526: 1–10. On Gautieri see G. Genè, "Necrologio di G. Gautieri," *Biblioteca italiana* 19, LXX (1833): 287–97.

95. Epistolario Brocchi, III, BCB.

96. B. de Maillet, *Telliamed, ou entretiens d'un philosophe indien avec un missionaire français sur la diminution de la mer, la formation de la terre, l'origine de l'homme* (Telliamed, or conversations of an Indian philosopher with a French missionary on the withdrawal of the sea, the formation of the earth, the origin of man) (Amsterdam, 1748).

97. P. J. G. Cabanis, *Rapports du physique et du moral de l'homme* (Relations of the physical and moral in man) (Paris, 1802).

98. E. Darwin, *Zoonomia; or, The Laws of Organic Life* (London, 1794–96). On Erasmus Darwin see D. King-Hele, *Doctor of Revolution: The Life and Genius of Erasmus Darwin* (London: Faber, 1977).

99. E. Darwin, *Zoonomia, ovvero leggi della vita organica*, Italian translation by G. Rasori (Milan: Pirotta and Maspero, 1803–1805). *Zoonomia* promptly provoked reactions in Italy on the part of some philosophers alarmed by the materialistic implications of the work: see F. Soave, "Esame de' principi metafisici della Zoonomia d'Erasmo Darwin (1804)" (Examination of the metaphysical principles of Erasmus Darwin's *Zoonomia*, 1804), *Memorie dell'Istituto Nazionale Italiano* 1 (1809): particularly 48ff. On Rasori see *Scienza medica e giacobinismo in Italia: L'impresa politico-culturale di Giovanni Rasori (1796–1799)* (Medical science and Jacobinism in Italy: Giovanni Rasori's political-cultural enterprise, 1796–1799), ed. G. Cosmacini (Milan: Angeli, 1982).

100. On phrenology and its diffusion see O. Temkin, "Gall and the Phrenological Movement," *Bulletin of the History of Medicine* 21 (1947): 275–321; G. Lanteri-Laura, *Histoire de la phrénologie* (History of phrenology) (Paris: PUF, 1970); *F. J. Gall (1758–1828) Naturforscher und Anthropologe* (F. J. Gall [1758–1828]: The natural scientist and anthropology), ed. E. Lesky (Bern: Huber, 1979); and R. Cooter, *Meaning of Popular Science: Phrenology and the Organization of Consent in Nineteenth-century Britain* (Cambridge: Cambridge University Press, 1985).

101. P. Moscati, *Delle corporee differenze essenziali che passano fra la struttura de' bruti, e la umana: Discorso accademico* (Of the essential bodily differences between the structure of animals and human beings) (Milan: Galeazzi, 1770). On the reception of this work see A. O. Lovejoy, "Kant and Evolution," in *Forerunners of Darwin, 1745–1859*, ed. B. Glass, O. Temkin, and W. L. Strauss, Jr. (Baltimore: Johns Hopkins Press, 1959), 173–206, especially 177–78; and L. Belloni, "Echi del 'Discorso accademico' di P. Moscati sull'uomo quadrupede: La recensione di Kant" (Echoes of P. Moscati's "Academic Discourse" on quadruped man: Kant's review), *Physis* 3 (1961): 167–72. For Moscati's relations with Brocchi, see Epistolario Brocchi, IV, BCB.

102. Gautieri, *Slancio*, 64–65.

103. "All animals therefore draw apart one from the other, and divide . . . into genera, species and families as a result of innumerable past reproductions and mixtures. They therefore seem distinct from each other only because we cannot trace the various changes which little by little, in the course of infinite centuries, served to shape them differently" (ibid., 67).

104. L. Oken, *Lehrbuch der Naturphilosophie* (Textbook of natural philosophy) (Jena: Frommand, 1809–11). For the dissemination of Oken's ideas in Italy, see chap. 2 below.

105. Gautieri, *Slancio*, 28.

106. On Kielmeyer and the theory of recapitulation, see W. Coleman, "Limits of the Recapitulation Theory: Carl Friedrich Kielmeyer's Critique of the Presumed Parallelism of Earth History, Ontogeny, and the Present Order of Organisms," *Isis* 64 (1973): 341–50. On Naturphilosophie and recapitulation theory see S. J. Gould, *Ontogeny and Phylogeny* (Cambridge, Mass.: Belknap, 1977), particularly chap. 3. See also O. Temkin, "German Concepts of Ontogeny and History around 1800," *Bulletin of the History of Medicine* 24 (1950): 227–46.

107. *Conchiologia* 1: 240.

108. A. O. Lovejoy, *The Great Chain of Being* (Cambridge: Harvard College, 1936); Gould, *Ontogeny and Phylogeny*, 17–28.

109. C. Bonnet, *La palingénésis philosophique* (Geneva: Philibert et Chirol, 1769).

110. *Zibaldone*, MS 34.C.16, BCB, s.v. "Natura."

111. Blumenbach, *Manuel d'histoire naturelle*, 1: 10–12.

112. J. B. Lamarck, *Système des animaux sans vertèbres . . . précédé du discours d'ouverture du cours de zoologie, donné dans le Muséum national d'histoire naturelle, l'an VIII de la République* (System of invertebrate animals . . . preceded by the opening discourse of the zoology course given in the National Museum of Natural History, in the eighth year of the Republic) (Paris, 1801).

113. J. B. Lamarck, *Philosophie zoologique* (Paris, 1809).

114. See *Zibaldone*, MS 34.C.16, BCB, s.v. "Petrificati," where Brocchi quotes from J. B. Lamarck, "Considérations sur quelques faits applicables à la théorie du globe . . . " (Considerations on some facts applicable to the theory of the globe), *Annales du Muséum d'histoire naturelle* 13 (1805): 26–52.

115. Burkhardt, *The Spirit of System*, 112.

116. Ibid., chap. 6, especially 145–46.

117. Brocchi, "Osservazioni sulle spelonche di Adelsberg in Carniola," 275–91.

118. Ibid., 275.

119. Lamarck, *Philosophie zoologique*, part 1, chap. 7, 242.

120. P. Configliachi and M. Rusconi, *Del Proteo anguino di Laurenti: Monografia* (On Laurenti's proteus: A monograph) (Pavia: Fusi, 1819).

121. Ibid., 102.

122. Ibid., 99.

123. Ibid., 105.

124. Brocchi, "Osservazioni sulle spelonche di Adelsberg," 283.

125. Ibid., 283–84.

126. See Larber, *Elogio storico di G. B. Brocchi*, 66–79. *Giornale esteso in Egitto, nella Siria e nella Nubia da G. B. Brocchi* (Journal written in Egypt, Syria, and Nubia by G. B. Brocchi) (5 vols.) was published posthumously (Bassano: Roberti, 1841–43).

127. See Brocchi's correspondence with the two men in Epistolario Brocchi, IV, BCB. The French reception of *Conchiologia*, which goes beyond our concerns here, must have been very favorable. A letter dated 1819 from Cuvier, de Jussieu, and Bruguière to a malacologist living in Tuscany expressed their high esteem for Brocchi's work and asked him to send them specimens of shells described there that were missing from the collections of the Muséum d'histoire naturelle (Cuvier, de Jussieu, and Bruguière to Joseph Antoiz, Mar. 22, 1819, Autografoteca Campori,

Biblioteca Estense, Modena, Italy). The library of the Muséum National d'Histoire Naturelle has an early nineteenth-century manuscript (MS 871) containing a partial translation of *Conchiologia* into French, to which Martin J. S. Rudwick called my attention.

128. See Buckland to Brocchi, 1 June 1818, Epistolario Brocchi, II, BCB; and Parolini to Brocchi, 13 July 1817, Epistolario Brocchi, IV, BCB. On Buckland, see A. Rupke, *The Great Chain of History: William Buckland and the English School of Geology (1814–1849)* (Oxford: Clarendon Press, 1983).

129. See Granville to Brocchi, 16 Nov. 1816, Epistolario Brocchi, III, BCB.

130. [L. Horner], review of *Conchiologia fossile subappennina*, *Edinburgh Review* 26 (1816): 156–80. For the identification of the author, see Horner to Brocchi, 30 Dec. 1816, Epistolario Brocchi, III, BCB. In this letter Horner describes *Conchiologia* as "one of the most interesting [works] that has appeared since Geology began to be studied as a branch of true science." On Horner see *Dictionary of National Biography* (London: Oxford University Press, reprint 1949–50) 9: 1265–66. For Horner's activity in the Geological Society see P. J. Weindling, "Geological Controversy and Its Historiography: The Prehistory of the Geological Society of London," in *Images of the Earth: Essays in the History of the Environment Sciences*, ed. L. J. Jordanova and R. S. Porter (Chalfont St. Giles: British Society for the History of Science, 1979), 248–71. For Horner's activity within the British Association for the Advancement of Science, see J. Morrell and A. Thackray, *Gentlemen of Science* (Oxford: Clarendon Press, 1981), 56.

131. [Horner], review of *Conchiologia*, 157.

132. Ibid., 176, 180.

133. Ibid., 180. Brocchi's arguments for the recent origin of human beings are found in *Conchiologia* 1: 36–49, 213–15.

134. Ideas very like Brocchi's are also discussed in [R. E. Grant], "Observations on the Nature and Importance of Geology," *Edinburgh New Philosophical Journal* 1 (1826): 293–302, especially 298, which, however, does not name Brocchi; see P. Corsi, "The Importance of French Transformist Ideas for the Second Volume of Lyell's *Principles of Geology*," *British Journal for the History of Science* 11 (1978): 221–44, especially 238. In the interpretation of fossils, Grant preferred Lamarck's hypothesis ("Observations," 297).

135. C. Lyell, *Principles of Geology (1830–1833)*, 4th ed. (London: Murray, 1835). On the role of Brocchi's geological ideas in Lyell's work, see L. G. Wilson, *Charles Lyell, The Years to 1841*: The Revolution in Geology (New Haven: Yale Unversity Press, 1972), 218–19. For Lyell's utilization of the history of geology delineated by Brocchi in *Conchiologia*, see P. J. McCartney, "C. Lyell and G. B. Brocchi: A Study in Comparative Historiography," *British Journal for the History of Science* 60 (1979): 175–89. For the basic theoretical project of Lyell's *Principles*, see Lyell to Murchison, Jan. 15, 1829, in *Life, Letters and Journals of Sir Charles Lyell* (London: Murray, 1881) 1: 234, and M. J. S. Rudwick, "The Strategy of Lyell's *Principles of Geology*," *Isis* 61 (1970): 5–33.

136. *Life of Sir Charles Lyell* 1: 199–202, 206, 233, 240–45.

137. Lyell, chap. 8 in vol. 3 of *Principles of Geology*.

138. Ibid., 105.

139. Ibid., 106.

140. Ibid., 109.

141. See *Life of Sir Charles Lyell* 1: 245–46.

142. Lyell, *Principles of Geology*, 3: 140. Understandably, Lyell did not adequately recognize this affinity between his own perspective and Brocchi's when, after his conversion to evolutionism, he emphasized his earlier opposition to Brocchi's particular ideas on *the causes* of extinction; see C. Lyell, *The Geological Evidences of the Antiquity of Man*, 2d ed. (London: Murray, 1863; reprint, Westmead: Gregg, 1970), 393–94.

143. Lyell, *Principles of Geology*, 1: Summary.
144. D. Kohn, "Theories to Work By: Rejected Theories, Reproduction, and Darwin's Path to Natural Selection," *Studies in History of Biology* 4 (1980): 67–170.
145. C. Darwin, *Geological Notes (1835)*, ms. quoted in Kohn, "Theories to Work By," 70.
146. C. Darwin, *Journal of Researches into the Geology and Natural History of the Various Countries Visited by H. M. S. Beagle* (London: Colburn, 1839), 212.
147. See C. Darwin, "The Red Notebook," pp. 129–33, in *Charles Darwin's Notebooks, 1836–1844*, ed. P. H. Barrett, P. J. Gautrey, S. Herbert, D. Kohn, and S. Smith (London: British Museum, Natural History, and Cambridge University Press, 1987), 62–63.
148. Kohn, "Theories to Work By," 77–78; M. J. S. Hodge, "Darwin and the Laws of the Animate Part of the Terrestrial System (1835–1837): On the Lyellian Origins of His Zoonomical Explanatory Program," *Studies in History of Biology* 7 (1982): 1–106.
149. C. Darwin, "Notebook B," in Barrett et al., *Darwin's Notebooks 1836–44*, 187.
150. Kohn, "Theories to Work By," 79.
151. C. Limoges, *La sélection naturelle* (Paris: PUF, 1970), particularly chap. 2.
152. On environmentalism in natural sciences and medicine in the eighteenth and nineteenth centuries, see L. J. Jordanova's important essay "Earth Science and Environmental Medicine: The Synthesis of the Late Enlightenment," in Jordanova and Porter, *Images of the Earth*, 129–46.
153. See O. Heer, *Le monde primitif de la Suisse* (The primitive world of Switzerland), trans. I. Demole (Geneva: Georg, 1872), 757–58.
154. Nevertheless, Brocchi's book, and his ideas on species, continued to circulate in Italy during the nineteenth century. *Conchiologia* was reprinted in 1843 (Milan: Silvestri); the chapter on species was republished, along with the part of *Conchiologia* devoted to the history of geology, in G. B. Brocchi, *Riflessioni sul perdimento delle specie e Discorso sui problemi dello studio della conchiologia fossile italiana* (Reflections on the loss of species and discourse on problems of the study of Italian fossil conchology) (Rome: Perino, 1885). Also dealing with Brocchi's ideas on species were Stoppani, *Atti della festa commemorativa per il primo centenario della nascita di G. B. Brocchi . . .* , 15–48, and Camerano, "Materiali per la storia della zoologia in Italia nella prima metà del secolo XIX," no. 486: particularly 9–11.
155. D. Rosa, *Ologenesi: Nuova teoria dell'evoluzione e della distribuzione geografica dei viventi* (Hologenesis: New theory of evolution and of the geographical distribution of living beings) (Florence: Bemporad, 1918), 8–9.
156. Ibid., vii, x.
157. Ibid., 8, 21.
158. Ibid., 90, 159.
159. The analogies between Brocchi's theories and Rosa's did not escape contemporaries; see Camerano, "Materiali per la storia della zoologia in Italia nella prima metà del secolo XIX," no. 486: 9.

TWO. MAPPING THE LABYRINTH

1. The vast literature on the subject includes T. A. Appel, *The Cuvier-Geoffroy Debate: French Biology in the Decades before Darwin* (New York: Oxford University Press, 1987); F. Bourdier, "Geoffroy Saint-Hilaire versus Cuvier: The Campaign for Paleontological Evolution (1825–1838)," in *Towards a History of Geology*, ed. C. J. Schneer (Cambridge: MIT Press, 1969), 36–61; and W. Coleman, *Georges Cuvier, Zoologist: A Study in the History of Evolution Theory* (Cambridge: Harvard University Press, 1964), especially chap. 6.
2. I adopt here T. A. Appel's view that the theme of transformism had a limited but not negligible role in the Cuvier-Geoffroy controversy; see Appel, *The Cuvier-*

Geoffroy Debate, particularly 154, 173. On Geoffroy's *partial* adhesion to Lamarckian positions, see ibid., 132, 136.

3. Appel, *The Cuvier-Geoffroy Debate*, 233ff.

4. For an account of the life of Carlo Luciano Bonaparte (1903–1957), see the entry by F. Bartoccini and M. Cappelletti Alippi in *Dizionario Biografico degli Italiani* (Rome: Enciclopedia Italiana, 1960–), s.v. "C. L. Bonaparte." See also G. Petit, in *Dictionary of Scientific Biography* (New York: Scribner, 1970–78), s.v. "C. L. Bonaparte." The Italianized form of Charles Lucien Bonaparte's name is used here, as he himself used it during the two decades he spent in Italy.

5. C. L. Bonaparte, "Sulla seconda edizione del Regno Animale del Barone Cuvier" (On the second edition of Baron Cuvier's *Règne animal*), *Annali di storia naturale* 4 (1830) (actually published 1831, see n. 67 below): 3–26, 159–220, 303–89. A lengthy summary of the article also appeared in German in Lorenz Oken's journal: C. L. Bonaparte, "Bemerkungen über die 2te Ausgabe von Cuvier's Thierreich," *Isis*, no. 11 (1833): columns 1041–99.

6. This aspect of Linnaeus's work is examined by J. L. Larson, *Reason and Experience: The Representation of Natural Order in the Work of Carl von Linné* (Berkeley and London: University of California Press, 1971). See C. Linnaeus, *Philosophia botanica* (Vindobonae: Trattnern, 1770), § 156, on the image of the "Ariadne's thread" required to find a way through the "chaos" of living forms. The image became a topos for all authors who dealt with classification.

7. See C. Darwin, *On the Origin of Species*, reprinted from the original 1859 edition, with an introduction by Ernst Mayr (Cambridge: Harvard University Press, 1966), 411–34.

8. Ibid., chap. 2.

9. For France see, e.g., F. Dagognet, *Le catalogue de la vie* (The Catalogue of life) (Paris: PUF, 1970), chap. 2; and B. Balan, *L'ordre et le temps: L'anatomie comparée et l'histoire des vivants au XIXe siècle* (Order and time: Comparative anatomy and the history of living organisms in the nineteenth century) (Paris: Vrin, 1979), particularly 151–207. For England, see, for example, the vast literature on Darwin, his precursors, and the impact of his work on the British scientific community listed in D. Kohn, ed., *The Darwinian Heritage* (Princeton: Princeton University Press, 1985), 1021–99. A valuable general assessment focusing particularly on the relations between Darwin's theory and the scientific debate in progress in England can be found in D. Ospovat, *The Development of Darwin's Theory: Natural History and Natural Selection, 1838–1859* (Cambridge: Cambridge University Press, 1981).

10. Bonaparte, "Sulla seconda edizione," 3.

11. G. Cuvier, *Le Règne animal distribué d'après son organisation* (The animal kingdom arranged according to its organization), 2d ed. (Paris: Déterville, 1829). Apropos of this work and its place in Cuvier's scientific writings, see Coleman, *Georges Cuvier*, 12, 94–97.

12. Bonaparte, "Sulla seconda edizione," 10.

13. Ibid., 5.

14. Ibid.

15. Ibid., 6–7.

16. Ibid., 6: cf. Cuvier, *Règne animal*, 1: 69–70.

17. Bonaparte, "Sulla seconda edizione," 11–12. Similar phrases can be found on pp. 196, 217, 220, 360.

18. Cuvier's attitude toward the animal "series," or "chain of beings," is delineated in Coleman, *Georges Cuvier*, 147–51.

19. Bonaparte, "Sulla seconda edizione," 11–12.

20. Bonaparte deals with geographical distribution ibid., 19, 165n, 193, 197, 219, 305, 328, 330.

21. For a vivid description of Cuvier's working habits, as reported by his con-

temporary Charles Lyell, see Coleman, *Georges Cuvier*, 13–14, and Mrs. Lyell, *Life, Letters, and Journals of Sir Charles Lyell* (London: Murray, 1888), 1: 249–50.

22. See the accusations of inaccuracy in Bonaparte, "Sulla seconda edizione," 4, 168, 172, 195, 198, 206, 307, 327n, 346, 352.

23. Ibid., 4.

24. An account of Cuvier's prestige, and of the intertwining of scientific, academic, and political factors that sustained it, is given in D. Outram, *Georges Cuvier: Vocation, Science and Authority in Post-revolutionary France* (Manchester: Manchester University Press, 1984).

25. See n. 4 above for Bonaparte's biography. A detailed bibliography of Bonaparte's writings is given in *Notice sur les travaux zoologiques de C. L. Bonaparte* (On the zoological works of C. L. Bonaparte) (Paris: Bachelier, 1850). A competent and impassioned illustration of Bonaparte's contribution to ornithology is provided by E. Stresemann, *Ornithology from Aristotle to the Present*, in a translation from the original German (1951), with an introduction and an epilogue by E. Mayr (Cambridge: Harvard University Press, 1975), 153–69. Stresemann may go a little too far when he claims that Bonaparte was "already inspired by the theory of evolution" (p. 169), but his estimation of Bonaparte's merits confirms how much Bonaparte had to contribute to the development of taxonomy in the second quarter of the nineteenth century even without explicitly endorsing evolution, which he did not do in the 1830s and 1840s. (His later opinions on the species problem are described in the concluding section of this chapter.) Bonaparte's numerous publications dating from when he was in the United States include C. L. Bonaparte, "Observations on the Nomenclature of Wilson's Ornithology," *Journal of the Philadelphia Academy of Sciences* 3 (1823): 340–71; 4 (1824): 25–66, 163–89, 251–77; 5 (1825): 57–107, and "The Genera of North American Birds and a Synopsis of the Species Found within the Territory of the United States, Systematically Arranged in Orders and Families," *Annals of the Lyceum of Natural History of New York* 2 (1828 [but "read January 24, 1826"]): 7–28, 293–451; and, as a continuation of A. Wilson's work by the same title, *American Ornithology*, 4 vols. (Philadelphia: Carey and Lee, 1825–33). See also M. J. Brodhead, "The Work of Charles Lucien Bonaparte in America," *Proceedings of the American Philosophical Society* 122 (1978): 198–203. For a portrayal of the academy itself, see P. A. Gerstner, "The Academy of Natural Sciences of Philadelphia, 1812–1850," in *The Pursuit of Knowledge in the Early American Republic*, ed. A. Oleson and S. C. Brown (Baltimore: Johns Hopkins University Press, 1976), 174–93; and C. M. Porter, "The Concussion of Revolution: Publications and Reform of the Early Academy of Natural Sciences, Philadelphia," *Journal of the History of Biology* 12 (1979): 273–92.

26. On Luciano Bonaparte, see A. Pietromarchi, *Luciano Bonaparte principe romano* (Luciano Bonaparte, Roman prince) (Rome: Città Armoniosa, 1981).

27. C. L. Bonaparte, "Faunula et florula viterbenses" (Small fauna and small flora of Viterbo), Papiers Bonaparte, vol. 2549, Muséum d'histoire naturelle, Paris (hereafter PBMHN). The manuscript bears the words "Cet apperçu [*sic*] . . . valut à son auteur à l'âge de 17 ans sa première inscription dans un album académique: celui des Ardents de Viterbe."

28. C. L. Bonaparte, "Faunae romanae prodromus . . . " [Romae, 1822], PBMHN, vol. 2549.

29. C. L. Bonaparte, "Specchio comparativo delle ornitologie di Roma e di Filadelfia" (Comparative synopsis of the ornithologies of Rome and Philadelphia), *Nuovo giornale de' letterati* 14 (1827): 161–85; 15 (1827): 3–29, 95–120; C. L. Bonaparte, *A Geographical and Comparative List of the Birds of Europe and North America* (London: Voorst, 1838).

30. The role of geographical distribution in the formulation of Darwin's theory is described by C. Limoges, *La sélection naturelle* (Natural selection) (Paris: PUF,

1970); and R. A. Richardson, "Biogeography and the Genesis of Darwin's Ideas on Transmutation," *Journal of the History of Biology* 14 (1981): 1–41. Apropos of "biogeography," see G. Nelson, "From Candolle to Croizat: Comments on the History of Biogeography," *Journal of the History of Biology* 11 (1978): 269–305; and M. P. Kinch, "Geographical Distribution and the Origin of Life: The Development of Early Nineteenth-century British Explanations," *Journal of the History of Biology* 13 (1980): 91–119.

31. See n. 25 above.

32. The history of the idea in philosophy and science is traced by A. O. Lovejoy, *The Great Chain of Being* (Cambridge: Harvard College, 1936). The concept of an animal "series," "scale," or "chain" of beings in eighteenth-century biology is dealt with in J. Roger, *Les sciences de la vie au XVIIIe siècle: La génération des animaux de Descartes à l'Encyclopédie* (Life sciences in the eighteenth century: The generation of animals from Descartes to the *Encyclopédie*), 2d ed. (Poitiers: Collin, 1971); and G. Solinas, *Il microscopio e le metafisiche: Epigenesi e preesistenza de Cartesio a Kant* (The microscope and metaphysics: Epigenesis and preexistence from Descartes to Kant) (Milan: Feltrinelli, 1967).

33. See, respectively, J. F. Blumenbach, *Manuel d'histoire naturelle* (Manual of natural history) (Metz: Collignon, 1803), 1: 10–12, and Coleman, *Georges Cuvier*, 147–51.

34. On Lamarck and the organic series see R. W. Burkhardt, Jr., *The Spirit of System, Lamarck and Evolutionary Biology* (Cambridge: Harvard University Press, 1977), particularly 52, 125. On Isidore Geoffroy Saint-Hilaire see J.-L.-A. Quatrefages, "Éloge historique de M. Geoffroy Saint-Hilaire" (Historical tribute to M. Geoffroy Saint-Hilaire), *Bulletin de la Société Impériale d'acclimatation* 9 (1862): 257–78; and "Éloge historique par J. B. Dumas" (Historical tribute by J. B. Dumas), *Mémoires de l'Académie des sciences*, 2d ser., 38 (1873): 178–212. On Blainville see T. A. Appel, "Henri de Blainville and the Animal Series: A Nineteenth Century Chain of Being," *Journal of the History of Biology* 13 (1980): 291–319, and G. Laurent, "La paléontologie de de Blainville (1777–1850): Support ou rouine du fixisme?" (Blainville's paleontology: Defense or demolition of immutability?), *Histoire et nature* 12–13 (1978): 83–96. See also the articles collected in the monographic issue devoted to Blainville, *Revue d'histoire des sciences* 32 (1979).

35. Bonaparte, *Genera of North American Birds*, 8.

36. See n. 17 above.

37. Bonaparte, *Genera of North American Birds*, 23; according to Bonaparte, Juan Ignacio Molina's *Vultur jota* (black vulture) "forms the transition from the American to the European subgenus *Percnopterus*."

38. On Camillo Ranzani (1775–1841) see C. Politi, *Discorso intorno alla vita ed agli studi dell'abate Camillo Ranzani* (Discourse on the life and studies of Abbot Camillo Ranzani) (Bologna: Sassi e Amoretti, 1842); A. Bertoloni, "Elogio storico del monsignore Camillo Ranzani" (Historical tribute to Monsignor Camillo Ranzani), *Memorie della Accademia delle Scienze dell'Istituto di Bologna* 4 (1853): 225–59; and G. Montalenti, in *Enciclopedia italiana*, 1949 ed., s.v. "C. Ranzani."

39. Ranzani to Bonaparte, 20 Aug. 1828, Correspondence Bonaparte, no. 2790, Muséum d'histoire naturelle, Paris (hereafter CBMHN).

40. See above, chap. 1, n. 136.

41. Blainville to Ranzani, 26 (or 28?) Apr. 1823, Carteggio Ranzani, 2086, Biblioteca Universitaria, Bologna (hereafter CRBUB). Cf. C. Ranzani, *Elementi di zoologia* (Elements of zoology) (Bologna: Nobili, 1819–26).

42. Bonaparte to Swainson, 24 July 1830, Swainson Correspondence, Linnean Society, London.

43. Bonaparte to Ranzani, 30 July 1829, CRBUB, 2086.

44. Bonaparte to Ranzani, 3 Sept. 1829, CRBUB, 2086.

45. Ibid.
46. Bonaparte, "Sulla seconda edizione," 4.
47. See above, n. 24.
48. Bonaparte, "Sulla seconda edizione," 4.
49. Bonaparte to Ranzani, 3 Sept. 1829, CRBUB, 2086.
50. Say to Bonaparte, 5 July 1830, CBMHN, no. 3088.
51. Bonaparte to Ranzani, 16 Apr. 1828, CRBUB, 2086. For some aspects of Say's activity in this context, see C. M. Porter, " 'Subsilentio': Discouraged Works of Early Nineteenth-century American History," *Journal of the Society for the Bibliography of Natural History* 9 (1979): 109–19.
52. On Savi see *Alla memoria di Paolo Savi* (In memory of Paolo Savi) (Pisa: Nistri, 1871).
53. Paolo Savi, *Ornitologia toscana* (Tuscan ornithology) (Pisa: Nistri, 1827–31), especially viii–xii, xxi. See also Savi to Bonaparte, 17 Dec. 1828, CBMHN, no. 2958.
54. See Coleman, *Georges Cuvier*, 95.
55. This is the impression one gets from going through the *Annali di storia naturale*.
56. Ranzani, *Elementi di zoologia*. For the European echoes of this work, see, e.g., H. de Blainville, "De l'ancienneté des Primatès à la surface de la terre" (On the antiquity of primates on earth), in H. de Blainville, *Ostéographie (Mammifères, Primatès)* (Paris: Bertrand, 1841), 11.
57. Ranzani, *Elementi*, 1: 100ff.
58. Ibid., 104.
59. The notes in CRBUB, 2086, 1.D, testify to the scrupulous reading Ranzani had given Lamarck's most significant evolutionary writings.
60. Ranzani, *Elementi*, 1: 108.
61. The renewed popularity in the early nineteenth century of the idea of the "spontaneous" generation of organisms is described in J. Farley, *The Spontaneous Generation Controversy from Descartes to Oparin* (Baltimore: Johns Hopkins University Press, 1977), chaps. 3, 4.
62. Ranzani, *Elementi*, 1: 19–21.
63. See Ranzani's notes for his lectures on anthropological subjects in CRBUB, 2086, 1.E; and C. Ranzani, in *Dizionario universale della conversazione e della lettura*, ed. L. Carrer (Padua: Minerva, 1839), s.v. "Antropolito" (Fossil man), 31: 1699–1706.
64. Bonaparte to Ranzani, 3 Sept. 1829, CRBUB, 2086.
65. Ranzani to Bonaparte, 7 July 1828, CBMHN, no. 2792.
66. Bonaparte to Ranzani, 28 July 1828, CRBUB, 2086. For further evidence of Bonaparte's conception of the role of criticism in scientific work, see Bonaparte to Ranzani, 16 June 1830, ibid.
67. Various statements to that effect are found in the 1830–31 correspondence between Bonaparte and Ranzani (e.g., Bonaparte to Ranzani, 18 Apr. 1831). As for the delay in publishing "Sulla seconda edizione," the correspondence reveals that an early draft of the long review of Cuvier's book was in Ranzani's hands by fall 1829. After finally receiving permission to publish the paper, in September 1830 Bonaparte sent the first part of a later version for printing. The proofs were ready in November, but printing of the article was not completed until summer 1831. Causes of the delays included the political troubles of 1831, which affected Bologna as they did many other cities in Europe, and in which the printer of the *Annali*, Marsigli, was involved.
68. See Bonaparte to Ranzani, 29 Apr. and 14 May 1831, CRBUB, 2086.
69. See the introduction to *The Letters of Georges Cuvier*, ed. D. Outram (Chalfont St. Giles: British Society for the History of Science, 1980). For the correspondence between Ranzani and Cuvier, see CRBUB, 2086.
70. Pentland to Ranzani, 24 July 1824, CRBUB, 2086.

71. Savi to Bonaparte, 29 May and 5 July 1831, CBMHN, nos. 2970, 2972.
72. C. L. Bonaparte, *Saggio di una distribuzione metodica degli animali vertebrati* (Essay on a systematic distribution of vertebrates) (Rome: Boulzaler, 1831).
73. In his review, Bonaparte commented on the *Règne animal* page by page up to approximately the second volume, fishes excluded. However, his only remark on the introduction in which Cuvier had expounded his "philosophy of zoology" was as generous as it was general and was contradicted by the rest of the review. It read, "I shall not comment on the Introduction, which deserves nothing but admiration for its profundity of thought and lucidity of expression. It is impossible to say more, and to say as much in fewer words" (Bonaparte, "Sulla seconda edizione," 14).
74. Bonaparte, *Saggio di una distribuzione metodica*.
75. Bonaparte, "Sulla seconda edizione,'' 10.
76. Ibid., 76.
77. This is the implication of later declarations by Bonaparte, e.g., that Cuvier was "a greater anatomist than zoologist" (C. L. Bonaparte, "Coup d'oeil sur l'ordre des Pigeons" [A glance at the order of Pigeons], *Comptes rendus des séances de l'Académie des sciences* 39 [1854]: 870).
78. See above, n. 17 and the corresponding text.
79. Cuvier, *Règne animal*, 1: 174.
80. Bonaparte, "Sulla seconda edizione," 22; see also ibid., 162.
81. Ibid., 196.
82. V. Donati, *Della storia naturale marina dell'Adriatico* (On the marine natural history of the Adriatic Sea) (Venice: Storti, 1750), xxi: "in each of these orders or classes nature forms its series and has there its imperceptible passages from link to link in its chain. Besides, the links of one chain are so closely connected to those of another that natural progressions are more like a net than a chain, as the various threads are woven together, so to speak, having reciprocal communication, correlation, and union."
83. This was also a way of asserting his own competence in the field of American species: see Bonaparte, "Sulla seconda edizione," 193ff., 207.
84. Ibid., 165n, 330, 342–43.
85. Ibid., 6: "It may bother some to see Man, that miracle of creation, grouped with *Apes* in the same order, although we have no repugnance against placing Man and apes together in the same Class. To preserve the necessary niceties let Man be a separate class, a Kingdom apart, if you like, because *Reason* is the feature that perpetually distinguishes us from every other animal. But, given the overall features at stake, such separations are not in harmony with the rest of the system." See also Bonaparte, *Saggio di una distribuzione metodica*, 5–6, and C. L. Bonaparte, "General Synopsis of Mammalia Inhabiting North America," in J. D. Godman, *American Natural History*, 3d ed. (Philadelphia: Hogan and Thompson, 1836), 271–75.
86. Bonaparte, "Sulla seconda edizione," 19. Some significant aspects of this routine in the case of ornithology, the discipline most assiduously cultivated by Bonaparte, are dealt with in P. L. Farber, "The Development of Taxidermy and the History of Ornithology," *Isis* 68 (1977): 550–66, and P. L. Farber, "The Development of Ornithological Collections in the Late Eighteenth and Early Nineteenth Centuries and Their Relationship to the Emergence of Ornithology as a Scientific Discipline," *Journal of the Society for the Bibliography of Natural History* 9 (1980): 391–94.
87. On center and periphery in the international scientific community, and on the characterization of these two notions from the standpoint of the sociology of science, see R. von Gizycki, "Centre and Periphery in the International Scientific Community: Germany, France and Great Britain in the Nineteenth Century," *Minerva* 11 (1973).
88. This question in relation to the early nineteenth-century British scientific

community is discussed by S. F. Cannon, *Science in Culture* (New York: Science History Publication, 1978), chaps. 5, 6, where the vast literature on the subject is mentioned.

89. Savi to Bonaparte, 21 Dec. 1829, CBMHN, no. 2966.

90. See above, n. 53.

91. Ranzani to Bonaparte, 25 May 1829 and 5 Aug. 1829, CBMHN, nos. 2795, 2796.

92. Examples in Ranzani to Bonaparte, 20 Feb. 1827 and 5 Aug. 1829, CBMHN, nos. 2786, 2796.

93. See above, n. 4.

94. On Bonaparte's role in the establishment of the annual congresses of Italian scientists (and for literature on the subject), see G. Pancaldi, "Cosmopolitismo e formazione della comunità scientifica italiana, 1828–1839" (Cosmopolitanism and the formation of the Italian scientific community), *Intersezioni* 2 (1982): 331–43.

95. Exemplary studies on institutions of this kind established in Britain include J. Morrell and A. Thackray, *Gentleman of Science: Early Years of the British Association for the Advancement of Science* (Oxford: Clarendon Press, 1981); and R. MacLeod and P. Collins, eds., *The Parliament of Science: The British Association for the Advancement of Science, 1831–1981* (Northwood: Science Reviews, 1981). See also S. G. Kohlstedt, *The Formation of the American Scientific Community: The American Association for the Advancement of Science, 1848–1860* (Urbana: University of Illinois Press, 1976).

96. Proceedings were regularly published covering the meetings from 1839 to 1847, which we will deal with below. Since the city hosting the meeting was also in charge of publishing the Acts, separate bibliographic information is given for each volume. The essential literature on these congresses includes A. Hortis, *Le riunioni degli scienziati italiani prima delle guerre dell'independenza (1839–1847)* (Meetings of the Italian scientists before the wars of independence, 1839–1847) (Città di Castello: Leonardo da Vinci, 1922); A. Mancini, "Note e ricerche sul Congresso di Pisa del 1839" (Notes and researches on the Pisa Congress of 1839), *Annali della Scuola Normale Superiore di Pisa* 8 (1939): 205–25; F. Bartoccini and S. Verdini, *Sui congressi degli scienziati* (On the scientists' congresses) (Rome: Edizioni dell'Ateneo, 1952); G. C. Marino, *La formazione dello spirito borghese in Italia* (The formation of the bourgeois spirit in Italy) (Florence: La Nuova Italia, 1974); Pancaldi, "Cosmopolitismo e formazione della comunità scientifica italiana"; and G. Pancaldi, ed., *I congressi degli scienziati italiani nell'età del positivismo* (The meetings of the Italian scientists in the Age of Positivism) (Bologna: CLUEB, 1983).

97. *Atti della seconda riunione degli scienziati italiani tenuta in Torino (1840)* (Proceedings of the second meeting of Italian scientists held in Turin, 1840) (Turin: Cassone e Marzorati, 1941), 240–42. On Filippo De Filippi, see M. Lessona, *Naturalisti italiani* (Italian naturalists) (Rome: Sommaruga, 1884), 161–206.

98. *Atti della seconda riunione*, 240. For further testimonies on the circulation in Italy of Isidore Geoffroy's ideas on parallel series, see *Atti della terza riunione degli scienziati italiani tenuta in Firenze nel settembre del 1841* (Proceedings of the third meeting of Italian scientists held in Florence in September 1841) (Florence: Galileiana, 1841), 332–33.

99. Ibid., 240–41. See F. De Filippi, *Sunto di alcune osservazioni sull'embriogenia de' pesci* (Summary of some observations on the development of fishes) (Milan: Bernardoni, 1845). On Mauro Rusconi see G. Montalenti, in *Enciclopedia italiana*, 1949 ed., s.v. "M. Rusconi."

100. See above, chap. 1.

101. On recapitulation theory and its relevance to the history of evolutionary thought, see S. J. Gould, *Ontogeny and Phylogeny* (Cambridge, Mass.: Belknap, 1977).

102. Von Baer's embryological work and its implications for biology are discussed in D. Ospovat, "The Influence of Karl Ernst von Baer's Embryology, 1828–1859: A

Reappraisal in Light of Richard Owen's and William B. Carpenter's *Palaeontological Application of 'Von Baer's Law,'* " *Journal of the History of Biology* 9 (1976): 1–28.

103. J. F. Meckel, *Manuale d'anatomia generale e patologica* (Manual of general and pathological anatomy), Italian translation of *Handbuch der pathologischen Anatomie* (Milan: Giusti, 1825–26; Naples: Manzi, 1826–27).

104. Meckel, *Manuale d'anatomia*, 48–49.

105. On Filippo Parlatore see G. Negri, "F. Parlatore," *Nuovo giornale botanico italiano* 34 (1927): 972–99; and G. Landucci, *L'occhio e la mente: Scienza e filosofia nell'Italia del secondo Ottocento* (The eye and the mind: Science and philosophy in Italy in the second half of the nineteenth century) (Florence: Olschki, 1987), 75–135.

106. F. Parlatore, *Lezioni di botanica comparata* (Course of comparative botany) (Florence: Società tipografica, 1843).

107. See ibid., 10.

108. Ibid., 6–9. The ferment in evolutionary ideas in German biology at that time is described by O. Temkin, "The Idea of Descent in Post-Romantic German Biology: 1848–1858," in *Forerunners of Darwin, 1745–1859*, ed. B. Glass, O. Temkin, and W. L. Strauss (Baltimore: Johns Hopkins University Press, 1959), 323–55.

109. Parlatore, *Lezioni*, 35, 11.

110. Ibid., 40–41.

111. Ibid., 38.

112. Ibid., 43–44.

113. On Spinola, see R. Gestro, "Ricordo di M. Spinola" (Recollection of M. Spinola), *Annali del Museo civico di storia naturale* (Genoa) 47 (1915): 33.

114. *Atti della terza riunione degli scienziati italiani*, 393.

115. Ibid.

116. Ibid., 389–90: Bonaparte reported that Oken "did not share the distinguished zoologist [Hermann] Schlegel's inclination to group together as many living forms as possible. On the contrary, he complained that there were reverberations of that fatal inclination even in Italy."

117. For Lorenz Oken's principles of classification and their circulation in Italy, see L. Oken, "Idee sulla classificazione filosofica dei tre regni della natura" (Ideas on the philosophical classification of the three kingdoms of nature), *Il Politecnico* 2 (1840): 97–123, as well as Oken's correspondence with Bonaparte and Carlo Porro (see below, n. 129). On the figure of Oken in general, see P. C. Mullen, "The Romantic as Scientist: Lorenz Oken," *Studies in Romanticism* 14 (1977): 381–99.

118. *Atti della settima adunanza degli scienziati italiani tenuta in Napoli dal 20 settembre al 5 di ottobre del MDCCCXLV* (Proceedings of the seventh meeting of Italian scientists held in Naples from September 20 to October 5, 1845) (Naples: Fibreno, 1846), 690–91.

119. On Owen's special position with respect to evolutionary thought, see R. MacLeod, "Evolutionism and Richard Owen, 1830–1868: An Episode in Darwin's Century," *Isis* 56 (1965): 259–80. MacLeod describes Owen as "something of a bridge between the morphology of the first half-century and the evolutionism of the last," 280. On this same aspect of Owen's work, see also J. H. Brooke, "Richard Owen, William Whewell and the 'Vestiges,' " *British Journal for the History of Science* 10 (1977): 132–45, and especially E. Richards, "A Question of Property Rights: Richard Owen's Evolutionism Reassessed," *Journal for the History of Science* 20 (1987): 129–71.

120. *Atti della ottava riunione degli scienziati italiani tenuta in Genova da XIV al XXIX settembre MDCCCXLVI* (Proceedings of the eighth meeting of Italian scientists held in Genoa from 14 to 29 September 1846) (Genoa: Ferrando, 1847), 447. See R. Owen, *On the Archetype and Homologies of the Vertebrate Skeleton* (London: n.p., 1848). Perhaps recalling how interested Italian scientists had been in his ideas during the 1840s,

in 1873—that is, well into the Darwinian era—Owen chose to circulate in Italy a letter, addressed to Giuseppe Bianconi, in which he asserted his own role "in establishing the hypothesis of the origin of species" (Owen to Bianconi, 11 Dec. 1873, *Atti della Società Italiana di Scienze Naturali* 18 [1874]: 30–33).

121. On Costa, see F. del Giudice, "Cenni biografici del socio O. G. Costa" (Biographical notes on member O. G. Costa), *Atti del R. Istituto d'Incoraggiamento di Napoli*, 2d ser., 5 (1868): 21–36 (with a list of 126 publications by Costa).

122. O. G. Costa, *Prolusione al corso di zoologia per l'anno scolastico 1842–1843* (Introductory lecture to the zoology course for the academic year 1842–43) (Naples: Filiatre-Sebuzio, 1842), 16.

123. Ibid., 15.

124. Ibid., 16–17.

125. *Atti della terza riunione*, 383. On Porro and his correspondence on file at the Museo Civico di Storia Naturale, Milan, see M. Schiavone, "Passim di lettere inedite di A. e C. Porro" (Selections from A. and C. Porro's unpublished letters), *Il Risorgimento* 30 (1978): 81–93.

126. *Atti della quarta riunione degli scienziati italiani tenuta in Padova nel settembre del MDCCCXLII* (Proceedings of the fourth meeting of Italian scientists held in Padua in September 1847) (Padua: Tipi del Seminario, 1843), 190–93. See also C. Porro, *Malacologia terrestre e fluviale della provincia comasca* (Terrestrial and fluvial malacology in the province of Como) (Milan: Guglielmini e Redaelli, 1838), vii. G. Olivi had already dealt with the "modifications incurred by Beings according to the circumstances," with reference to certain shells, in *Zoologia adriatica* (Adriatic zoology) (Bassano: n.p., 1792), 18–21.

127. *Atti della quarta riunione*, 190.

128. See C. Porro, "Studii su talune variazioni offerte da molluschi fluviali e terrestri a conchiglia univalve" (Studies on some variations in univalve-shelled fluvial and terrestrial mollusks), *Memorie della Reale Accademia delle Scienze di Torino*, 2d ser., tome 1 (1839): 219–56. Cf. I. Geoffroy Saint-Hilaire, *Histoire générale et particulière des anomalies de l'organisation chez l'homme et les animaux ou traité de tératologie* (General and detailed history of anomalies of organization in man and animals, or treatise on teratology) (Paris: Baillière, 1832–36).

129. For this latter project of Porro's, see his correspondence with Lorenz Oken, in Corrispondenza Porro, Museo Civico di Storia Naturale, Milan, especially Oken to Porro, 6 May 1843, and the part of that bibliography that was actually published: C. Porro, *Note per una bibliografia malacologica* (Notes for a malacological bibliography) (Milan: Guglielmini e Redaelli, 1841).

130. *Atti della terza riunione*, 383.

131. For Linnaeus, see C. Linneaus, *Philosophia botanica* (Vindobonae: Trattnern, 1770), §§ 159–62. For Buffon, see Buffon, *Histoire naturelle* (Natural history) (Paris: Imprimerie Royale, 1749), 1: 13.

132. Porro, "Studii su talune variazioni," 38.

133. *Atti della quarta riunone*, 193.

134. See *Atti della terza riunione*, 394: Massimiliano Spinola declared that he believed instead "that the natural system may exist," but he held that "it cannot be composed except by the analytical method."

135. F. Parlatore, *Come possa considerarsi la botanica nello stato attuale delle scienze naturali* (How botany can be considered in the present state of natural sciences) (Florence: Piatti, 1842), 9.

136. Ibid., 7.

137. Ibid., 10. Parlatore's historical reconstruction evidently overlooked Cuvier's repeated attacks on the "chain of beings," which is indicative of the renewed popularity of that idea, Cuvier's condemnation notwithstanding.

138. Parlatore, *Lezioni*, chap. 3.

139. Ibid., 59.
140. Ranzani, *Elementi*, 1: 19.
141. Ibid., 7–8, 108.
142. See above, chap. 1.
143. J. B. Lamarck, *Ricerche intorno alle cause de' principali avvenimenti fisici* . . . (Venice: Bertazzoni, 1795–96). The publisher presented the Italian translation as a contribution to the debate on the new "pneumatic theory," that is, on Lavoisier's chemistry, and specified that by publishing the book, he—unlike Lamarck—did not mean to defend the earlier chemical theories.
144. F. Baldassini, ed., *Storia naturale degli animali invertebrati del sig. Cavaliere De Lamarck compendiata ed arricchita di note* (Natural history of invertebrates by Lamarck, summarized with the addition of notes) (Pesaro: Nobili, 1834). It is worth recalling here that Cuvier's reflections on "les révolutions du globe" had circulated in Italy a few years before, through a translation by Ignazio Paradisi (G. Cuvier, *Discorso su le rivoluzioni del globo* [Discourse on the revolutions of the earth] [Florence: Conti, 1828]). Paradisi provided an interpretation of Cuvier's work intended to emphasize Cuvier's agreement with the Mosaic tradition. See also I. Paradisi, *Riflessioni su le rivoluzioni del globo* (Reflections on the revolutions of the earth) (Rome: Salviucci, 1830).
145. Baldassini, *Storia naturale*, 21, 30.
146. *Dizionario classico di storia naturale* (Classical dictionary of natural history) (Venice: Tasso, 1831–43). The influence of the French edition of this dictionary on the diffusion of transformist concepts is described by P. Corsi, "The Importance of French Transformist Ideas for the Second Volume of Lyell's *Principles of Geology*," *British Journal for the History of Science* 11 (1978): 221–44, especially 228–29. On Bory and Lamarck see P. Corsi, *The Age of Lamarck: Evolutionary Theories in France, 1790–1830* (Berkeley and Los Angeles: University of California Press, 1988), 218–29.
147. Ranzani to Bonaparte, 27 Dec. 1830, CBMHN, no. 2807. On Ranzani's careful reading of Lamarck, see n. 59 above.
148. On Bonelli, see B. Baccetti and P. Omodeo, in *Dizionario Biografico degli Italiani* (Rome: Istituto della Enciclopedia Italiana, 1960–), s.v. "F. A. Bonelli."
149. See L. Camerano, "Contributo alla storia delle teorie Lamarckiane in Italia: Il corso di zoologia di Franco Andrea Bonelli" (Contribution to the history of Lamarckian theories in Italy: Franco Andrea Bonelli's zoology course), *Atti della R. Accademia delle Scienze di Torino* 37 (1902): 455–64; "Materiali per la storia della zoologia in Italia nella prima metà del secolo XIX: I manoscritti di F. A. Bonelli" (Materials for the history of zoology in Italy in the first half of the nineteenth century: F. A. Bonelli's manuscripts), *Bollettino dei Musei di Zoologia ed Anatomia comparata della R. Università di Torino* 21 (1906), nos. 535, 536; 23 (1908), nos. 579, 586, 591; 24 (1909), nos. 601, 606. On Bonelli and Lamarck see P. Corsi, " 'Lamarckiens' et 'Darwiniens' á Turin" ("Lamarckians" and "Darwinians" in Turin), in *De Darwin au Darwinisme: Science et idéologie*, ed. Y. Conry (Paris: Vrin, 1983), 49–67, 51–56.
150. See Camerano, "Contributo," 4. Another naturalist who was a student of Lamarck's for a time, and to some extent his follower, was Giosuè Sangiovanni, the director of the Naples Zoological Museum in the 1830s. On Sangiovanni, see P. Omodeo, "Documenti per la storia delle scienze naturali al principio del XIX secolo" (Documents for the history of natural sciences at the beginning of the nineteenth century), *Bollettino di zoologia* 16 (1949): 107–17, 131–37.
151. On Matteucci, see F. Selmi, *C. Matteucci* (Turin: UTET, 1862); N. Bianchi, *C. Matteucci e l'Italia del suo tempo* (C. Matteucci and the Italy of his time) (Turin: Bocca, 1874); and C. Pighetti, "Carlo Matteucci e il Risorgimento scientifico" (Carlo Matteucci and the scientific Risorgimento), *Quaderni di storia della scienza e della medicina*, Università di Ferrara, 1976.

152. C. Matteucci, *Discorso sopra gli elementi del progresso della scienza dell'organismo* (Florence: Galileiana, 1835).

153. Ibid., 15.

154. C. Matteucci, *Discorso sopra gli elementi* . . . (Forlì: Casali, 1839), 2.

155. See above, n. 128.

156. I. Geoffroy Saint-Hilaire, *Histoire générale*, 3: 610 and n.

157. Although there are no recent systematic studies on the Italian scientific community, this is the impression to be had from the testimony of contemporaries such as A. de Candolle, *Histoire des sciences et des savants depuis deux siècles* (History of the sciences and scientists in the last two centuries) (Geneva: Georg, 1873), especially 176–77. See also Pancaldi, "Cosmopolitismo."

158. F. De Filippi, *Regno animale* (Milan: Vallardi, 1852).

159. Ibid., 50.

160. L. Camerano, "Materiali per la storia della Zoologia in Italia nella prima metà del secolo XIX" (Materials for the history of zoology in Italy in the first half of the nineteenth century), *Bollettino dei Musei di Zoologia ed Anatomia comparata della R. Università di Torino* 20, no. 486 (1905): especially 33–36.

161. De Filippi, *Regno Animale*, 245.

162. Agreement between the new biological theories and religious tradition was a constant concern of De Filippi's, as is shown by many of his writings both before and after the publication of Darwin's *Origin of Species*.

163. De Filippi, *Regno animale*, 247.

164. Ibid., 260.

165. See F. De Filippi, "L'uomo e le scimie [*sic*]: Lezione pubblica detta in Torino la sera dell'11 gennaio 1864" (Man and monkeys: Public lecture delivered in Turin the evening of 11 January 1864) (Milan: Daelli, 1864), especially 42–43.

166. F. C. Marmocchi, "Della creazione degli animali, o zoogenia" (On the creation of animals, or zoogeny), 3d part, section 1, § 4 of *Prodromo della storia naturale generale e comparata d'Italia* (Florence: Soc. Editrice, 1844–53), 765–66. On this work see D. Rosa, "La 'Zoogenia' di F. C. Marmocchi (1853)" (F. C. Marmocchi's *Zoogeny* [1853]), *Bollettino dei Musei di Zoologia ed Anatomia comparata della R. Università di Torino* 6, no. 95 (1891).

167. Marmocchi, *Prodromo*, 766–67.

168. Ibid., 769.

169. Ibid., 772–73.

170. Ibid., 771–76.

171. F. Baldassini, *Intorno all'analisi ragionata dei lavori di G. Cuvier preceduta dal suo elogio fatta da P. Flourens* (On the reasoned analysis of G. Cuvier's works, prefaced by a tribute by P. Flourens) (Pesaro: Nobili, 1856). Cf. P. Flourens, *Analyse raisonnée des travaux de Georges Cuvier* (Paris: Paulin, 1841).

172. Baldassini, *Intorno all'analisi*, 62–63. In the 1850s Baldassini was not the only one interested in exonerating Lamarck of the charge of pantheism. G. B. Pianciani made a similar attempt, in the Jesuit organ *Civiltà cattolica*; see [G. B. Pianciani], "Cosmologia: Della origine delle specie organizzate" (Cosmology: On the origins of organized species), *Civiltà cattolica*, year 9, vol. 7, 4th ser. (July 1860): particularly 165–69.

173. See D. Paoli, *Del moto intestino delle parti de' solidi* (On the internal movements of the parts contained in solid bodies) (Pesaro: Gavelli, n.d.).

174. For the importance of this tradition in British culture and its relationship to Darwin's theory, see Limoges, *La sélection naturelle*, and Ospovat, *Development of Darwin's Theory*.

175. Some of Gaspare Brugnatelli's thoughts in his *Trattato delle cose naturali* (1837) might be considered an exception if they were not so typical of the eighteenth-

century tradition of reflections of this sort (see Camerano, "Materiali," no. 486: 27–30).

176. Olivi, in *Zoologia adriatica*, had prefaced his work with some "Reflections on zoological geography." At the Italian scientists' congresses, Pietro Calcara of Palermo had dealt with the geographical distribution of mollusks and connected his studies with the problem of the "epochs of nature" (see *Atti della settima adunanza degli scienziati italiani*, 769).

177. M. J. S. Rudwick, *The Meaning of Fossils: Episodes in the History of Paleontology*, 2d ed. (New York: Science History Publications, 1976), 207ff.; Appel, "Henri de Blainville and the Animal Series," 319. Equally important for the viewpoint described here are some of Dov Ospovat's observations on the inadequacy of the evolutionism/creationism dichotomy in representing the situation of natural history studies in the 1850s; see D. Ospovat, "Perfect Adaptation and Teleological Explanation: Approaches to the Problem of the History of Life in the Mid-nineteenth Century," *Studies in History of Biology* 2 (1978): 33–56, particularly 49–50.

178. Bonaparte, "Coup d'oeil sur l'ordre des pigeons," 870–71.

179. C. L. Bonaparte, "Considérations sur l'espèce" (Considerations on species), *Revue et magazine de zoologie* (1856): 292–95, especially 292 (emphasis added). The article, which summarized a talk held at the congress of German ornithologists at Köthen, also appeared in German: C. L. Bonaparte, "Betrachtungen über die Species," *Journal für Ornithologie* 4 (1856): 257–59. For Isidore Geoffroy's views on the same subject, see I. Geoffroy Saint-Hilaire, "Resumé des vues sur l'espèce organique émises par les principaux naturalistes français du XVIIIe siècle et du commencement du XIXe" (Synopsis of views on organic species by the leading French naturalists of the eighteenth century and the beginning of the nineteenth), offprint of the *Histoire naturelle générale des règnes organiques*, tome 2, part 2, at the Bibliothèque centrale du Muséum d'histoire naturelle of Paris, 33–40.

Bonaparte died in 1857, and the historian of science will therefore never know how he would have reacted to Darwin's *Origin*. As for Darwin, only the descriptive aspect of Bonaparte's work drew his attention. He did, however, note Bonaparte's classic references to principles such as that of the "balancing of organs," formulated by Étienne Geoffroy Saint-Hilaire (see Darwin's marginal notes in his copy of Bonaparte, "Coup d'oeil," in the Darwin Library, Cambridge University Library).

THREE. INTRODUCING NATURAL SELECTION

1. C. Darwin, "Autobiography," in C. Darwin and T. H. Huxley, *Autobiographies*, ed. G. De Beer (London: Oxford University Press, 1974), 84. Stressing the fact that his ideas enjoyed greater success in Germany than in France, Darwin had occasion to note: "It is curious how nationality influences opinion" (*Life and Letters of Charles Darwin*, ed. F. Darwin [London: Murray, 1888; Johnson Reprint, 1969], 3: 118).

2. Exceptions pertaining to the history of biology include F. A. Stafleu, *Linnaeus and the Linnaeans: The Spreading of Their Ideas in Systematic Botany, 1735–1789* (Utrecht: Oostheork, 1971); *The Comparative Reception of Darwinism*, ed. T. F. Glick (Austin: University of Texas Press, 1974), a collection of pioneering essays in the area, recently reprinted with a new preface (Chicago and London: University of Chicago Press, 1988); R. C. Maulitz, *Morbid Appearances: The Anatomy of Pathology in the Early Nineteenth Century* (Cambridge and New York: Cambridge University Press, 1987); J. Harwood, "National Styles in Science: Genetics in Germany and the United States between the World Wars," *Isis* 78 (1987): 390–414; and "The Migration of Science and Medicine," a group of papers included in British Society for the History of

Science and the History of Science Society, *Program, Papers and Abstracts for the Joint Conference*, Manchester, England, 11–15 July 1988, 188–220. Reflections on how science circulates in different national contexts can be found in R. G. A. Dolby, "The Transmission of Science," *History of Science* 15 (1977): 1–43; M. Crosland and C. W. Smith, "The Transmission of Physics from France to Britain, 1800–1840," *Historical Studies in the Physical Sciences* 9 (1978): 1–61; and M. Crosland, "History of Science in a National Context," *British Journal for the History of Science* 10 (1977): 95–113.

3. See some classic reflections on the subject in R. K. Merton, "The Normative Structure of Science" [1942], in R. K. Merton, *The Sociology of Science*, ed. N. W. Storer (Chicago: University of Chicago Press, 1973), 267–78.

4. Although Glick's collection (see n. 2) did not include a chapter devoted specifically to Italy, Italy is dealt with there by H. W. Paul, "Religion and Darwinism: Varieties of Catholic Reaction," in Glick, *Comparative Reception of Darwinism*, 403–36. Since then a number of studies on the diffusion of Darwinism in Italy have appeared: G. Benasso, "Materiali per una storia dell'evoluzionismo italiano: Da Bonelli a De Filippi: 1811–1864" (Materials for a history of Italian evolutionism: From Bonelli to De Filippi, 1811–1864), *Atti della Accademia Roveretana degli Agiati: Contributi della classe di scienze matematiche, fisiche e naturali* 14–15, B (1976): 3–106; "Materiali . . . : Un approccio al Darwinismo, 1864–1900" (Materials . . . : An approach to Darwinism), ibid. 16–17, B (1978): 73–151; G. Landucci, *Darwinismo a Firenze: Tra scienza e ideologia (1860–1900)* (Darwinism in Florence: Between science and ideology [1860–1900]) (Florence: Olschki, 1977); G. Pancaldi, *Charles Darwin: "Storia" ed "Economia" della natura* (Charles Darwin: "History" and "economy" of nature) (Florence: La Nuova Italia, 1977), 161–206; P. Rossi, introduction to A. Fogazzaro, *Ascensioni umane* (Human ascensions) (Milan: Longanesi, 1977); A. Cavalli, "Scienza e romanzo nel secondo Ottocento italiano" (Science and fiction in the second half of the nineteenth century in Italy), *Otto-Novecento* 2, no. 5 (1978): 37–65; E. Garin, "Il positivismo italiano alla fine del secolo XIX fra metodo e concezione del mondo" (Italian positivism at the end of the nineteenth century between method and world-view), *Giornale critico della filosofia italiana* 59 (1980): 1–27; V. Roda, "Evoluzionismo e letteratura 'fin de siècle' " (Evolutionism and *fin de siècle* literature), *Atti dell'Accademia delle Scienze dell'Istituto di Bologna, Memorie*, 79 (1980–81); G. Landucci, "Il darwinismo in Italia" (Darwinism in Italy), in *La cultura italiana tra Otto e Novecento e le origini del nazionalismo* (Florence: Olschki, 1981), 103–87; *Charles Darwin–Anton Dohrn Correspondence*, ed. C. Groeben, with an introduction by G. Montalenti (Naples: Macchiaroli, 1982); G. Montalenti, "Il darwinismo in Italia" (Darwinism in Italy), *Belfagor* 38 (1983): 65–78; F. M Scudo, "Darwin e vari darwinismi: Nota storico-bibliografica con particolar riguardo all'Italia" (Darwin and various Darwinisms: Historical-biographical note with special reference to Italy), *Rivista della libreria* 96 (1983): 188–202; P. Corsi and P. Weindling, "Darwinism in France, Germany, and Italy," in *The Darwinian Heritage*, ed. D. Kohn (Princeton: Princeton University Press, 1985), 683–729.

5. See A. de Candolle, *Histoire des sciences et des savants depuis deux siècles* (History of sciences and scientists in the past two centuries) (Geneva: Georg, 1873), 176–77.

6. See G. Pancaldi, "Scientific Internationalism and the British Association," in *The Parliament of Science: The British Association for the Advancement of Science, 1831–1981*, ed. R. MacLeod and P. Collins (Northwood: Science Reviews, 1981), 145–69; and G. Pancaldi, "Cosmopolitismo e formazione della comunità scientifica italiana (1828–1839)" (Cosmopolitanism and the making of the Italian scientific community), *Intersezioni* 2 (1982): 331–43.

7. The Linnean Society was founded in 1788; see *Rules and Orders of the Linnean Society* (London: Linnean Society, 1788). The Geological Society was founded in

1807; see H. B. Woodward, *The History of the Geological Society of London* (London: Geological Society, 1907). The Zoological Society was recognized as an autonomous institution in 1829; see *A Record of the Progress of the Zoological Society of London during the Nineteenth Century* (London: Zoological Society, 1901). All three societies had their headquarters in London.

An analogous movement fostering the foundation of specialist societies developed in Italy in the 1850s and 1860s. The Società Geologica, with headquarters in Milan, was active from 1855 (see its proceedings, vol. 1 [1855–59]); it took the name of Società Italiana di Scienze Naturali in January 1860. In 1861 Giovanni Canestrini described the situation of Italian scientific societies as follows: "It seems to me that for the progress of science it would be better if instead of various societies, each pursuing *all the natural sciences*, there existed individual societies, each devoted to its own special field. This should be done especially now in Italy, where there are no longer a number of separate states, each of which previously had to have its own academy. If in addition to these specialist societies a central society were also necessary, to collect and apply the results of all the special societies, it seems to me still a difficult problem to solve" (Canestrini to Emilio Cornalia, 11 May 1861, Archivio del Museo civico di storia naturale di Milano, hereafter MCSN). In 1866 Canestrini would promote the foundation of the Società dei Naturalisti di Modena (see *Annuario* 1 [1866]) and in 1872 the foundation of the Società Veneto-Trentina di Scienze Naturali; see *Statuto della Società . . .* (Padua: Sacchetto, 1872).

8. A telling example is provided by [R. Chambers], *Vestiges of the Natural History of Creation* (London: Churchill, 1844), with ten editions in nine years; see M. Millhauser, *Just before Darwin: Robert Chambers and "Vestiges"* (Middletown: Wesleyan University Press, 1959).

9. See below, chap. 6.

10. For the biography and scientific work of Giovanni Canestrini (1835–1900), see "Giovanni Canestrini," in *Memorie dell'I. R. Accademia di scienze lettere ed arti degli Agiati in Rovereto, pubblicate per commemorare il suo centocinquantesimo anno di vita* (Rovereto: Grigoletti, 1901), 847 (a brief autobiographical note); P. Buffa, "G. Canestrini," *Atti della Società Veneto-Trentina di Scienze Naturali* 4 (1907): 1–7; V. Largajolli, "G. Canestrini," *Bullettino della Società degli Studenti Trentini* 2, no. 4 (1900); P. Lioy, "Commemorazione di G. Canestrini," *Atti del Reale Istituto Veneto di Scienze, Lettere ed Arti* 62 (1902–1903): 45–67; *Nel centenario della nascita di G. Canestrini (26-12-1835–26-12-1935)* (On the hundredth anniversary of the birth of G. Canestrini, 26 December 1835–26 December 1935) (Trent: Saturnia, 1935); P. Pasquini, "G. Canestrini 1835–1900," *Studi Trentini di Scienze Naturali* 17 (1936) (offprint); U. D'Ancona, *L'opera di Giovanni Canestrini nella zoologia del suo tempo* (The works of Giovanni Canestrini in the zoology of his time) (*Quaderni Pro Cultura* [Trent], no. 2, 1950); B. Baccetti and U. Corsini, in *Dizionario Biografico degli Italiani* (Rome: Istituto della Enciclopedia Italiana, 1960–), s.v. "G. Canestrini"; S. Casellato, "Il darwinismo a Padova: G. Canestrini" (Darwinism in Padua: G. Canestrini), *Atti dell'Accademia Roveretana degli Agiati*, 6th ser., 21–22 (1981–82): 51–68.

11. The appellation was Paolo Mantegazza's and is reported in G. Canestrini, *Per l'evoluzione: Recensioni e nuovi studi* (For evolution: Reviews and new studies) (Turin: UTET, 1894), 179.

12. See T. Kuhn, *The Structure of Scientific Revolutions*, 2d ed. (Chicago: University of Chicago Press, 1969), especially chaps. 2–4.

13. This information on the international reception of the *Origin*, like the particulars that follow immediately, is taken from R. B. Freeman's valuable *Works of Charles Darwin: An Annotated Bibliographical Handlist*, 2d ed. (Folkestone: Dawson, Archon Books, 1977).

14. Ibid., 83. Besides the classic texts edited by T. F. Glick (see n. 2 above), studies

of the diffusion of Darwinism in national contexts other than Italy include the following: *El darwinismo en España* (Darwinism in Spain), ed. D. Nuñez (Madrid: Castalia, 1969); Y. Conry, *L'introduction du darwinisme en France au XIXe siècle* (The introduction of Darwinism in nineteenth-century France) (Paris: Vrin, 1974); P. Roome, "The Darwin Debate in Canada, 1860–1880," in *Science, Technology, and Culture in Historical Perspective*, ed. A. Knafla, M. S. Staum, and T. H. E. Travers (Calgary, Alberta: University of Calgary, 1976), 183–234; H. W. Paul, *The Edge of Contingency: French Catholic Reaction to Scientific Change from Darwin to Duhem* (Gainesville: University Presses of Florida, 1979); A. Kelly, *The Descent of Darwin: The Popularization of Darwinism in Germany, 1860–1914* (Chapel Hill: University of North Carolina Press, 1981); A. Santucci, "Darwin, Spencer e la filosofia sociale americana nella seconda metà dell'Ottocento" (Darwin, Spencer, and American social philosophy in the second half of the nineteenth century), *Il pensiero politico* 15 (1982): 48–73; P. J. Bowler, "Scientific Attitudes to Darwinism in Britain and America," in Kohn, *Darwinian Heritage*, 641–81; Corsi and Weindling, *Darwinism*, 683–729; A. Z. Ziadat, *Western Science in the Arab World: The Impact of Darwinism, 1860–1930* (London: Macmillan, 1986); A. Vucinich, *Darwin in Russian Thought* (Berkeley and Los Angeles: University of California Press, 1988); D. P. Todes, *Darwin without Malthus: The Struggle for Existence in Russian Evolutionary Thought* (New York and Oxford: Oxford University Press, 1989).

15. See Freeman, *Darwin Handlist*.

16. C. Darwin, *Origine des espèces*, French translation by C. Royer (Paris: Gauillaumin, 1862). On Clémence Royer see J. Harvey, " 'Strangers to Each Other': Male and Female Relationships in the Life and Work of Clémence Royer," in *Uneasy Careers and Intimate Lives: Women in Science, 1789–1979*, ed. P. G. Abir-Am and D. Outram (New Brunswick, N.J.: Rutgers University Press, 1987), 147–71, and the literature mentioned there.

17. C. Darwin, *Sull'origine delle specie per elezione naturale, ovvero conservazione delle razze perfezionate nella lotta per l'esistenza*, Italian translation based on the third English edition of the *Origin of Species*, by G. Canestrini and L. Salimbeni (Modena: Zanichelli, 1864). This and the following quotations are taken from the note "To the reader," signed by the two translators. An anastatic reprinting of this first Italian translation has been published, with a preface by G. Montalenti, by Zanichelli (Bologna, 1982).

18. In spite of their criticisms of the French translation, Canestrini and Salimbeni evidently referred to it continually. Thus in the title they translated Darwin's *selection* with *elezione*, the Italian equivalent of the French *élection*, which Royer reluctantly changed to *selection* only in the second edition (1866). Canestrini instead kept *elezione* even in his last writings in the 1890s. The term *selezione* was not found in Italian dictionaries of the 1860s, and when its existence was recognized—to the best of my knowledge in 1872, in the fourth volume of N. Tommaseo and B. Bellini, *Dizionario della lingua italiana* (Dictionary of the Italian language) (Turin: UTET, 1865–79)—it was actually done with polemical reference to Darwin's theory. Here is Tommaseo and Bellini's definition-invective: "*Selezione*. Term with which the scientists of bestiality and muck, in order to deny human liberty, affirm it by attributing it to all things [an allusion to the dictionary's definition of *elezione* as "the exercise of free will"]. They say that *Man and every thing have created themselves through selection*, but they do not explain how this elective affinity can be reconciled with that necessity they consider the universal tyrant" (Tommaseo and Bellini, *Dizionario* 4: 775). On the ambiguity caused by the use of *élection* in French, see Conry, *L'introduction du darwinisme*, 265ff. The English *selection*, too, though established around 1859 in its present sense, created some ambiguity that might have suggested that Darwin attributed a true choice to "Nature." See Darwin's amendments in subse-

quent editions of the *Origin* to correct this misinterpretation: *The Origin of Species by Charles Darwin: A Variorum Text*, ed. M. Peckham (Philadelphia: University of Pennsylvania Press, 1959), 165.

Some errors passed from the French translation into the Italian, such as *metafisiche* (metaphysical) for *metaforiche* (metaphorical), after the French *métaphisiques*, in the key expression in which Darwin specified the metaphorical (hardly metaphysical!) nature of the term *natural selection;* see the 1864 Italian translation, 58. The error was eliminated in 1875 in the second Italian edition of the *Origin,* amended by Canestrini (see below, n. 29).

19. Darwin had conceived of the *Origin* as a popular book: "I think my book will be popular to a certain extent (enough to ensure [against] heavy loss) amongst scientific and semi-scientific men," Darwin to J. D. Hooker, 2 Apr. 1859, in F. Darwin, *Life and Letters of Darwin,* 2: 153. His commercial success confirmed that the work had reached a wide audience.

20. See, for instance, G. Canestrini, "Intorno alla teoria della trasformazione delle specie ed all'origine dell'uomo" (On the theory of the transmutation of species and the origin of man), *Annuario filosofico del libero pensiero* (1867), supplement to the periodical *Il libero pensiero: Giornale dei razionalisti,* which was printed in Milan.

21. See G. Canestrini to Giorgio Jan, 25 July 1863, MCSN.

22. *Archivio per la zoologia, l'anatomia e la fisiologia* (Archive for zoology, anatomy, and physiology). The periodical led an afflicted existence. The first issue appeared in Genoa in 1861, edited by Canestrini, G. Doria, P. M. Ferrari, and M. Lessona; the second was printed in Modena in 1863, edited by Canestrini and Doria; the third, in 1864, was edited by Canestrini alone. A second series, this too edited by Canestrini alone, began in 1869 but was suspended the following year. Its founders intended that the *Archivio* bring its readers up to date on news of what was going on abroad, permitting prompter circulation of information than was provided by the academies' traditional "Acts" (see Canestrini to Cornalia, 11 May 1861, MCSN, and the presentation of the first issue, *Archivio* [1861]. Both goals remained largely unrealized.

23. L. Salimbeni, *Sulla eterogenia ovvero sulla generazione spontanea* (On heterogeneity, or, On spontaneous generation) (Modena: Zanichelli, 1863). See also L. Salimbeni, *Il microscopio diretto a determinare e prevenire la malattia del baco da seta* (The microscope aimed at detecting and preventing disease in the silkworm) (Modena: Zanichelli, 1868).

24. Salimbeni, *Sulla eterogenia,* 8: "The Creator chose to assign [simpler animals] such varied systems of generation in order to show the wise observer that microscopic creatures can reveal His glory and His omnipotence no less than the starry sky."

25. See *Catalogo ragionato delle edizioni Zanichelli, 1859–1959* (Annotated catalogue of the books published by Zanichelli, 1859–1959) (Bologna: Zanichelli, 1959), vol. 1 (the only volume published, covering 1859–1905).

26. Cf. Canestrini, "Intorno alla teoria della trasformazione."

27. G. Grimelli, *Sulla divisione originaria dell'umanità e circa la supposta derivazione dell'uomo* (On the original division of humankind and the supposed derivation of man) (Bologna, Zanichelli, 1866); and G. G. Bianconi, *La théorie darwinienne et la Création dite indépendante* (Darwin's theory and "independent" creation) (Bologna: Zanichelli, 1874).

28. Zanichelli Publishers appear not to have kept any files on the size of the editions of its early publications. In Nicola Zanichelli's manuscript papers in the library of the Archiginnasio in Bologna, I found no information on the first Italian translation of the *Origin.* For data on English editions, see Freeman, *Darwin Handlist.*

29. G. Canestrini, "Al lettore" (To the Reader), in C. Darwin, *Sulla origine delle*

specie per elezione naturale . . . , translation of the sixth English edition, ed. G. Canestrini (Turin: UTET, 1875).

30. M. Lessona, preface to C. Darwin, *L'origine dell'uomo*, trans. M. Lessona (Turin: UTET, 1871). On Lessona see below, chap. 6.

31. Cf. "Statuten der Kaiserlich-Königlichen zoologisch-botanischen Gesellschaft in Wien" (Statutes of the Kaiserlich-Königlichen zoologisch-botanischen Gesellschaft in Vienna), *Verhandlungen des zoologisch-botanischen Vereins in Wien* 8 (1858): xi–xiv. On medical and natural history teaching in Vienna of the time, see E. Lesky, *Die wiener medizinische Schule im 19. Jahrhundert* (The Vienna medical school in the nineteenth century) (Vienna: Böhlaus, 1965).

32. G. Canestrini, "Zur Kritik des Müller'schen Systems der Knochenfische" (Criticism of Müller's system of teleosts), *Verhandlungen* 9 (1859): 119–26.

33. G. Canestrini, "Zur Systematik und Charakteristik der Anabatinen" (On the systematics and characters of Anabantidae), *Verhandlungen* 10 (1860): 697–712, especially 697.

34. Canestrini, "Zur Systematik."

35. In the first (1861) issue of the *Archivio* that Canestrini helped edit, Darwin was indirectly mentioned as the author of the theory of "natural selection" in Richard Owen's letter to *Annals and Magazine of Natural History* (June 1861), translated by De Filippi for the *Archivio*.

36. G. Canestrini, "I pleuronettidi del Golfo di Genova" (The pleuronectids of the Gulf of Genoa), *Archivio per la zoologia, l'anatomia e la fisiologia* 1 (1961): 1–44.

37. G. Canestrini, "Intorno allo sviluppo del Dactylopterus volitans C. V. ed al genere Cephalacanthus" (On the development of *Dactylopterus volitans* . . .), ibid., 45–51.

38. G. Canestrini, "Note ittiologiche" (Ichthyological notes), *Archivio* 3 (1864): 107. Cf. C. Darwin, *On the Origin of Species* [1859], facsimile of the first edition, with an introduction by Ernst Mayr (Cambridge: Harvard University Press, 1966), chaps. 1, 2.

39. G. Canestrini, "Prospetto critico dei pesci d'acqua dolce d'Italia" (Critical outline of Italian freshwater fishes), *Archivio* 4 (1866): 47–187, especially 52.

40. G. Canestrini, notes to C. Darwin, *Sulla origine delle specie* (Turin: UTET, 1875), 441–80, especially 447.

41. Ibid.

42. See Canestrini's and Lessona's letters to Darwin in Darwin Papers, Cambridge University Library. For the correspondence between Darwin and Canestrini, see below, n. 122.

43. *Rivista contemporanea* 20, no. 8 (Jan. 1860): 140.

44. *La civiltà cattolica*, 4th ser., 9, no. 7 (July 1860): 280. Cf. F. J. Pictet, "Sur l'origine de l'espèce, par C. Darwin," *Bibliothèque universelle de Genève—Archives des sciences naturelles* 7 (1860): 233–55.

45. *Il Politecnico* 9, no. 49 (July 1860): 110–12.

46. F. De Filippi, "L'uomo e il diluvio: Lettera a E. Littré" (Man and the flood: Letter to E. Littré), *Rivista contemporanea* 7, no. 19 (1859): 76–96.

47. [G. B. Pianciani], "Cosmogonia: Della origine delle specie organizzate" (Cosmogony: On the origin of organized species), *La civiltà cattolica*, 4th ser., 9, no. 7 (July 1860): 165ff. This article was part of a series of articles on the same subject begun in 1858.

48. Pictet, "Sur l'origine," 234.

49. See above, n. 45.

50. *Rivista italiana di scienze, lettere ed arti, colle effemeridi della pubblica istruzione*, no. 30 (22 Apr. 1861): 517.

51. See above, chap. 2.

52. Darwin, *On the Origin of Species*, 420.
53. G. Canestrini, "Intorno ai lofobranchi adriatici" (On Adriatic lophobranchians), *Atti del Regio Istituto Veneto di Scienze, Lettere e Arti*, 3d ser., 16 (1871): 1047–67.
54. Ibid., 1055.
55. Ibid.
56. See ibid., 1057: "[In sea horses] the caudal fin is useless, or nearly so, and if it existed in *calamostoma*, having been inherited from other fishes, in sea horses it has undergone the effects of *that law that condemns useless organs first to become rudimentary, then to disappear in adults, and finally to vanish even in embryos*" [emphasis added].
57. P. J. Vorzimmer, *Charles Darwin: The Years of Controversy—The Origin of Species and Its Critics, 1859–1882* (Philadelphia: Temple University Press, 1970).
58. R. A. von Koelliker, "Ueber die Darwin'sche Schöpfungstheorie" (On Darwin's theory of creation), *Zeitschrift für wissenschaftliche Zoologie* 14 (1864): 179–181. For Canestrini's attitude, see G. Canestrini, *Origine dell'uomo* (Origin of man) (Milan: Brigola, 1866), 6–12. For Huxley's reactions to Koelliker, see T. H. Huxley, "Criticism on *The Origin of Species*" [1864], in *Darwiniana*, now in vol. 2 of Huxley's *Collected Essays* (New York: Greenwood Press, 1968), 80–106. Darwin's attitude toward Koelliker's criticisms coincided with Huxley's; cf. *Life and Letters of Charles Darwin* 3: 29–30. Huxley took Koelliker's objections, which saw Darwin's theory as a reproposal of a teleological view of nature, and used them to reiterate that, on the contrary, Darwin's "selection" had dealt finalism "a mortal blow" (Huxley, *Darwiniana*, 82).
59. Darwin, *On the Origin of Species*, 488.
60. On this and similar episodes, see L. Eiseley, *Darwin's Century: Evolution and the Men Who Discovered It* (New York: Doubleday, 1958); A. Ellegord, *Darwin and the General Reader: The Reception of Darwin's Theory of Evolution in the British Periodical Press* (Göteborg: Acta Universitatis Gotheburgensis, 1958); G. Himmelfarb, *Darwin and the Darwinian Revolution* (1959; New York: Norton, 1968); W. Irvine, *Apes, Angels and Victorians: A Joint Biography of Darwin and Huxley* (Cleveland: Meridian, 1959); J. G. Greene, *The Death of Adam: Evolution and Its Impact on Western Thought* (Ames: Iowa University Press, 1959); and especially I. B. Cohen, "Three Notes on the Reception of Darwin's Ideas on Natural Selection (Henry Baker Tristram, Alfred Newton, Samuel Wilberforce)," in Kohn, *Darwinian Heritage*, 589–607.
61. See above, chap. 2.
62. F. De Filippi, *L'uomo e le scimie* [sic]: *Lezione pubblica detta in Torino la sera dell'11 gennaio 1864* (Milan: Daelli, 1864). On the popular reception see below, chap. 6. Camerano reported that De Filippi felt his famous lesson may have been influenced even more by Richard Owen and Thomas Huxley than by Darwin (Camerano, "La vita scientifica di M. Lessona" [M. Lessona's scientific life], *Memorie della Reale Accademia delle Scienze di Torino* 45 (1896): 331–88, especially 367).
63. See above, n. 46.
64. See above, chap. 2.
65. De Filippi to Cornalia, 11 Jan. 1864, MCSN.
66. See G. Canestrini, *La evoluzione della teoria della discendenza: Discorso per l'inaugurazione dell'anno scolastico 1897–1898 dell'Università di Padova* (The evolution of the theory of the descendence: Speech for the inauguration of the academic year 1897–1898 of the University of Padua) (Padua: Randi, 1897), 11: "It was unwise to begin with the disclosure of the part of the theory that, by dealing directly with man, stirs many emotions, making impartial judgment difficult."
67. T. H. Huxley, *Man's Place in Nature and Other Anthropological Essays* [1863], now vol. 7 of T. H. Huxley, *Collected Essays* (New York: Greenwood, 1968). On this work of Huxley's, see W. L. Straus, Jr., "Huxley's Evidence as to Man's Place in

Nature: A Century Later," in *Medicine Science and Culture: Historical Essays in Honour of Owsei Temkin*, ed. G. Stevenson and R. T. Multhauf (Baltimore: Johns Hopkins University Press, 1868), 161–67; and J. G. Paradis, *T. H. Huxley: Man's Place in Nature* (Lincoln: University of Nebraska Press, 1978), chap. 4. On the relations between Darwin and Huxley, see M. Bartholomew, "Huxley's Defence of Darwin," *Annals of Science* 32 (1975): 525–35. See also E. Eng, "T. H. Huxley's Understanding of 'Evolution,' " *History of Science* 16 (1978): 291–303. For a detailed and convincing discussion of how Darwin's and Huxley's views of biology differed, see M. A. Di Gregorio, *T. H. Huxley's Place in Natural Science* (New Haven and London: Yale University Press, 1984).

68. C. Lyell, *The Geological Evidences of the Antiquity of Man*, 2d ed. (London: Murray, 1863; reprint, Westmead: Gregg, 1970). This work of Lyell's elicited a prompt response in Italy, especially by the offices of the geologist Giovanni Capellini, who had been in contact with Lyell since 1857; see Capellini's correspondence, Biblioteca dell'Archiginnasio, Bologna. On Capellini's anthropology lessons at the University of Bologna, see L. Foresti, *Una lezione del prof. G. Capellini sull'antichità dell'uomo* (A lecture by Prof. G. Capellini on the antiquity of man) (Bologna: Vitali, 1863). See also G. Capellini, *Ricordi* (Memoirs), 2 vols. (Bologna: Zanichelli, 1914).

69. C. Vogt, *Vorlesungen über den Menschen, seine Stellung in der Schöpfung und in der Geschichte der Erde* (Lectures on man, his place in the creation and in the history of the earth) (Giessen: n.p., 1863).

70. T. H. Huxley, *Prove di fatto intorno al posto che tiene l'uomo nella natura*, trans. Pietro Marchi, with a preface by the translator (Milan: Treves, 1869). On the debate on man's origin, see P. J. Bowler, *Theories of Human Evolution: A Century of Debate, 1844–1944* (Baltimore: Johns Hopkins University Press, 1986), especially parts 2 and 3.

71. On the rapid development of studies of this kind in those years, see L. Pigorini, *Bibliografia paleoetnologica italiana dal 1850 al 1871* (Italian paleoethnological bibliography, 1850–1871) (Parma: Rossi-Ubaldi, 1871); and P. Riccardi, *Saggio di un catalogo bibliografico antropologico italiano* (Attempt at an Italian anthropological bibliographical catalogue) (Modena: Vincenzi e Nipoti, 1883). Confirmation of Canestrini's interest in terramare is found in his correspondence with Cornalia preserved at the Museum of Natural History in Milan: "I am continually excavating in the terramare, and as soon as I have an ample collection of objects I hope that we can agree to make an exchange of these objects" (Canestrini to Cornalia, 16 May 1864, MCSN).

72. G. Canestrini, "Sopra due teschi umani scavati nelle terremare del modenese" (On two human skulls unearthed in the terramare near Modena), *Archivio* 3 (1865): 337–38; "Riflessioni sulle nostre terremare" (Reflections on our terramare), *Il Panaro: Gazzetta di Modena*, no. 51 (1865); "Oggetti trovati nelle terremare del modenese" (Objects found in the terramara near Modena), *Annuario della Società dei naturalist di Modena* 1 (1866): 1–12, 91–152; and "Sopra due crani antichi trovati nell'Emilia" (On two ancient skulls found in Emilia), ibid. 2 (1867): 1–6.

73. Canestrini, "Oggetti trovati," 151.

74. See Darwin, *On the Origin of Species*, 109.

75. On Strobel see V. Strobel, "Biobibliografia del naturalista Pellegrino von Strobel" (Biobibliography of the naturalist Pellegrino von Strobel), *Atti dell'Accademia Roveretana degli Agiati* 18–19, B (1980): 199–217.

76. G. Canestrini, *Origine dell'uomo* (Milan: Brigola, 1866). See also G. Canestrini, "L'antichità dell'uomo: Lezione popolare detta in Modena li 22 marzo 1866" (The antiquity of man: Popular lecture delivered in Modena, 22 March 1866) (Modena: Vincenzi, 1866).

77. G. G. Bianconi, *La teoria dell'uomo-scimmia esaminata sotto il rapporto dell'organizzazione* (The ape-man theory examined in relation to organization) (Bologna: Gamberini e Parmeggiani, 1864). A copy of a later work by Bianconi, *La théorie darwinienne* (see n. 27), is preserved in the Darwin Library in the Cambridge University Library. A handwritten comment by Darwin indicates that he skimmed the first part but found "nothing of importance" there. On Bianconi see V. Martucci, "Un interlocutore italiano di Darwin: Giuseppe Bianconi e la 'creazione indipendente,' " *Physis* 20 (1978): 349–55.

78. See above, chap. 2.

79. See Huxley, *Man's Place in Nature*, 125ff.

80. Bianconi, *Teoria dell'uomo-scimmia*, 18, 38.

81. Canestrini, *Origine dell'uomo*, 67.

82. De Filippi, *L'uomo e le scimie*, 49–50.

83. Canestrini, *Origine dell'uomo*, 96.

84. Ibid., 100.

85. See Darwin, *On the Origin of Species*, 111ff. On the formation and significance of the principle of divergence in Darwin's theory, see D. Ospovat, *The Development of Darwin's Theory: Natural History, Natural Theology and Natural Selection, 1838–1859* (Cambridge: Cambridge University Press, 1981), especially chaps. 7, 8; and D. Kohn, "Darwin's Principle of Divergence as Internal Dialogue," in Kohn, *Darwinian Heritage*, 245–57.

86. Canestrini, *Origine dell'uomo*, 104.

87. See Darwin, *On the Origin of Species*, 336–37.

88. In 1864, Alfred Russel Wallace had dealt with the problem of the origin of human beings as viewed through the theory of natural selection, but he had attributed a role to intellectual capacities in the recent evolutionary history of the human species that Darwin found excessive and inconsistent with his theory. See A. R. Wallace, "The Origin of Human Races and the Antiquity of Man Deduced from the Theory of Natural Selection," *Journal of the Anthropological Society of London* (1864): clviii–clxx; A. R. Wallace, *Letters and Reminiscences*, ed. J. Marchant (New Haven: Yale University Press, 1972).

89. C. Darwin, *The Descent of Man, and Selection in Relation to Sex* (London: Murray, 1871; Princeton: Princeton University Press, 1981).

90. Cf. L. Büchner, *Sechs Vorlesungen über die Darwin'sche Theorie* (Six lectures on Darwin's theory) (Leipzig: Thomas, 1868); E. Haeckel, *Natürliche Schöpfungs-Geschichte* (Natural history of creation) (1868; Berlin: Reimer, 1909).

91. G. Canestrini, "Caratteri anomali e rudimentali in ordine all'origine dell'uomo," *Annuario della Società dei Naturalisti in Modena* 2 (1867): 81–99.

92. Ibid., 84–85.

93. Ibid., 87.

94. Darwin, *Descent of Man*, 1: 125.

95. Ibid., 194–95.

96. Ibid., 201–22.

97. G. Canestrini, *Per l'evoluzione*, 141.

98. Cf. ibid., 142–44.

99. Ibid., 149.

100. Ibid., 163.

101. Ibid., 164–65. For Canestrini's use of *elezione* (election) to translate Darwin's *selection*, see n. 18 above.

102. Ibid., 153.

103. Ibid., 171.

104. On the subject see, e.g., R. C. Olby, *Origins of Mendelism* (London: Constable, 1966), particularly 54–62.

105. Darwin, *On the Origin of Species*, 81.

106. Ibid., chap. 5.

107. Vorzimmer, *Darwin: Years of Controversy*, 95.

108. "Variability from the indirect and direct action of the external conditions of life, and from use and disuse," was, according to Darwin, one of the great "laws" of the living world (*On the Origin of Species*, 489–90).

109. G. Canestrini, *La teoria di Darwin criticamente esposta* (Darwin's theory expounded critically) (Milan: Dumollard, 1880), 112.

110. Darwin, *On the Origin of Species*, 142–43.

111. Ibid.

112. Canestrini, *Teoria dell'evoluzione*, 148.

113. See Darwin, *On the Origin of Species*, 7: Knight had claimed that the increased variability of domestic species might depend in some way on the excess of available food compared with the conditions in nature.

114. P. Lucas, *Traité philosophique et physiologique de l'hérédité naturelle* (Philosophical and physiological treatise on natural heredity) (Paris: Baillière, 1847–50). See Darwin, *On the Origin of Species*, 12, 175.

115. See, e.g., I. Geoffroy Saint-Hilaire, *Histoire générale et particulière des anomalies de l'organisation chez l'homme et les animaux ou traité de tératologie* (General and detailed history of the anomalies of organization in man and animals, or, Treatise on teratology), 3 vols. (Paris: Baillière, 1832–36), 3: 832–36.

116. See Darwin, *On the Origin of Species*, 143ff., and the literature cited there.

117. See Vorzimmer, *Darwin: Years of Controversy*, chap. 5; and Olby, *Origins of Mendelism*, 61–62.

118. Canestrini, *Teoria dell'evoluzione*, 44.

119. See, e.g., J. A. Secord, "Nature's Fancy: Charles Darwin and the Breeding of Pigeons," *Isis* 72 (1981): 163–86.

120. G. Canestrini, "Intorno alla ereditarietà dei caratteri individuali" (On the inheritance of individual characters), *Rivista di filosofia scientifica* 1 (1881).

121. Darwin, *On the Origin of Species*, 87ff.; and Darwin, "Sexual Selection," part 2 of *Descent of Man*.

122. As is shown by Canestrini's letters to Darwin dated 13 Mar. and 8 Apr. 1868, Darwin Papers, Cambridge University Library, vol. 86. From the correspondence between Darwin and Canestrini, we know of seven letters from Canestrini to Darwin, in the Darwin Papers, vol. 86 and 161, and two letters from Darwin to Canestrini, 17 May 1880 and 26 Aug. (1880?), preserved by a descendant of the Canestrini family, Dr. Sandro Onestinghel of Milan. See *A Calendar of the Correspondence of C. Darwin*, ed. F. Burkhardt and S. Smith (New York and London: Garland, 1985). I am grateful to Dr. Onestinghel for allowing me to examine Darwin's two letters to Canestrini.

123. On the subject see, in addition to the letters mentioned in the previous note, Canestrini to Cornalia, 8 Mar. (?) 1868, MCSN. Later Canestrini would publish a handbook on beekeeping: G. Canestrini, *Apicoltura* (Apiculture) (Milan: Hoepli, 1880).

124. A. R. Wallace, "On the Phenomena of Variations and Geographical Distribution, as Illustrated by the Papilionidae of the Malayan Archipelago," *Transactions of the Linnean Society* 25 (1865); see Vorzimmer, *Darwin: Years of Controversy*, 191ff. For the epistolary debate between Darwin and Wallace on the subject, see Wallace, *Letters and Reminiscences*, 177ff.

125. G. Canestrini, "Caratteri sessuali secondari della tinca" (Secondary sexual characteristics of the tench), *Atti della Società Veneto-Trentina di Scienze Naturali residente in Padova* 1, no. 2 (1872). The copy of this article by Canestrini, preserved in the Darwin Offprint Collection, Cambridge University Library, confirms that Dar-

win took careful note of certain facts illustrated by Canestrini that could be reconciled with the theory of sexual selection (see Darwin General Collection, no. 830). See also G. Canestrini, "Caratteri sessuali secondari degli aracnidi" (Secondary sexual characteristics of arachnids), *Atti della Società Veneto-Trentina* 1, no. 3 (1873). This article was also carefully annotated by Darwin (see Darwin General Collection, Cambridge University Library, no. 805).

126. G. Canestrini, notes to C. Darwin, *Sull'origine delle specie per elezione naturale*, 453.

127. Canestrini, *Per l'evoluzione*, 110.

128. On Darwin's attitude toward the problem of mind from an evolutionary standpoint, see H. E. Gruber, *Darwin on Man: A Psychological Study of Scientific Creativity*, 2d ed. (Chicago: University of Chicago Press, 1981), especially part 3. See also G. Pancaldi, *Charles Darwin: "Storia" ed "economia" della natura* (Charles Darwin: "History" and "economy" of nature) (Florence: La Nuova Italia, 1977), 32ff.

129. G. Canestrini, *L'indirizzo dell'odierna biologia* (The trend of biology today) (Padua: Randi, 1882), 20–21.

130. This is how Darwin expressed it in the *Descent of Man*, 2: 396: "In the lower division of the animal kingdom, sexual selection seems to have done nothing: such animals are often affixed for life to the same spot, or have the two sexes combined in the same individual, or what is still more important, their perceptive and intellectual faculties are not sufficiently advanced to allow of the feelings of love and jealousy, or of the exertion of choice. When, however, we come to the Arthropoda and Vertebrata, even to the lowest classes in these two great Subkingdoms, sexual selection has effected much; and it deserves notice that we here find the intellectual faculties developed, but in two very distinct lines, to the highest standard, namely in the Hymenoptera (ants, bees, etc.) amongst the Arthropoda, and in the Mammalia, including man, amongst the Vertebrata."

131. C. Darwin, *The Variation of Animals and Plants under Domestication* (London: Murray, 1868) 2: chap. 28. Italian translation: *Variazioni degli animali e delle piante allo stato domestico*, trans. G. Canestrini (Turin: UTET, 1876).

132. *More Letters of Charles Darwin*, ed. F. Darwin (New York: Appleton, 1903; New York: Johnson, 1972), 1: 360ff.

133. See Canestrini, *Teoria di Darwin criticamente esposta*, 210.

134. See Conry, *Introduction du darwinisme en France*, 318ff.

135. See Canestrini, *La teoria di Darwin criticamente esposta*.

136. P. Mantegazza, "Carlo Darwin e il suo ultimo libro" (Charles Darwin and his latest book), *Nuova antologia di scienze, lettere e arti* 3 (1868): 70–89. For Buccola's viewpoint and that of other Italian authors on this subject, see V. Martucci, "Il discusso fascino di una ipotesi: La pangenesi di Darwin e gli studiosi italiani (1868–1888)" (The controversial appeal of a hypothesis: Darwin's pangenesis and Italian scientists, 1868–1888), *History and Philosophy of the Life Sciences* 3 (1981): 243–57. On the interesting figure of Gabriele Buccola, see N. Dazzi, "Gabriele Buccola," in G. Cimino and N. Dazzi, eds., *Gli studi di psicologia in Italia: Aspetti teorici, scientifici e ideologici*, Quaderni di storia e critica della scienza (Pisa, Domus Galilaeana), n.s., 9 (1980): 23–39.

137. Canestrini to Buccola, 14 May 1879, in Buccola correspondence, Biblioteca Comunale di Palermo.

138. For evidence to that effect, see Canestrini, *Per l'evoluzione*, chap. 5.

139. Ibid., 52.

140. A similar opinion was expressed by D'Ancona, *Opera di Giovanni Canestrini*, 20.

141. G. and R. Canestrini, *Batteriologia* (Bacteriology) (Milan: Hoepli, 1880); and

G. Canestrini, "Le rivelazioni della batteriologia" (The revelations of bacteriology), *Atti del R. Istituto Veneto di scienze, lettere ed arti*, 7th ser., 1 (1890): 837–56.

142. See G. and R. Canestrini, preface to *Batteriologia*.

143. Canestrini, *Per l'evoluzione*.

144. Ibid., 52, 55, 58.

145. Ibid., 141.

146. G. Canestrini, *La evoluzione della teoria della discendenza* (The evolution of the theory of descendence) (Padua: Randi, 1897).

147. On Roux and relevant bibliography, see F. B. Churchill, in *Dictionary of Scientific Biography*, ed. C. C. Gillispie (New York: Scribner, 1970–78), s.v. "Wilhelm Roux."

148. Canestrini, *Evoluzione della teoria della discendenza*, 29.

149. Ibid., 20.

150. Ibid., 26.

151. See H. Spencer, *The Inadequacy of Natural Selection* [1893], now in *The Works of Herbert Spencer* (1905; reprint, Osnabrück: Zeller, 1966–67) 17: 1–69. Cf. Canestrini, *Per l'evoluzione*, chap. 4. On Weismann and Spencer's dispute, see F. B. Churchill, "The Weismann-Spencer Controversy over the Inheritance of Acquired Characters," in *Human Implications of Scientific Advance: Proceedings of the XVth International Congress of the History of Science*, ed. E. G. Forbes (Edinburgh: Edinburgh University Press, 1978), 451–68. On neo-Lamarckism at the turn of the century in France, see J. Roger, "La filosofia dei neolamarckiani francesi" (The philosophy of French neo-Lamarckians), in *Scienza e filosofia nella cultura positivistica*, ed. A. Santucci (Milan: Feltrinelli, 1982), 234–44; and the monographic issue of *Revue de Synthèse* 100, nos. 95, 96 (1979). For an excellent survey of Darwinism and Lamarckism around 1900, see P. J. Bowler, *The Eclipse of Darwinism* (Baltimore: Johns Hopkins University Press, 1983).

152. Canestrini, *Evoluzione della teoria della discendenza*, 18.

153. On the important role played by the disciplines, as organized areas of research, in the history of the sciences, see *Perspectives on the Emergence of Scientific Disciplines*, ed. G. Lemaine et al. (Chicago: Morton and Aldine, 1976); and R. E. Kohler, "Discipline History," in *Dictionary of the History of Science*, ed. W. F. Bynum et al. (London: Macmillan, 1981), 104. Studies on nineteenth-century Darwinism have not paid much attention to these disciplinary aspects. For an important exception see W. Coleman, "Morphology between Type Concept and Descent Theory," *Journal of the History of Medicine* 31 (1976): 149–75.

154. Up to now the transmission of Darwinism has been studied mainly in this wider perspective. This is particularly true for Italy. A great deal remains to be done, however, for the history of the reactions to Darwin's theory in the different scientific disciplines as they developed within the various national contexts.

155. On these events see the works cited above, n. 60.

156. It is worth recalling how Canestrini perceived the institutional situation of recently introduced biological disciplines in Italy in 1890: "To tell the truth, confining ourselves to the past decade, our discoveries on the cause of malaria and the various forms of Proteus are of prime importance; but it is also true that other discoveries of greater worth have been made by foreigners. The reason for our inferiority, in my modest opinion, is to be sought in the present state of higher education, which has long been in need of reform. In Italy bacteriology is taught by *liberi docenti*, so that few devote themselves to it expressly and exclusively. Our bacteriologists are for the most part anatomist-pathologists, clinicians, veterinarians, or naturalists, who apply themselves to this discipline only as much as their chief occupation allows them to. It would also help to reflect that easy discoveries are a thing of the past, and that new ones will not be made without great sacrifice of time, and will require the aid of adequate means for which we here, unfortunately, have reason

to envy the well-equipped laboratories of foreign schools" (Canestrini, "Rivelazioni della batteriologia," 855).

157. See J. Huxley, *Evolution: The Modern Synthesis* (London: Allen and Unwin, 1942).

158. See E. Mayr, "The Role of Systematics in the Evolutionary Synthesis," in *The Evolutionary Synthesis: Perspectives on the Unification of Biology*, ed. E. Mayr and W. B. Provine (Cambridge: Harvard University Press, 1980), 123–36; and E. Mayr, *Principles of Systematic Zoology* (New York: McGraw-Hill, 1969), 51–53.

FOUR. DARWIN'S THEORY AND DESIGN

1. C. Darwin, *The Various Contrivances by Which Orchids Are Fertilised by Insects* [1862] (hereafter *Fertilisation of Orchids*), 2d ed. (London: Murray, 1877; reprint, with a new foreword by M. Ghiselin, Chicago: University of Chicago Press, 1984), 1. Unless otherwise noted, all page references are to this edition. This and Darwin's other major botanical works, such as *On the Movements and Habits of Climbing Plants* (1865), *Insectivorous Plants* (1875), *The Effects of Cross- and Self-fertilization in the Vegetable Kingdom* (1875), *The Different Forms of Flowers* (1877), and *The Power of Movement in Plants* (1880), were translated into Italian by Giovanni Canestrini, most often with the help of Pier Andrea Saccardo, and published by the Unione Tipografica Torinese between 1878 and 1884. Darwin's botanical works have not yet been studied in as great detail as his other works. Studies on Darwin the botanist include K. Goebel, "The Biology of Flowers," in *Darwin and Modern Science*, ed. A. C. Seward (Cambridge: Cambridge University Press, 1910), 401–23; H. L. K. Whitehouse, "Cross- and Self-fertilisation in Plants," in *Darwin's Biological Work*, ed. P. R. Bell (Cambridge: Cambridge University Press, 1959), 207–61; G. Wichler, "Darwin als Botaniker" (Darwin the botanist), *Sudhoffs Archiv für Geschichte der Medizin und der Naturwissenschaften* 44 (1960): 289–313; P. J. Vorzimmer, "Charles Darwin and Blending Inheritance," *Isis* 54 (1963): 371–90; G. Basalla, "Darwin's Orchid Book," in *Proceedings of the 10th International Congress of the History of Science (Ithaca NY, 1962)* (Paris: Hermann, 1964), 971–74; L. Baillaud, "Le mémoire de Charles Darwin sur les plantes grimpantes" (Charles Darwin's essay on climbing plants), *Archives internationales d'histoire des sciences* 19 (1966): 235–46; R. B. Freeman, "Charles Darwin on the Routes of Male Humble Bees," *Bulletin of the British Museum (Natural History) Historical Series* 6 (1968): 177–89; Y. Conry, *Correspondence entre Charles Darwin et Gaston de Saporta* (The Charles Darwin–Gaston de Saporta correspondence) (Paris: PUF, 1972); M. Allan, *Darwin and His Flowers* (London: Faber and Faber, 1977); J. Browne, "Darwin's Botanical Arithmetic and the 'Principle of Divergence,' 1854–1858," *Journal of the History of Biology* 13 (1980): 53–89; and D. M. Porter, "Darwin's Missing Notebooks Come to Light," *Nature* 291 (1981): 13, on the botanical collections assembled by Darwin during the journey of the *Beagle*.

2. Darwin, *Fertilisation of Orchids*, 2.

3. See C. Darwin, *Autobiography*, in C. Darwin and T. H. Huxley, *Autobiographies* (London: Oxford University Press, 1974), 32–33, 50. There is an extensive literature on the relations between Darwin's theory of evolution and British natural theology, of which I will mention only C. Limoges, "Darwinisme et adaptation" (Darwinism and adaptation), *Revue des questions scientifiques* 116 (1970): 353–74; D. Ospovat, "Perfect Adaptation and Teleological Explanation: Approaches to the Problem of the History of Life in the Mid-nineteenth Century," *Studies in History of Biology* 2 (1978): 33–56; D. Ospovat, *The Development of Darwin's Theory, Natural History, Natural Theology, and Natural Selection, 1838–1859* (Cambridge: Cambridge University Press, 1981); E. Manier, chap. 5 of *The Young Darwin and His Cultural Circle* (Dordrecht: Reidel, 1978); J. Moore, *The Post-Darwinian Controversies* (Cam-

bridge: Cambridge University Press, 1979); and N. C. Gillespie, *Charles Darwin and the Problem of Creation* (Chicago: University of Chicago Press, 1979).

4. A. Gray, review of *Fertilisation of Orchids* (1862), *American Journal of Science and Arts* 34 (1862): 139.

5. A. Gray, *Darwiniana* [1876], ed. A. H. Dupree (Cambridge, Mass.: Belknap, 1963). On the relations between Gray and Darwin see A. H. Dupree, *Asa Gray, 1810–1888* (Cambridge, Mass.: Belknap, 1959), especially 276ff., and Moore, *Post-Darwinian Controversies*, especially chap. 11.

6. P. J. Bowler, "Darwinism and the Argument from Design," *Journal of the History of Biology* 10 (1977); 29–43. See the important contributions of T. Lenoir, *The Strategy of Life: Teleology and Mechanics in Nineteenth-century German Biology* (Dordrecht: Reidel, 1982); and P. F. Rehbock, *The Philosophical Naturalists: Themes in Early Nineteenth-century British Biology* (Madison: University of Wisconsin Press, 1983).

7. See chap. 2 above.

8. Evidence of Darwin's esteem for Delpino can be found in his letters to Delpino, his comments in the margins of Delpino's publications (see below), and his correspondence with other scientists. See, e.g., *More Letters of Charles Darwin*, ed. F. Darwin (New York: Appleton, 1903), 2: 388. On the life and scientific work of Federico Delpino (1833–1905), see *Onoranze a F. D. nel suo settantesimo compleanno* (In honor of F. D. on his seventieth birthday) (Naples, 17 Dec. 1903) (Palermo: Priulla, 1904); A. Borzì, "F. D.," *Nuovo giornale botanico italiano*, n.s., 12 (1905): 417–39; "Commemorazione del socio F. D.," *Rendiconti della R. Accademia dei Lincei* 14 (1905): 462–78; F. Morini, "Commemorazione di F. D.," *Rendiconto delle sessioni della R. Accademia delle Scienze dell'Istituto di Bologna*, n.s., 9 (1904–1905): 113–45; L. Macchiati, *Cenno biografico del Prof. F. D.* (Savona: Bertolotto, 1905); O. Penzig, *Commemorazione di Delpino* (Genoa: Ciminago, 1905); F. Cavara, "F. D.," *Annuario della R. Università di Napoli* (1905–1906): 467–74; M. Geremicca, *L'opera botanica di F. D.* (Naples: n.p., 1908), the most extensive monograph, with a 492-item bibliography of Delpino's writings; A. Anile, *F. D.* (Chiavari: Devoto, 1922); and M. Cappelletti Alippi, in *Dizionario Biografico degli Italiani* (Rome: Enciclopedia Italiana, 1960–), s.v. "F. D." (forthcoming). On botany in Italy in the second half of the nineteenth century, see P. A. Saccardo, *La botanica in Italia* (Venezia, 1895–1901; reprint, Bologna: Forni, 1971); G. B. Grassi, "Botanica," part 2 of *I progressi della biologia e delle sue applicazioni pratiche conseguiti in Italia nell'ultimo cinquantennio* (Rome: Accademia dei Lincei, 1911), 89–109; and O. Mattirolo, "Ciò che hanno fatto i botanici itialiani nell'ultimo cinquantennio e ciò che dovrebbero fare" (What Italian botanists have accomplished in the last fifty years and what they need to accomplish) (5th meeting, Rome, 1911), in *Atti della S.I.P.S.* (Rome: Società Italiana per il Progresso delle Scienze, 1912), 497–521.

9. The publications that Delpino sent Darwin, containing many of Darwin's comments, are preserved at the Cambridge University Library. For the other material quoted, see below, nn. 12, 25.

10. C. Darwin, "Provisional Hypothesis of Pangenesis," chap. 27 in *The Variation of Animals and Plants under Domestication* (London: Murray, 1868).

11. F. Delpino, "Relazione sull'apparechio della fecondazione nelle asclepiadee. Aggiuntevi alcune considerazioni sulle cause finali e sulla teoria di Carlo Darwin intorno all'origine delle specie" (Report on the fertilization mechanism in asclepiadeae, with the addition of some considerations on final causes and Charles Darwin's theory on the origin of species), *Gazzetta medica di Torino*, 2d ser., 15 (1865): 372–74, 382–84, 390–91, 398–400.

12. F. Delpino, "Sulla darwiniana teoria della pangenesi," *Rivista contemporanea* 17 (1869), vol. 56: 196–204; vol. 57: 25–38. See F. Delpino, "On the Darwinian Theory of Pangenesis," *Scientific Opinion* 2 (1869): 365–67, 391–93, 407–408. Darwin had

the English translation done at his own expense and found a journal to publish it. This emerges from Darwin's letter to Delpino of 24 April 1869 (Library of the American Philosophical Society, 376). Both Darwin and Delpino kept a copy of the letter (Cambridge University Library, Darwin Papers [hereafter DAR] 143, and Delpino family papers, Rome). Delpino gave the original to an American friend. Seven letters in all from Darwin to Delpino are known of, and nineteen from Delpino to Darwin. Delpino's original letters to Darwin, and some copies that Darwin kept of his own letters to Delpino, are on file in DAR, vols. 77, 111, 143, 162; only the one mentioned above is at the American Philosophical Society. Six letters from Darwin to Delpino (four originals and two copies) are in the possession of Ms. Anna Barone, Rome. See *A Calendar of the Correspondence of C. Darwin*, ed. F. Burkhardt and S. Smith (New York and London: Garland, 1985).

13. Darwin's brief reply appeared in *Scientific Opinion* 2 (1869): 426; the Italian translation, with further comments by Delpino, appeared in *Rivista europea* 1 (1869): 118–24.

14. C. Darwin, *The Variation of Animals and Plants under Domestication*, 2d ed. (London: Murray, 1875), 2: 350. St. G. J. Mivart made ample use of Delpino's criticisms of pangenesis in *On the Genesis of Species* (London: Macmillan, 1871), 212ff. There were personal contacts between Delpino and Mivart in 1869 (see Delpino to Darwin, 15 Nov. 1871, Cambridge University Library, DAR 162).

15. I summarize here the basic concepts of the pangenesis hypothesis as they were laid out by Darwin in the first edition of *Variation*.

16. Considerations on the persistence of these Lamarckian elements in Darwin, and even more so in many of his followers, such as Canestrini, have already been made in chap. 3, with bibliographical references on the subject.

17. Darwin, *Variation* (1868), 2: 404.

18. Ibid.

19. D. Kohn, "Theories to Work By: Rejected Theories, Reproduction, and Darwin's Path to Natural Selection," *Studies in History of Biology* 4 (1980): 67–170; M. J. S. Hodge, "Darwin and the Laws of the Animate Part of the Terrestrial System (1835–1837): On the Lyellian Origins of His Zoonomical Explanatory Program," *Studies in History of Biology* 6 (1982): 1–106.

20. M. J. S. Hodge, "Darwin, as a Lifelong Generation Theorist," in *The Darwinian Heritage*, ed. D. Kohn (Princeton: Princeton University Press, 1985), 207–43.

21. Delpino, "Sulla darwiniana teoria della pangenesi." For other Italian reactions to pangenesis, in addition to what has already been said in chap. 3 in regard to Canestrini, see V. Martucci, "Il discusso fascino di una ipotesi: La pangenesi di Darwin e gli studiosi italiani (1868–1888)" (The debated appeal of a hypothesis: Darwin's pangenesis and Italian scientists), *History and Philosophy of the Life Sciences* 3 (1981): 243–57.

22. Delpino, "On the Darwinian Theory of Pangenesis," 366.

23. Ibid., 367. "The final cause of the sexes is most evident," Delpino emphatically declared on the same page.

24. Ibid.

25. Descendants of the Delpino family, Rome, preserve part of Federico Delpino's library. As can be seen from Delpino's annotated copy, he read Darwin's *Origin of Species* in Clémence Royer's French translation (Paris: Gauillaumin, 1862). Delpino had a limited command of English, as seen from his transcription of some of Darwin's letters in the possession of the Delpino family. In Delpino and Darwin's correspondence, each wrote in his own language. Darwin, who did not read Italian, had Delpino's letters and articles translated by his wife, Emma.

26. Delpino, handwritten comment in Darwin, *Origin*, the French translation cited, Delpino private family archives, 280.

27. Ibid.

28. Ibid., 292, emphasis added.
29. Ibid., 115, 118.
30. Ibid., 120.
31. Ibid., 298.
32. Ibid., 116.
33. Delpino, "On the Darwinian Theory of Pangenesis," 408.
34. Ibid., 407.
35. Ibid.
36. Darwin, handwritten comment in Delpino, "On the Darwinian Theory of Pangenesis," p. 407 of the copy in the Cambridge University Library, Darwin Offprint Collection, Review Collection, 125a (see Darwin's annotation on p. 365: "All marked very good").
37. Delpino, "On the Darwinian Theory of Pangenesis," 408.
38. *Rivista europea* 1 (1869): 122–23.
39. Darwin, handwritten comment in Delpino, "Sulla darwiniana teoria della pangenesi," p. 124 of the copy in the Darwin Review Collection (see n. 36), 126.
40. Delpino, comments to Darwin's reply in *Rivista europea* 1 (1869): 124.
41. Ibid. In what may have been his first letter to Darwin (Delpino to Darwin, 5 Sept. 1867, DAR 162), Delpino declared that he wanted to interpret the theory of pangenesis "in a spiritualistic perspective." (He repeatedly used the expressions *spiritualism, dualism,* and *vitalism* interchangeably.) Delpino's position might be described as "spiritualistic naturalism," adopting an expression that V. Cappelletti proposed for Ernst von Baer in *Entelechìa: Saggi sulle dottrine biologiche del secolo decimonono* (Entelechy: Essays on nineteenth-century biological doctrines) (Rome: Università degli Studi, Istituto di Filosofia, 1965), 85ff.
42. Delpino, "On the Darwinian Theory of Pangenesis," 408.
43. *Scientific opinion* 2 (1869): 426; now in *The Collected Papers of Charles Darwin,* ed. P. H. Barrett (Chicago: University of Chicago Press, 1977), 2: 158–60; an Italian translation was published in *Rivista europea* 1 (1869): 119–22.
44. C. Darwin, *On the Origin of Species,* reprint of the first (1859) edition, with an introduction by E. Mayr (Cambridge: Harvard University Press, 1966), 91–92.
45. Ibid., 94, emphasis added.
46. Ibid., 95. For the significance of these ideas of Darwin's in the history of ecology, see the literature mentioned by F. N. Egerton, "A Bibliographical Guide to the History of General Ecology and Population Ecology," *History of Science* 15 (1977): 189–215. See also D. Worster, *Nature's Ecology: The Roots of Ecology* (San Francisco: Sierra Club, 1977).
47. Delpino, handwritten comment in Darwin, *On the Origin of Species,* the Delpino family's copy of the French translation (cf. n. 25 above), 130.
48. Darwin, *Fertilisation of Orchids.*
49. Ibid., 37.
50. C. K. Sprengel, *Das entdeckte Geheimniss der Natur im Bau und in der Befruchtung der Blumen* (The secret of nature in the construction and fertilization of flowers revealed) (Berlin: Veiweg, 1793) (a reprint in four installments, ed. P. Knuth, appeared in the series Die Klassiker der exakten Wissenschaften (Leipzig: Engelmann, 1894). On Sprengel's biography and scientific work see L. J. King, "C. K. Sprengel," in *Dictionary of Scientific Biography,* ed. C. C. Gillispie (New York: Scribner, 1970–78), 12: 587–91. See also J. von Sachs, *History of Botany (1530–1860)* (1875; English translation, Oxford: Clarendon Press, 1890): 414–22. For the research on the relations between flowers and insects prior to Sprengel, see J. Lorch, "The Discovery of Nectar and Nectaries and Its Relation to Views on Flowers and Insects," *Isis* 69 (1978): 514–33.
51. Darwin acknowledged his debt to Sprengel in the introduction to *Fertilisation of Orchids.* His copy of Sprengel's work (now at the Darwin Library, Cambridge

University Library), dated August 1841, contains notes in Darwin's hand in which he expresses his disagreement with a number of explanations proposed by Sprengel: "all the passage a priori reasoning," "mere conjecture" (p. 423); "no real explan[ation]" (p. 111); "has no notion of advantage of intermarriage" (p. 18).

52. Sprengel, *Das entdeckte Geheimniss*, 404–405.

53. Darwin, *Fertilisation of Orchids*, 37.

54. Ibid.

55. Ibid., 42.

56. Darwin, *Fertilisation of Orchids* (1862), 49–51.

57. H. Müller, *Die Befruchtung der Blumen durch Insekten und die gegenseitigen Anpassungen Beider* (The fertilization of flowers by insects, and their reciprocal adaptations) (Leipzig: Engelmann, 1873).

58. Delpino, "Relazione sull'apparechio della fecondazione nelle asclepiadee."

59. Ibid., 399.

60. F. Delpino, "Pensieri sulla biologia vegetale, sulla tassonomia, sul valore tassonomico dei caratteri biologici, e proposta di un genere nuovo della famiglia delle labiate," (Thoughts on plant biology, taxonomy, the taxonomic value of biological characters, and the proposal of a new genus of the labiate family), *Il nuovo cimento* 25 (1867): 284–304, 321–98.

61. Ibid., 284, 296.

62. F. Delpino, "Sugli apparecchi della fecondazione nelle piante antocarpe (fanerogame): Sommario di osservazioni fatte negli anni 1865–1866" (On the fertilization apparatuses in anthocarps [phanerogams]: Summary of observations made in the years 1865–1866) (Florence, Cellini, 1867); "Ulteriori osservazioni e considerazioni sulla dicogamia nel regno vegetale" (Further observations and considerations on dichogamy in the plant kingdom), *Atti della Società Italiana di Scienze Naturali* 11 (1868): 265–332; 12 (1869): 21–141, 179–233; 13 (1870): 167–205; 16 (1873): 151–349; 17 (1874): 266–407.

63. Delpino, "Ulteriori osservazioni," 16: 166–270.

64. See D'Arcy W. Thompson's English translation of H. Müller's 1873 treatise *The Fertilisation of Flowers*, with a preface by Charles Darwin (London: Macmillan, 1883). See also P. Knuth's treatise *Handbook of Flower Pollination* (Oxford: Clarendon Press, 1906–1909), originally published as *Handbuch der Blütenbiologie*, 3 vols. in 3 parts (Leipzig, 1893).

As for Italy, it would be interesting to establish whether the tradition of ecological studies begun by Delpino was incorporated in the new tradition—in many ways so remote from Delpino's concerns—that in the twentieth century led to the important contributions of Vito Volterra. I am grateful to Francesco M. Scudo for calling my attention to this still-unresolved question in the history of ecology in Italy; see F. M. Scudo, "Vito Volterra and Theoretical Ecology," *Theoretical Population Biology* 2 (1971): 1–23; and *The Golden Age of Theoretical Ecology, 1923–1940*, ed. F. M. Scudo and J. R. Ziegler (Berlin: Springer, 1978). See also E. Luzi, "Vito Volterra e le applicazioni della matematica alla biologia" (Vito Volterra and the applications of mathematics to biology), unpublished dissertation, University of Bologna, 1980–81.

65. Delpino, "Ulteriori osservazioni," 12: 129.

66. H. Müller, "Ueber die Anwendung der Darwin'schen Theorie auf Blumen und blumenbesuchende Insekten" (On the application of Darwin's theory to flowers and the insects that visit them), *Correspondenzblatt des Naturhistorischen Vereins für Rheinland und Westphalen* 6 (1869): 43–66.

67. H. Müller, "Applicazione della teoria darwiniana ai fiori ed agli insetti visitatori dei fiori," translated and annotated by F. Delpino, *Bullettino della Società Entomologica Italiana* 2 (1870): 140–59, 228–40, 155–56.

68. Delpino, "Ulteriori osservazioni," 12: 129.

69. See also C. Darwin, "Notes on the Fertilisation of Orchids," *Annals and Magazine of Natural History,* 4th ser. (1869): 141–59; now in *Collected Papers of Charles Darwin* 2: 138–56.

70. Hermann Müller to Federico Delpino, 11 Dec. 1970, Delpino family papers, Rome.

71. Some time before, Darwin had sent Delpino an abstract of his "Notes," for which Delpino thanked him in Delpino to Darwin, 9 Oct. 1869, Cambridge University Library, DAR 162.

72. Delpino to Darwin, 7 Jan. 1871, Cambridge University Library, DAR 111.

73. Müller, *Die Befruchtung der Blumen,* 421–25; on nectarless flowers, 85. The attack on Delpino's finalism was dropped in the English translation promoted by Darwin (see n. 64 above).

74. Delpino, "Ulteriori osservazioni," 16: 269.

75. Ibid., 270.

76. Ibid., 266.

77. Darwin, *Fertilisation of Orchids,* 41ff.

78. Ibid., 42.

79. Ibid., 44 (cf. 1st ed. [1862], p. 53).

80. Ibid., 43–44.

81. Darwin, *Origin,* 91.

82. F. Delpino, "Rapporti tra insetti e tra nettarii estranuziali in alcune piante" (Relations between insects and extranuptual nectaries in some plants), *Bullettino della Società Entomologica Italiana* 6 (1874), offprint.

83. Ibid.

84. Darwin, *On the Origin,* 91.

85. Delpino, "Rapporti tra insetti e tra nettarii estranuziali," 13.

86. C. Darwin, *The Effects of Cross- and Self-fertilisation in the Vegetable Kingdom* (London: Murray, 1876), 402–404.

87. Ibid., 403.

88. C. Darwin, *The Different Forms of Flowers on Plants of the Same Species* (London: Murray, 1877).

89. Ibid., chap. 8, 310–45.

90. F. Delpino, "Sull'opera 'La distribuzione dei sessi nelle piante e la legge che osta alla perennità della fecondazione consanguinea' del prof. Federico Hildebrand. Note critiche" (On Professor Frederic Hildebrand's essay "Sexual distribution in plants and the law that prevents self-fertilization": Critical notes), *Atti della Società Italiana di Scienze Naturali* 10 (1867); the offprint with Darwin's handwritten notes is in the Cambridge University Library, Darwin Offprint Collection, General Collection 548 (mentions hereafter refer to this offprint).

91. Ibid., 30.

92. Darwin, *Different Forms of Flowers,* 337ff.

93. Ibid., 338.

94. Ibid.

95. Delpino, "Sull'opera *La distribuzione dei sessi,*" 11n.

96. Darwin Offprint Collection, General Collection, 548.

97. Darwin, *Different Forms of Flowers,* 344–45.

98. Ibid., 344.

99. F. Delpino, "Studi sopra un lignaggio anemofilo delle Composte, ossia sopra il gruppo delle Artemisiacee" (Studies on the descent of wind-pollinated *Compositae,* or Artemisias) (Florence: Cellini, 1871), offprint.

100. On the subject see S. S. Schweber's essay "Darwin and the Political Economists: Divergence of Character," *Journal of the History of Biology* 13 (1980): 195–289. See also G. Pancaldi, chap. 2 in part 1 of *Charles Darwin: "Storia" ed "economia" della natura* (Charles Darwin: "History" and "Economy" of nature) (Florence: La Nuova

Italia, 1977); and "Charles Darwin e il pensiero sociale: Alcune prospettive storiografiche recenti" (Charles Darwin and social thought: Some recent historiographic perspectives), *Il pensiero politico* 15 (1982): 222–30. On Darwinism, economy, teleology, and the origin of sexes in a perspective that ranges from Darwin to contemporary biology, see M. T. Ghiselin, *The Economy of Nature and the Evolution of Sex* (Berkeley and Los Angeles: University of California Press, 1974).

101. Delpino, "Studi sopra un lignaggio anemofilo," 23.

102. Darwin, handwritten comment in Delpino, "Studi sopra un lignaggio anemofilo," Cambridge University Library, Darwin Offprint Collection, General Collection, 715, p. 23.

103. M. J. S. Rudwick, "Charles Darwin in London: The Integration of Public and Private Science," *Isis* 73 (1982): 186–206. For further reflections on the subject, see M. J. S. Rudwick, introduction to *The Great Devonian Controversy: The Shaping of Scientific Knowledge among Gentlemanly Specialists* (Chicago: University of Chicago Press, 1985).

104. The conclusion I have drawn leaves unanswered the question of *when* Darwin broke away from the tradition of natural theology in which he had been raised. According to Ospovat (*Development of Darwin's Theory*), the split came later than is usually assumed. On the other hand, my conclusion raises doubts about Moore's claims in chap. 11 of his *Post-Darwinian Controversies*. In his treatment of the relations between Darwin and Gray, Moore holds that even after 1859 Darwin was essentially in agreement with Gray on the issue of teleology. This seems hard to defend in the light of the relations between Darwin and Delpino on finalism examined here.

105. See Gray's own testimonial (16 Feb. 1963) in *Letters of Asa Gray*, ed. J. L. Gray (London: Macmillan, 1893), 498.

106. Delpino, "Sull'opera *La distribuzione dei sessi*," 7n.

107. Alphonse de Candolle to Darwin, 31 July 1877, in C. Baehni, "Correspondence de Charles Darwin et d'Alphonse de Candolle," *Gesnerus* 12 (1955): 103–56, especially 148.

108. Darwin to Candolle, 3 Aug. 1877 and 24 Jan. 1881, ibid., 150, 154. For some stimulating general reflections on Darwin's "ambiguity" toward teleology, see D. Kohn, "Darwin's Ambiguity: The Secularization of Biological Meaning," *British Journal for the History of Science* 22 (1989): 215–39.

109. It may be useful here to mention the authors of the older books found in the part of Federico Delpino's library still preserved by the Delpino family: J. J. Berzelius, Alphonse de Candolle, I. Geoffroy Saint-Hilaire, J. Liebig, J. V. Carus, H. G. Bronn, Georg Weber, D. A. Godron, and C. Lyell.

110. See chap. 2 above. Information on the earliest academic relations between Delpino and Parlatore can be gathered from Delpino's letters in the Carteggio Parlatore, Biblioteca Comunale di Palermo.

111. See Delpino, "Pensieri sulla biologia vegetale," 343–45, with long, approving quotations from G. R. Treviranus, *Die Erscheinungen und Gesetze des organischen Lebens* (The phenomena and laws of organic life) (Bremen: Heyse, 1831–33). Treviranus's ties with the Kantian or transcendental branch of Naturphilosophie, as opposed to the Hegelian and Schellingian branches, is argued by T. Lenoir, "The Göttingen School and the Development of Transcendental Naturphilosophie in the Romantic Era," *Studies in History of Biology* 5 (1981): 111–205, particularly 175ff. Lenoir partly adopts the map of Naturphilosophie suggested by D. von Engelhart, *Hegel und die Chemie* (Wiesbaden: Pressler, 1976). On Treviranus see also B. Hoppe, "Le concept de biologie chez G. R. Treviranus" (G. R. Treviranus's conception of biology), in *Colloque international Lamarck*, ed. J. Schiller (Paris: Blanchard, 1971), 199–237.

112. Delpino, "Ulteriori osservazioni," 12: 55n.

113. Dupree, *Asa Gray*, 46–47, does not, however, rule out that German Romantic philosophy may have had a certain influence on Gray as well.

114. Delpino, "Rapporti tra insetti e nettarii estranuziali," 13n.

115. See, for example, the passage added to the chapter on natural selection in the third edition of the *Origin*, where Darwin declares, "It is difficult to avoid personifying the word Nature; but I mean by Nature, only the aggregate action and product of many natural laws, and by laws the sequence of events as ascertained by us." See *The Origin of Species: A Variorum Text*, ed. M. Peckham (Philadelphia: University of Pennsylvania Press, 1959), 165.

116. F. Delpino, *Il materialismo nella scienza* (Genoa: Martini, 1881).

117. For a map of the diffusion in Italy, parallel to the spread of Darwinism, of themes from naturalism, monism, and materialism, see chap. 6 below. See also G. Landucci, *Darwinismo a Firenze: Tra scienza e ideologia (1860–1900)* (Darwinism in Florence: Between science and ideology [1860–1900] (Florence: Olschki, 1977); Pancaldi, chap. 2 of part 2 of *Darwin: "Storia" ed "economia" della natura*; G. Cosmacini, "Problemi medico-biologici e concezione materialistica della scienza" (Medical-biological problems and materialistic conceptions of science), in *Storia d'Italia, Annuali 3, Scienza e tecnica nella cultura e nella società dal Rinascimento a oggi*, ed. G. Micheli (Turin: Einaudi, 1980), 813–61; and G. De Liguori, *Materialismo inquieto: Vicende dello scientismo in Italia nell'età del positivismo, 1868–1911* (Uneasy materialism: Scientism in Italy in the Age of Positivism, 1868–1911) (Bari: Laterza, 1988).

118. Delpino, "On the Darwinian Theory of Pangenesis," 407.

119. See Delpino's other fervent and sometimes harsh public speeches: F. Delpino, *Disordini universitari: Cause e rimedi* (University unrest: Causes and remedies) (Bologna: Treves, 1892), and *Socialismo e storia naturale* (Socialism and natural history) (Naples: Tipografia dell'Università, 1895).

120. Delpino, *Materialismo nella scienza*, 13. Further testimonials of Delpino's brand of vitalism in the 1880s can be found in F. Delpino, "Le spiritualisme dans la science" (Spiritualism in science), *Revue internationale* 1 (1884): 5–33, which is in part a tolerant exchange with Canestrini, who upheld opposite views.

FIVE. MAN'S ANCESTORS AND CRIMINOLOGY

1. J. W. Burrow, *Evolution and Society: A Study in Victorian Social Theory* (Cambridge: Cambridge University Press, 1966), 19–21.

2. Ibid., 114.

3. On these subjects see R. M. Young, "Malthus and the Evolutionists: The Common Context of Biological and Social Theory," *Past and Present* 43 (1969): 109–45, and other papers now collected in R. M. Young, *Darwin's Metaphor: Nature's Place in Victorian Culture* (Cambridge: Cambridge University Press, 1985); G. Pancaldi, *Charles Darwin: "Storia" ed "economia" della natura* (Charles Darwin: The "history" and "economy" of nature) (Florence: La Nuova Italia, 1977), especially chap. 1 of part 2; M. J. S. Rudwick, "Transposed Concepts from the Human Sciences in the Early Work of Charles Lyell," in *Images of the Earth: Essays in the History of the Environmental Sciences*, ed. L. J. Jordanova and R. S. Porter (Chalfont St. Giles: British Society for the History of Science, 1978), 67–83; and S. S. Schweber, "Darwin and the Political Economists: Divergence of Character," *Journal of the History of Biology* 13 (1980): 195–289.

4. See Schweber, "Darwin and the Political Economists."

5. D. Kohn, "Theories to Work By: Rejected Theories, Reproduction, and Darwin's Path to Natural Selection," *Studies in History of Biology* 4 (1980): 67–170.

6. G. Jones, chap. 3 in *Social Darwinism and English Thought: The Interaction between Biological and Social Theory* (Brighton: Harvester, 1980).

7. R. C. Bannister, *Social Darwinism: Science and Myth in Anglo-American Social Thought* (Philadelphia: Temple University Press, 1979). For an additional map of social Darwinism and reflections on historiography, see A. La Vergata, "Biologia, scienze umane e 'darwinismo sociale': Considerazioni contro una categoria storiografica dannosa" (Biology, human sciences, and "social Darwinism": Considerations against a harmful historiographic category), *Intersezioni* 2 (1982): 77–97.

8. J. Durant, "The Meaning of Evolution: Post-Darwinian Debates on the Significance for Man of the Theory of Evolution, 1858–1908," unpublished doctoral dissertation, Cambridge University, 1977.

9. J. Durant, review of Bannister, *Social Darwinism, British Journal for the History of Science* 15 (1982): 76–77.

10. Considerations on social Darwinism in Italy can be found in G. Landucci, *Darwinismo a Firenze: Tra scienza e ideologia (1860–1900)* (Darwinism in Florence: Between science and ideology [1860–1900]) (Florence: Olschki, 1977); Pancaldi, chap. 2 in part 2 of *Darwin: "Storia" ed "economia" della natura*; G. Cosmacini, "Problemi medico-biologici e concezione materialistica nella seconda metà dell'Ottocento" (Medical-biological problems and materialistic conception in the second half of the nineteenth century), in *Storia d'Italia: Annali 3, Scienza e tecnica nella cultura e nella società dal Rinascimento ad oggi*, ed. G. Micheli (Turin: Einaudi, 1980); G. Montalenti, preface to C. Darwin, *L'origine delle specie*, anastatic reprinting of the 1864 edition of the *Origin* (Bologna: Zanichelli, 1982).

11. Of the vast literature on Lombroso's (1835–1909) anthropological and criminological work, see H. Kurella, *Cesare Lombroso: A Modern Man of Science*, translated from the German (London: Rebman, 1911); G. Lombroso-Ferrero, *Cesare Lombroso: Storia della vita e delle opere* (Cesare Lombroso: History of his life and works) (Turin: Bocca, 1915); M. E. Wolfgang, "C. Lombroso," in *Pioneers in Criminology*, ed. H. Mannheim (London: Stevens, 1960), 168–227; L. Bulferetti, *Cesare Lombroso* (Turin: UTET, 1975); F. Giacanelli, introduction to G. Colombo, *La scienza infelice: Il museo di antropologia criminale di Cesare Lombroso* (The sad science: Cesare Lombroso's museum of criminal anthropology) (Turin: Boringhieri, 1975); E. de Bernart and M. Tricarico, "Per una rilettura dell'opera di C. Lombroso" (For a rereading of C. Lombroso's work), *Physis* 18 (1976): 179–84; R. Nye, "Heredity or Milieu: The Formation of European Criminological Theory," *Isis* 67 (1976): 335–55; R. Villa, "Letture recenti di Lombroso" (Recent interpretations of Lombroso), *Studi storici* 2 (1977): 243–52; S. J. Gould, chap. 4 in *The Mismeasure of Man* (New York: Norton, 1981); and D. Pick, *Faces of Degeneration: A European Disorder, c. 1848–c. 1918* (Cambridge: Cambridge University Press, 1989), chap. 5, which is the most comprehensive and penetrating survey available in English on Lombroso's criminology considered within the context of late-nineteenth-century Italian society.

12. C. Lombroso, *L'uomo delinquente studiato in rapporto alla antropologia, alla medicina legale e alle discipline carcerarie* (The criminal man studied in connection with anthropology, forensic medicine, and prison studies) (Milan: Hoepli, 1876); Lombroso expanded the subsequent editions with the new material he was collecting, and to keep up with the developments of the discipline he termed *criminal anthropology*.

13. See Lombroso's address presented at the sixth International Congress of Criminal Anthropology (1906), in *Comptes-Redus du VIe Congrès international d'antropologie criminelle* (Turin: Bocca, 1908), xxxii.

14. C. Lombroso, "Esistenza di una fossa occipitale mediana nel cranio di un delinquente" (The existence of a median occipital fossa in the skull of a criminal), *Rendiconti del R. Istituto Lombardo di Scienze e Lettere*, 2d ser., 4 (1871): 37–41.

15. See R. B. Freeman, *The Works of Charles Darwin: An Annotated Bibliographical Handlist*, 2d ed. (Folkestone: Dawson, Archon Books, 1977), 129–30. C. Darwin, *The Descent of Man, and Selection in Relation to Sex* (London: Murray, 1871), reprint

with an introduction by J. T. Bonner and R. M. May (Princeton: Princeton University Press, 1981).

16. T. H. Huxley, *Man's Place in Nature* (1863; New York: Greenwood Reprint, 1968); C. Lyell, *The Geological Evidences of the Antiquity of Man; with Remarks on Theories of the Origin of Species by Variation* (1863; Westmead: Gregg International, 1970).

17. See chap. 3 above.

18. See M. Bartholomew, "Huxley's Defence of Darwin," *Annals of Science* 32 (1975): 525–35; and M. A. Di Gregorio, *T. H. Huxley's Place in Natural Science* (New Haven: Yale University Press, 1984). For additional references see chap. 3 above, n. 67.

19. See the conclusions to chaps. 2 and 3 above. See also P. Bowler, *The Non-Darwinian Revolution* (Baltimore: Johns Hopkins University Press, 1988).

20. Lombroso, "Esistenza di una fossa occipitale mediana."

21. In his first publication on the subject, Lombroso was cautious in delineating Villella's criminal attributes: he described him as "suspected of banditry" and reported that Villella had been convicted three times for theft and once for setting fire to a mill in connection with a burglary.

22. H. de Blainville, *Ostéographie* (Paris: Bertrand, 1839–41).

23. P. Gratiolet, *Anatomie comparée du système nerveux considéré dans ses rapport avec l'intelligence* (Comparative anatomy of the nervous system in relation to intelligence) (Paris: Baillière, 1857), 88–99, 247ff. This was the second volume of a work of which the first volume, by F. Leuret, was published in 1839. It should be noted that Lombroso, in his first important publication on the subject, did *not* mention B. A. Morel, whose works are sometimes regarded as having inspired him. On Morel see Pick, *Faces of Degeneration*, chap. 2.

24. Lombroso, "Esistenza di una fossa occipitale mediana," 39.

25. On F. J. Gall and on phrenology and its broad influence on nineteenth-century scientific culture, see G. Lanteri-Laura, *Histoire de la phrénologie: L'homme et son cerveau selon F. J. Gall* (The history of phrenology: Man and his brain according to F. J. Gall) (Paris: PUF, 1970), which occasionally also deals with the relations between phrenology and Lombroso. See also R. Cooter, *The Cultural Meaning of Popular Science: Phrenology and the Organization of Consent in Nineteenth-century Britain* (Cambridge: Cambridge University Press, 1985).

26. See the criticisms to this effect in F. Leuret, *Anatomie comparée du système nerveux considéré dans ses rapports avec l'intelligence* (Paris, Baillière, 1839), 556: "[Phrenologists] do not study the brain, only the skull; and when they want to describe a cerebral convolution, instead of showing it and allowing you to touch it, they show you a bony protuberance, a bump on the skull. . . . "

27. Lombroso, "Esistenza di una fossa occipitale mediana," 39: "above all, the shape of the wax cast of the cranial cavity, attesting to a very regular three-lobed cerebellum, as in a five-month fetus, convinces us that the indentation housed a median lobe of the cerebellum." This was one of the most controversial points of Lombroso's thesis, a point that, by 1875, had already been written about by Andrea Verga, Luigi Calori, Giulio Bizzozero, and others. Cf. C. Lombroso, "Della fossetta occipitale mediana in rapporto collo sviluppo del vermis cerebellare" (On the median occipital fossa in relation to the development of the vermis of the cerebellum), *Rivista sperimentale di freniatria* 2 (1876): 121–30.

28. Gould, *Mismeasure of Man*, 124.

29. Gratiolet, *Anatomie comparée*, 248–51.

30. See chap. 3 above.

31. See C. Darwin, *On the Origin of Species* (Cambridge: Harvard University Press, 1964), 25–26, and Darwin, *Descent of Man*, 173.

32. Huxley, *Man's Place in Nature*, 134.

33. C. Lombroso, "Delle relazioni fra funzioni encefaliche e riproduttive in alcuni

nevrotteri ed imenotteri" (On the relations between encephalic and reproductive functions in some neuroptera and hymenoptera), *Collettore dell'Adige* 3, nos. 65, 67, 70, 74, 75 (1853). The references hereafter are to the more accessible reprinting of this essay in C. Lombroso, *Psicologia e natura* (Psychology and nature), ed. Gina Lombroso (Turin: Bocca, 1927), 129–51 (the passages quoted here have been checked against the original edition).

34. Ibid., 129–33.

35. For the diffusion of these ideas in the Italian scientific community before Darwin, see chaps. 1 and 2 above.

36. See Stephen Jay Gould's major work on the history of recapitulation theory, *Ontogeny and Phylogeny* (Cambridge: Belknap, 1977), 120–25. On the circulation of Meckel's works in Italy, see chap. 2 above.

37. Lombroso, "Delle relazioni fra funzioni encefaliche e riproduttive," 146.

38. C. Lombroso, "Su la pazzia di Cardano," *Gazzetta medica italiana. Lombardia*, no. 4 (1855): 344n.

39. C. Lombroso, "Influenza della civiltà su la pazzia e della pazzia su la civiltà" (The influence of civilization on madness and of madness on civilization), *Gazzetta medica italiana. Lombardia*, no. 48 (1856); no. 5 (1857); no. 14 (1857).

40. C. Lombroso, "Ricerche su'l cretinesimo in Lombardia" (Research on cretinism in Lombardy), *Gazzetta medica italiana. Lombardia*, nos. 32, 40, 49 (1859): e.g., 334.

41. C. Lombroso, "Sul cretinismo negli animali" (On cretinism in animals), *Gazzetta medica italiana. Lombardia* (1860): 408–409.

42. On the relations between Marzolo and Lombroso, see G. Lombroso, chap. 2. in *C. Lombroso*. On Marzolo see M. Ceccarel, *Della vita e degli scritti di Paolo Marzolo* (On the life and writings of Paolo Marzolo) (Treviso: Priuli, 1870).

43. Kurella, *C. Lombroso*, 144 and passim; Bulferetti, *Cesare Lombroso*, especially chap. 2.

44. Since in this book I deal mainly with the diffusion of Darwin's ideas, I do not address in detail the issue of other possible sources of Lombroso's conception of atavism. Apropos of this, see G. Antonini, *I precursori di C. Lombroso* (C. Lombroso's precursors) (Turin: Bocca, 1900); *L'opera di Cesare Lombroso*, especially E. Morselli, *Cesare Lombroso e l'antropologia generale* (Cesare Lombroso and general anthropology), 1–31; and Pick, *Faces of Degeneration*, chap. 5.

45. Lombroso, "Influenza della civiltà su la pazzia," no. 14: 109–10.

46. Ibid.

47. The comparison of present-day "primitives," or "inferior peoples," with the animal ancestors of white races recurred in nearly every page of what Canestrini deemed Lombroso's most important anthropological work, *L'uomo bianco e l'uomo di colore: Letture sull'origine e le varietà delle razze umane* (The white man and the colored man: Readings on the origin and the varieties of human races) (Padua: Sacchetto, 1871). For Canestrini's opinion, see G. Canestrini, *Per l'evoluzione: Recensioni e nuovi studi* (For evolution: Reviews and new studies) (Turin: UTET, 1894), 180–81. For views on race in the Italian context, see chap. 6 below.

48. See, e.g., Lombroso, *L'uomo delinquente* (1876), 197, 245.

49. See C. Lombroso, *L'uomo delinquente in rapporto all'antropologia, alla giurisprudenza ed alla psichiatria* (Criminal man in relation to anthropology, law, and psychiatry), 5th ed. (Turin: Bocca, 1896–97), s.v. "Darwin" in the index. On Lombroso's "fearful quest for facts," see some interesting considerations in Giacanelli's introduction to Colombo, *La scienza infelice*, 15ff.

50. C. Lombroso, translator's preface to J. Moleschott, *La circolazione della vita: Lettere fisiologiche* (The circulation of life: Physiological letters) (Milan: Brigola, 1869), vi–vii.

51. C. Lombroso, "L'atavismo e la legge di convergenza degli organi nelle razze

e nelle specie" (Atavism and the law of convergence of organs in races and species), *Rivista di scienze biologiche* 1 (1899): 721–44. See also the contemporaneous essays on the problem of acquired characters reprinted in Lombroso, *Psicologia e natura*, 152–206.

52. C. Lombroso, introduction to A. MacDonald, *Criminology* (New York: Funk and Wagnalls, 1893), ii, iii. The book was dedicated to Lombroso, "the founder of criminology."

53. C. Lombroso, preface to *L'uomo delinquente* (1896–97), xviii–xix. On later developments of Lombroso's doctrine, which besides atavism gave epilepsy and the old idea of "arrested development" as additional, or occasionally alternative, characteristics typical of the "born delinquent," see G. Sergi, *I caratteri degenerativi nell'uomo secondo Cesare Lombroso* (Degenerative characters in man according to Cesare Lombroso), in *L'opera di Cesare Lombroso*, 32–38.

54. See C. Lombroso, *The Man of Genius* (London: Scott, 1891), 356–57. For a recent and well-documented approach to similar aspects of Darwin's biography, see R. Colp, Jr., *To Be an Invalid: The Illness of Charles Darwin* (Chicago: University of Chicago Press, 1977).

55. See S. Shapin and B. Barnes, "Darwin and Social Darwinism: Purity and History," in *Natural Order: Historical Studies of Scientific Culture*, ed. B. Barnes and S. Shapin (Beverly Hills and London: Sage, 1979), 125–42.

56. See above, n. 8.

57. For the diffusion of Lombroso's ideas in German-speaking countries, see H. Kurella's writings and his translations of Lombroso (Kurella, *Cesare Lombroso*). For English-speaking countries, see the translations mentioned in n. 11 above, as well as in C. Lombroso, introduction to MacDonald, *Criminology*; W. D. Morrison, introduction to C. Lombroso and G. Ferrero, *The Female Offender* (London: Fisher Unwin, 1895); C. Lombroso, introduction to A. Drähms, *The Criminal, His Personnel and Environment* (New York: Macmillan, 1900); C. Kelly, *The Italian Theory of Crime: Cesare Lombroso* (Cambridge: Hall, 1910); C. Lombroso, introduction to *Criminal Man* (New York and London: Putnam's, 1911); Wolfgang, *Cesare Lombroso*, 216–22. For the diffusion in Spanish-speaking countries, see indications in Villa, *Letture recenti di Lombroso*.

58. On naturalism in the Italian context, see chap. 2 above and chap. 6 below.

SIX. THE POPULAR RECEPTION

1. Paolo Lioy, in *Atti Parlamentari*, Camera dei Deputati, "Discussioni" (Debates of the House of Representatives), 1 Apr. 1881, 4922. On the limited circulation of Darwin's books in Italian translation, it should be remembered that only two editions of the *Origin of Species* were issued during the nineteenth century (1864 and 1875; the latter was reissued in 1915). The *Descent of Man* was more popular, with four impressions from 1872 to 1914. See *Un secolo di vita della Unione tipografico-editrice torinese, 1855–1954* (A century of life of the Torinese Publishing-Typographic Union UTET, 1855–1954) (Turin: UTET, 1974), 532–33.

2. Istituto Centrale di Statistica (ISTAT), *Sommario di statistiche storiche dell'Italia, 1861–1975* (Summary of historical statistics of Italy, 1861–1975) (Rome: ISTAT, 1976), 14.

3. For this and the following data on schools and universities, see Marzio Barbagli's fundamental study *Disoccupazione intellettuale e sistema scolastico in Italia, 1859–1973* (Intellectual unemployment and the school system in Italy, 1859–1973) (Bologna: il Mulino, 1974), especially 23, 29, 31–32, 62–64, 90. On related issues see V. Zamagni, "Istruzione e sviluppo economico in Italia, 1861–1913" (Education and economic development in Italy, 1861–1913), in P. Ciocca et al., *Lo sviluppo economico italiano 1861–1940* (Italian economic development, 1861–1940) (Bari: Laterza, 1973),

187–240; C. G. Lacaita, *Istruzione e sviluppo industriale in Italia, 1859–1914* (Education and industrial development in Italy, 1859–1914) (Florence: Giunti, 1973); and Marcello Rossi, *Università e società in Italia alla fine dell'1800* (University and society in Italy at the end of the nineteenth century) (Florence: La Nuova Italia, 1976).

4. ISTAT, *Sommario di statistiche storiche*, 58.

5. V. Castronovo, L. Giacheri Fossati, and N. Tranfaglia, *La stampa italiana nell'età liberale* (The Italian press in the liberal age) (Bari: Laterza, 1979), 11.

6. Only 2 percent of the population had suffrage rights in 1861, and 7 percent in 1895 (Castronovo, *La stampa italiana*, 9; and Barbagli, *Disoccupazione intellettuale*, 67).

7. A thorough description of feelings and expectations on this subject is to be found in the classic work by F. Chabod *La politica estera italiana dal 1870 al 1896* (Italian foreign policy, 1870–96) (Bari: Laterza, 1976), 248–55, 272–84, 287.

8. S. Woolf, *A History of Italy, 1700–1860* (London: Methuen, 1979), 471.

9. On d'Ondes Reggio and Italian Catholics in the 1860s and 1870s, see G. De Rosa, *Il movimento cattolico in Italia: Dalla Restaurazione all'età giolittiana* (The Catholic movement in Italy: From the Restoration to the Age of Giolitti) (Bari: Laterza, 1972), especially 37ff., 68ff.

10. On Mantegazza see G. Landucci, *Darwinismo a Firenze* (Darwinism in Florence) (Florence: Olschki, 1977), 107–27, and P. Govoni, "Paolo Mantegazza tra scienza e divulgazione" (P. Mantegazza between science and popularization), unpublished dissertation, University of Bologna, 1985–86.

11. *Atti Parlamentari*, Camera dei Deputati, "Discussioni," 20–21 Apr. 1866: 1763–93, 1788.

12. T. Vignoli, *Myth and Science* (London: Kegan Paul, 1882 [Ital. ed. 1879]), 37–38.

13. Ibid., 322. On Vignoli see Paolo Rossi, introduction to *L'età del positivismo* (The age of positivism), ed. Paolo Rossi (Bologna: Il Mulino, 1986), 14–15.

14. Vignoli, *Myth and science*, 322.

15. G. Landucci, "Scienza, religione ed editoria scolastica" (Science, religion, and educational publishing), in *Editori a Firenze nel secondo Ottocento*, ed. I. Porciani (Florence: Olschki, 1983), 183–229.

16. Ibid., 185.

17. F. De Sanctis, quoted in Landucci, "Scienza, religione ed editoria scolastica," 216–17.

18. See chap. 3 above.

19. On Capellini see chap. 3 above, n. 68.

20. Chap. 2 above.

21. Landucci, *Darwinismo a Florence*, 89ff.

22. The following information on Lessona is based on L. Camerano, "Michele Lessona: Notizie biografiche e bibliografiche" (Michele Lessona: Biographical and bibliographical information), *Bollettino dei Musei di zoologia ed anatomia comparata* (University of Turin) 9 (1984): 1–72. The success of the popular literature on science circulated by Lessona in the second half of the century can profitably be compared with the frustrations experienced by the publishers who had invested in the same kind of literature during the first half of the century. See L. Firpo, *Vita di Giuseppe Pomba da Turin, Libraio, tipografo, editore* (The life of Giuseppe Pomba of Turin, bookseller, typographer, and publisher) (Turin: UTET, 1975), 66–67.

23. *Descent of Man* (translated in 1871), *Journal of Researches* (1872), *The Formation of Vegetable Mould* (1882).

24. M. Lessona, *Volere è potere* (Florence: Barbera, 1873).

25. See P. Corsi, " 'Lamarckiens' et 'Darwiniens' à Turin (1812–1894)" ("Lamarckians" and "Darwinians" in Turin [1812–1894]), in *De Darwin au darwinisme: Science et idéologie*, ed. Y. Conry (Paris: Vrin, 1983), 49–67.

26. M. Lessona, *Carlo Darwin* (Rome: Sommaruga, 1883), 273–76.

27. M. Larizza Lolli, "Comte e l'Italia (1849–1857)" (Comte and Italy, 1849–1857), *Società e storia*, n. 24 (1984): 313–67.

28. S. Tommasi, "Il naturalismo moderno" (Modern naturalism) [1866], in S. Tommasi, *Il naturalismo moderno. Scritti vari*, ed. A. Anile (Bari: Laterza, 1913).

29. This was especially evident in the case of the philosopher Roberto Ardigò. See G. Pancaldi, *Charles Darwin: "Storia" ed "economia" della natura* (Charles Darwin: "History" and "economy" of nature) (Florence: La Nuova Italia, 1977), 188–89.

30. See, for example, B. Spaventa, "La legge del più forte" (The law of the strongest) [1874], in B. Spaventa, *Scritti filosofici* (Naples: Morano, 1900), 339–52.

31. Spaventa, *Principi di filosofia* (Principles of philosophy) (Naples: Ghio, 1867). On Spaventa and the important Hegelian tradition in Naples, see G. Oldrini, *La cultura filosofica napoletana dell'Ottocento* (Nineteenth-century Neapolitan philosophical culture) (Bari: Laterza, 1973); and G. Oldrini, *L'Ottocento filosofico napoletano nella letteratura dell'ultimo decennio* (Nineteenth-century philosophy in Naples in the literature of the last decade) (Naples: Bibliopolis, 1986).

32. De Rosa, *Il movimento cattolico*, 128, 160.

33. G. Bovio in *Atti Parlamentari*, Camera dei Deputati, "Discussioni," 2 Apr. 1881, 4929.

34. P. Lioy in *Atti Parlamentari*, Camera dei Deputati, "Discussioni," 2 Apr. 1881, 4923–28. On Lioy see S. Lanaro, *Società e ideologie nel Veneto rurale (1866–1898)* (Society and ideologies in rural Venetia [1866–1898]) (Rome: Edizioni di Storia e Letteratura, 1976), 161–99.

35. A. Sormani, "La nuova religione dell'evoluzionismo" (The new religion of evolutionism), *Rivista di filosofia scientifica*, 2d ser., 8 (1889): 513–40.

36. See E. Morselli, "La filosofia monistica in Italia" (Monistic philosophy in Italy), *Rivista di filosofia scientifica* 6 (1887): 1–36.

37. See E. Ferri, *Discordie positiviste del socialismo* (Positivistic disputes in socialism) (Palermo: Sandron, 1895), 10.

38. *Critica sociale* 2 (1892): 133–38.

39. "La conferenza di Ferri su 'La scienza e il socialismo' " (Ferri's lecture on "Science and Socialism"), *Lotta di classe*, 5–6 May 1894.

40. E. Ferri, *Socialismo e scienza positiva (Darwin-Spencer-Marx)* (Rome: Editrice Italiana, 1894).

41. E. Ferri, *Science and Socialism: Darwin-Spencer-Marx* (London: The Socialist Library, 1905).

42. A. Labriola, *Essays on the Materialistic Conception of History*, trans. C. H. Kerr (Chicago, 1903; reprint, New York: Monthly Review, 1966), 118–19.

43. Ibid., 120.

44. Ibid., 135.

45. The American translator grasped Labriola's methodological message: "The central and fundamental proposition of socialism is not any scheme for reconstructing society, on a cut-and-dried program, nor again is it any particular mathematical formula showing to what extent the laborer is robbed by the present system of the fruits of his labor; it is precisely this Historical Materialism, which Labriola has so admirably explained in the present work" (Kerr, preface to Labriola, *Materialistic Conception of History*).

46. E. Malatesta, *Anarchy* (London: The Freedom Press, 1974). The original Italian edition was published in 1891, in London, like the first English translation, published in installments in 1891–92.

47. *See Chiesa e religiosità in Italia dopo l'Unità, 1861–1878* (The church and religiosity in Italy after unification, 1861–1878), 3 vols. bound in 2 vols. (Milan: Vita e Pensiero, 1973), passim.

48. G. Casati, *L'Indice dei libri proibiti* (Milan and Rome: Pro Familia, 1936), 1: 25;

and F. H. Reusch, *Der Index der verbotenen Bücher* (1885; Aalen: Scientia, 1967), 1033–43.

49. Reusch, *Der Index*, 1036.

50. See chap. 1 above, n. 98.

51. Priests attracted by evolutionism, and critical of the resistance offered by many Catholics, could also incur the rigors of the Index. This happened to Raffaello Caverni, now known for his *Storia del metodo sperimentale in Italia* (History of the experimental method in Italy) (Reprint, Bologna: Forni, 1969, with a preface by Giorgio Tabarroni). His *De' nuovi studi della filosofia: Discorsi a un giovane studente* (On the new philosophical studies: Talks to a young student) was prohibited in 1878. Caverni publicly repented and retracted. See Reusch, *Der Index*, 1043; and V. Cappelletti and F. Di Trocchio, in *Dizionario biografico degli italiani* (Rome: Enciclopedia Italiana, 1960–), s.v. "R. Caverni."

52. See chap. 3 above, text corresponding to n. 47.

53. See E. E. Y. Hales, *Pio Nono: A Study in European Politics and Religion in the Nineteenth Century* (London: Eyre and Spottiswoode, 1954), 255–62; and A. Polverani, *Vita di Pio IX* (The life of Pius IX), 3 vols. (Rome: Pio IX, 1988), 3: 115–47. A few years later Pius IX defined the dogmas of the Immaculate Conception and of Papal Infallibility.

54. Chap. 4 above.

55. A. Fogazzaro, *Ascensioni umane* (Human ascensions) [3d ed., 1899] (Milan: Longanesi, 1977). On Fogazzaro's evolutionism see Paolo Rossi, introduction to Fogazzaro, *Ascensioni*, 7–44. On Fogazzaro and modernism see P. Scoppola, *Crisi modernista e rinnovamento cattolico in Italia* (Modernist crisis and Catholic renewal in Italy) (Bologna: il Mulino, 1961), 172–76. In an appendix Scoppola published a manuscript essay by the British-naturalized Catholic Friedrich von Hügel, containing an extremely sympathetic description of Charles Darwin's investigations (p. 377).

56. Pius X, "Lamentabili sane exitu," 3 July 1907, especially theses nos. 53, 58, 64. For an English translation, see B. M. G. Reardon, ed., *Roman Catholic Modernism* (London: Adam and Charles Black, 1970), 242–48.

57. Pius XII, "Humani generis," 12 Aug. 1950. Latin and Italian texts in *Rivista di filosofia neo-scolastica* 43 (1951): 3–29, especially 7, 25.

58. A. Gemelli, "Il significato storico della 'Humani generis' " (The historical significance of "Humani generis"), *Rivista di filosofia neo-scolastica* 43 (1951): 30–40, especially 37. For a recent assessment see T. Roszak, in *The Encyclopedia of Religion*, ed. M. Eliade, 16 vols. (London: Collier Macmillan, 1988), s.v. "Evolution," 5: 208–14, especially 210.

59. T. Poesche, *Die Arier* (The Aryans) (Jena: Costenoble, 1878), especially 184–95; K. Penka, *Origines Ariaceae* (Origins of the Aryans) (Vienna and Teschen: Proschaska, 1883), and K. Penka, *Die Herkunft der Arier* (Vienna and Teschen: Proschaska, 1886).

60. G. Sergi, *The Mediterranean Race: A Study of the Origin of European Peoples* (1st Italian ed., 1895; London: Scott, 1901). On Sergi, see G. De Liguori, *Materialismo inquieto* (Uneasy materialism) (Bari: Laterza, 1988), 126–47.

61. Sergi, *The Mediterranean Race*, v–vii.

62. See Sergi's testimonial in his *Crania Habessinica: Contributo all'antropologia dell'Africa Orientale* (Abyssinian skulls: Contribution to the anthropology of East Africa) (Rome: Loescher, 1912), 5, 116.

63. Just how sensitive anthropologists could be to the issues of Italian colonialism, and to the attempt to counteract the jealousy aroused in other European powers, can be seen from G. Sergi, *I Britanni* (The Britons), vol. 1 of *I mediterranei nel settentrione d'Europa* (Milan: Bocca, 1936), where he took pleasure in depicting

the ancient British populations as "a bud of the majestic Mediterranean tree" (p. 24).

64. See G. Sergi, *Africa* (Turin: Bocca, 1897), 402, and G. Sergi, *Europa* (Turin: Bocca, 1908), 539–40.

65. E. Morselli, *Antropologia generale* (General anthropology) (Turin: UTET, 1911), 1333–34. The book was partly made up of lectures delivered at the Università Popolare in Genoa. On Morselli see L. Rossi, "Enrico Morselli e le scienze dell'uomo nell'età del positivismo" (Enrico Morselli and human sciences in the Age of Positivism), special issue of *Rivista sperimentale di freniatria e medicina legale delle alienazioni mentali* (1984).

66. See, for example, the new editions of Charles Darwin's major works, published in the 1920s in Milan by Casa Editrice Sociale, which also published or republished works by Giovanni Canestrini, Félix Le Dantec, and Petr Kropotkin.

67. B. Croce, "Ciò che è vivo e ciò che è morto nella filosofia di Hegel" (1906) (What is alive and what is dead in Hegel's philosophy), in B. Croce, *Saggi filosofici*, 5th ed. (Bari: Laterza, 1967), 107–109. See also B. Croce, *A History of Italy, 1871–1915* (Oxford: Clarendon, 1929), 154, and B. Croce, *History of Europe in the Nineteenth Century* (London: Allen and Unwin, 1934), 256–57.

68. V. Pareto, *The Mind and Society* (London: Jonathan Cape, 1935), 492, 1230, 1475–76.

69. However, Pareto's criticism of some "degenerations" of Darwinism, which he thought amounted to reintroducing final causes in biology and the genetic fallacy in sociology, was discerning (ibid., 1344n, 1481n). It has been suggested that, through Pareto's and Gaetano Mosca's theories of the elite, social Darwinism may have contributed to the ideology of "permanent conflict" held by fascism. See A. Lyttelton, ed., *Italian Fascisms from Pareto to Gentile* (London: J. Cape, 1973), 12, 20. The matter must be left for assessment to a much-needed history of Italian science under fascism.

70. B. Mussolini, *Opera omnia*, ed. E. and D. Susmel, 36 vols. (Florence: La Fenice, 1951–61), 4: 243.

71. Ibid. 2: 8–10.

Index

39–54, 184n; charges of pantheism, 70, 71; decline of influence, 73; chain of beings, 187n

Darwin, C.: Lyell's and Brocchi's influence, 4, 35–38; reception of theory in Italy, 39–41, 78–86, 88; anthropology and human origins, 88–96; Canestrini and evolution of theory, 96–104; adaptation and natural selection in *Fertilisation*, 107–108; natural theology, 108–109, 204n; relation with Delpino, 109, 204n; Delpino and pangenesis, 109–17; Delpino and plant fertilization, 117–19, 121, 123–27, 129–36; Malthus's theory, 140; paradox of popularity, 152; references to Bonaparte, 190n; Wallace and human origins, 198n; sexual selection, 200n; debt to Sprengel, 205n–206n

Darwin, E.: Brocchi and species problem, 25; Gautieri's transformism, 26; books prohibited by Church, 164

Darwinism: usage of term, xi, xiii; disciplinary traditions and revolution, 104–106; Lombroso's criminal anthropology, 142–43, 145–46; Lombroso's evolutionism, 146–50; definition and popularization of evolutionism, 153; political uses, 154–156, 161–63; secularization of education, 156–58; popular literature, 158–59; philosophy and popularization, 159–61; Catholicism and secularization, 163–66; popular reaction against, 167–68

De Filippi, F.: natural system in zoology, 55; Lamarckian creationism, 68–69; Darwinism and human origins, 89

Delpino, F.: connection with Darwin, xiii, 109, 204n; Darwin and pangenesis, 109–17; Darwin and fertilization, 117–19, 121, 123–27, 129–36; religious interpretation of Darwin, 165; Darwin and finalism, 169; spiritualistic naturalism, 205n; tradition of ecological studies, 206n

De Luc, J.-A.: hypothesis on sea level change, 14

Diderot, D.: individual-species analogy, 24

Donati, V.: network as image, 51

Durant, J.: social Darwinism, 141

Ecology: Brocchi's and Lyell's theories of extinction, 34; Darwin and Delpino, 109, 119

Education: national unification, 153, 154; secularization and Darwinism, 155

Embryology: species problem and classification, 55–56; Lombroso's evolutionism, 147

England: reception of Brocchi, 32; scientific institutions compared to Italy, 77–78

Environment: Brocchi and species problems 31–32; Canestrini and role of variation in evolution, 97; Lombroso's atavism, 149

Environmentalism: Darwin and individual-species analogy, 36–37

Evolutionism: early impact of the *Origin*, 79–86, 88; Delpino's criticism of pangenesis, 112–14; Huxley and Darwin, 143; Lombroso and Darwin, 146–50; unification, 153–54; Lessona, 158–59; Fogazzaro's Christian, 165; 1951 encyclical letter, 165–66; race and anthropology, 166–67

Extinction: early hypotheses, 3–4; Brocchi's hypothesis, 5–8, 17–18, 20–28, 32–37; Brocchi and Lamarck, 28–29, 31–32

Ferrero, G.: socialism and Darwinism, 161

Ferri, E.: politics and evolutionism, 95, 162

Fertilization, plant: debate between Darwin and Delpino, 117–19, 121, 123–27, 129–36

Finalism: Müller and Darwinian theory of flowers, 126; Darwin and teleology, 133, 136, 169

Flourens, P.: chain-of-beings, 56; pantheism, 70

Fogazzaro, A.: religion and evolutionism, 165

Fossils: species problem, 3; Brocchi's extinction hypothesis, 17–18, 20–22; human, 89–90

France: translations of the *Origin*, 79; reception of Brocchi, 177n

Freeman, R. B.: translations of the *Origin*, 79

Galton, F.: pangenesis, 101; social Darwinism, 141

Gautieri, G.: species problem and individual-species analogy, 25–26

Geoffroy Saint-Hilare, E.: debate with Cuvier, 39, 73; classification compared with Bonaparte's, 50; chain of beings, 51; pantheism, 65, 70, 73

Geoffroy Saint-Hilare, I.: influence on Porro, 61; Lamarck's influence, 67–68

Geology: Brocchi's fieldwork and theory of the earth, 10–11; Brocchi's hypothesis on sea level change, 12–17; Brocchi and Lamarck, 28; Horner on Brocchi, 32–33

Goether, W.: Parlatore and comparative botany, 56

Gould, S. J.: recapitulation theory, 27; Lombroso's theory, 145

Gratiolet, L. P.: Lombroso's sources, 143, 145

Gray, A.: review of *Fertilisation*, 108; Delpino's criticism of pangenesis, 113; Darwin and fertilization of nectarless flowers, 123; teleology and fertilization, 124; Darwin and finalism, 133

Greenough, G. B.: and Brocchi, 32

Haeckel, E.: theory of recapitulation, 26; Canestrini on Darwinism, 103–104; Delpino and teleology, 135

GIULIANO PANCALDI is Professor of the History of Science and Director of the Center for the History of Universities and Science, University of Bologna.